WORLD LITERACY SCENARIO

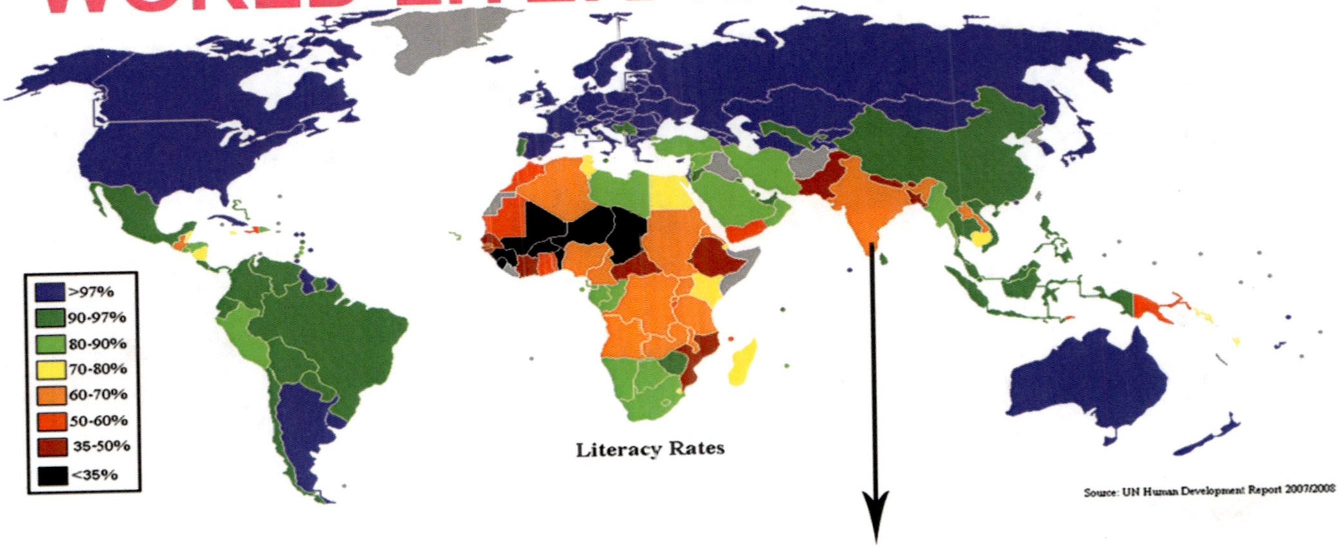

Of the 179 Countries in the WORLD, INDIA Stands at 147th position with 66% in literacy Source: UNDP Report, 2009 **2011 Census - 74.04%**

Andhra Pradesh Stands at 31th Position with 67.66% (2011 Census) of 28 States and 7 UTs

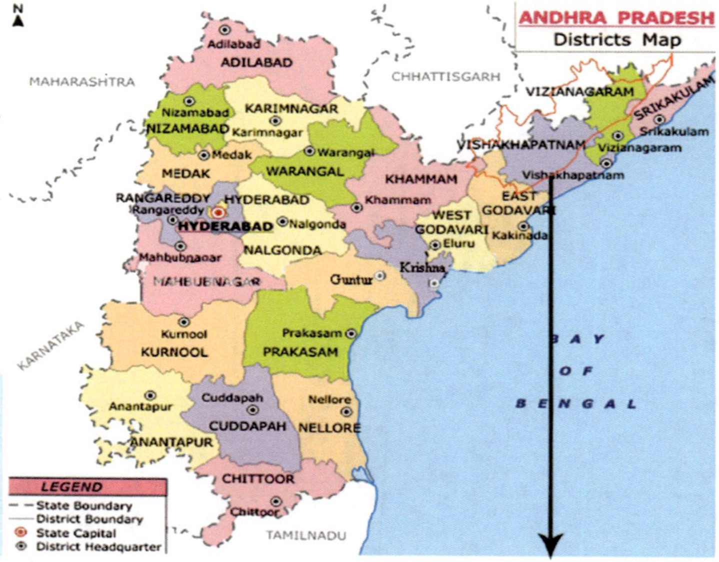

North Coastal AP(SKLM, VZM,VSKP) Districts Average Literacy rate as per the 2011 Census 63.16%

Right to Education Act 2009

Its Implementation as to Social Development in India

Prof. K. Vijaya Kumar

AKANSHA PUBLISHING HOUSE
NEW DELHI • GUWAHATI • VISAKHAPATNAM

AKANSHA PUBLISHING HOUSE
4649-B/21, Ansari Road
Darya Ganj, New Delhi - 110 002
Ph.: 23263193 / 9811582579 / 09435116718
Fax: 011-23263193
Email: ektabooks@yahoo.com
www.akanshapublishinghouse.com

Right to Education Act 2009: Its Implementation as to Social Development in India

First Published 2012
ISBN 978-81-8370-327-7

PRINTED IN INDIA

Published by Akansha Publishing House, New Delhi and Printed at Harmain Offset, Delhi.

Dedicated to
Economically Weaker Sections and Socially Disadvantaged Children

Contents

Foreword

This is the first attempt made in the country and it is a gigantic task for the Government of India to fulfill the task. The implementation of Right to Education Act, 2009, represents a momentous step forward in our 100-year struggle for universalisation of elementary education. It is commendable to notice that it is perhaps the most significant piece of legislation passed by the UPA Government. In its purview, millions of children, regardless of creed, colour and caste will now become accessible. It will serve as the springboard for emanicipating the deprived sections of our society.

The main targets of the Study are backward areas, tribal areas and weaker sections of the society, which have become victims of illiteracy, hunger and disease. Also, they have become vulnerable to exploitation and poverty. If the same trend continues, we cannot achieve the desired literacy level in the near future. As such, we have to achieve the goal of universalisation of elementary education in a short period of time, in the context of our National Development.

In this backdrop, Indian people, especially belonging to deprived and weaker sections of the society, are grateful to our beloved Prime Minister, Dr. Manmohan Singh and Chairperson Mrs. Sonia Gandhi and our Hon'ble Minister for HRD Mr. Kapil Sibal as well as Union Minister of State, Madam, Purandhareswari, all of whom, along with other Parliament members, took the initiative to plan for a powerful, prosperous and intelligent Bharat. All doubts of the vociferous groups and critics are cleared by the Prime Minister's assurance that financial constraints will not hamper the implementation of the RTE Act in inspiring a great beginning.

Finally, the main aim of the study is to achieve the goal of Right to Education for children in a specific period of time, as part of national endeavour of development and implement the right to education bill and make it successful, so that, it is the duty of every right-thinking citizen to mobilize those who are not eager to get their children educated.

I have so far done some fundamental field work and have collected primary data, while telecasting real conditions, including the state of running schools, along with parental responses, coupled with teachers' attitudes and cross-sections of the public.

In this connection, I am screening a 45 minutes documentary film which provide some insights into the formulation of tribal, rural and urban slum children denied of education. I believe that this work will be useful in the implementation stage of the Right to Education Act.

Prof. K. Vijaya Kumar

List of Pictures

1

Right to Education Act 2009: Its Implementation as to Social Development in India

Introduction

Right to live is a fundamental right as without education none can lead a decent and dignified life. Education is the most important instrument of social change. It is essential for human development as well as social development. Indian constitution enshrines justice, social, economic and political equality of status and opportunity to all the country men.

Education and institutions of learning are crucial both to creation of individual capabilities and also strong social responses that might help us meet these challenges. Education and learning contribute not just to livelihood and marketable skill but also nurture the sensibilities needed for human well-being. Education is the most important ingredient for socio-economic development without which the people of specially weaker sections, viz, scheduled castes, scheduled tribes, and vulnerable groups. As such education helps to build capabilities that promote just and equitable social and political arrangements.

Articles 21, 21A, 41 and 45 read together enjoin the same. In the world nations, ours is identified as the biggest democratic country. Our culture, our civilization and our social values are attendant with our democratic values. In such a fair democracy it is not a wrong to anticipate educational equality irrespective of social inequality.

In the world's largest democracies it is natural to hope for equal educational opportunities. In spite of attaining 74.04% literacy it is a disturbing fact that still a vast majority of people in India are illiterate. If the problem had been tackled right from the early years of our independence, it would not have assumed this much magnitude, what vociferous groups say. But some others say that it is economic slow down.

The economic slow down did not spare many countries, yet let us compare with our neighboring countries like Sri Lanka, China, Taiwan and Singapore which are forward in education than India. Nevertheless our government showed interest even now and brought out enactment as "Right to Education Act" making the elementary education as free and compulsory for our children between 6 to 14 age group. Unfortunately this Act is not being enforced so strictly as it is designed for education. It is an unforgettable fact that education is linked up with integrity and development of the country.

Education, as one of the important social indicators, is directly linked with social and economic development of a society. Despite its importance, education continues to be a neglected area at the policy-formulation level. Even after 65 years of planning and providing enormous funding, achievement of total literacy remains a distant dream. Due to low level of literacy at the national level, disparities existing across regions, inclusive of gender-bias among various social segments is of a serious concern. Education is recognized as a basic input for empowerment of the individual and overall development of the society. As such, Elementary Education has become a fundamental right under Article 21, 21(A) of the Indian Constitution (86th Amendment) Act 2002, RTE ACT came into force from 01.04.2010.

The Right to Education Act ensures access to education for children from weaker sections and disadvantaged groups. The main objectives of the act are to be achieved for universalisation of elementary education in a short period of time as follows:

- To enroll the non-enrolled children
- To stop the dropout rate from the school
- To provide infrastructural facilities
- To maintain pupil - teacher ratio
- Providing quality education
- Achieving 100 % school enrolment and retention
- Providing girl child education
- Capacitating teachers to be effective as facilitators of learning
- Promoting culture of reading
- Equipping children with skills for life
- Providing conducive learning environment
- Community participation that support learning.

Presently the major problem is private schools Vs Government schools. Today we are facing a great problem that schools run by the private people, challenging the government schools are bringing down the standard of education in government schools as observed by PRATHAM (2011) report and declared in their annual reports and in consequence the poorest of the poor, Scheduled Castes, Scheduled Tribes and female children are remaining the sufferers.

The private investors could understand that education is the better business to earn profits in multiways on the name of various fees like building fee, identity cards, Mid-day Meal, Hostel Facilities, Uniforms including shoes which all yield greater profits to these commercial minded people.

A number of private schools, in the name of quality education which is in most cases a dubious claim-fleece the parents under one guise or the other. With attractive names like Concept schools, Indo-American schools they have successfully transformed education, into one resounding financially successful business. When their claims are aided by mind boggling publicity stunts, it is natural that even parents who can't afford them to join the children into these schools. In the name of providing quality of education by the dubious private schools exploiting the parents and the government and they will take the law into their hands.

Therefore the "Right to Education Act 2009" is to be enforced strictly for which everyone in the country should work for the same as laws do not make the children go to school.

The tender minded children prone to surprise and feel pleasure to see the natural gifts of rain and rainbow and indulge themselves in overwhelming rejoicement are really expected to be great minds in course of their growth. But we have to feel sorry about their plight to become slaves in the mighty hands as bonded child labour and slavery and suffering from hunger and illiteracy without their due prosperity.

In fact, a successful education policy forms the bedrock of all fields of national development, political, economic, technical, scientific, social and environmental. Education is the foundation for a vibrant democracy in which informed citizens exercise their franchise to support the internal growth of the nation and its constructive role in the world community. It is the foundation for growth in productivity, income and employment opportunities, and for the development, application and adaptation of science and technology to enhance the quality of life. Education is the foundation for access to the benefit of the information revolution that is opening up vistas in the whole world. Education is also the foundation for improved health care and nutrition.

Generally, at the start of a very young age, children learn to develop and use their mental, moral and physical powers, which they acquire through various types of education. Education is commonly referred to as the process of learning and obtaining knowledge at school, in a form of formal education. However, the process of education does not start only when a child first attends school. Education begins at home. One does not only acquire knowledge from a teacher; one can also learn and receive knowledge from a parent or a family member and even only an acquaintance. In almost all societies, attending school and receiving an education is extremely vital and necessary, if one wants to achieve success.

Education is important not only for the full development of one's personality, but also for the sustained growth of the nation. *Elementary education in India,* therefore, is the foundation stone on which the development of every citizen and the nation as a whole hinges. But making *primary education* available for all in India has also been one of the major challenges for the government. Moreover, the quality of elementary education in India has also been a major cause of worry for the government.

Elementary Education And Literacy: The role of eduction in facilitating social and economic progress is well recognized. It opens up opportunities leading to both individual and group entitlements. Education, in its broadest sense of development of youth, is the most crucial input for empowering people with skills and knowledge and giving them access to productive employment in future, improvements in education are not only expected to enhance efficiency but also augment the overall quality of life. The highest priority on education as a central instrument for achieving rapid and inclusive growth. It presents a comprehensive strategy for strengthening the education sector covering all segments of the education pyramid. Elementary education, that is, classes I-VIII consisting of primary (I-V) and upper primary

(VI-VIII) is the foundation of the pyramid in the education system and has received a major push through the Sarva Shiksha Abhiyan (SSA).

Elementary education in India means eight years of schooling from the age of six. The government has made elementary education compulsory and free. But, the goal of universal elementary education in India has been very difficult to attain till now. Therefore, we have to introduce innovative ways of universalizing elementary education in India.

Right from the beginning we have made a decent progress in several dimensions. In this regard we feel proud as we belong to India which has produced world class scientists, engineers, doctors, bureaucrats, politicians and journalists. And also we have sent satellites and rockets into space. And further we can say that we have increased average life expectancy from 30 to 65 years.

The opportunities offered are very limited. Sometimes, there are not enough resources to provide schooling. Furthermore, because parents need their children to help them to work in factories, do odd jobs, or just do farm work.

Education for Empowerment of Weaker Sections and Disadvantaged Groups

To 'empower' a person, literarily speaking is to give power to the person. Power here does not mean a mode of domination over others, but a sense of internal strength and confidence to face life. The real empowerment is defined as re-distribution of social, economic, political, power and control of resources in favour of weaker sections. As such elementary education is treated as a fundamental right.

Education and health are two important variables for individual development as well as social development. Privatization of education, privatization of health care and other liberalization policies are affecting people in this way.

Under these circumstances the small want to develop, they cannot develop. A small (poor) man wants to send his child to English medium school not government school (where large scale of absenteeism of teachers, a dim view of school system and also abysmal quality of education). English medium school and speaking in English fills elation in fathers, who are not educated. They want their children to be better than themselves in terms of educational status. So where to get money? and how to get money? is the problem of weaker and downtrodden.

There is equally convincing set of data to shows that we have a long way to go. Today, India is home to the largest number of illiterates in the world with over 300 million illiterate people as per statistics. When we compare with the other developed and developing countries, out of the 179 countries in the world, India stands 147th rank with 66 % literacy as per the 2009 statistics (Source: *United Nations Development Programme* (UNDP) report 2009). Even if we compare with our sister countries, China stands 83rd rank with 93.3 % whereas Sri Lanka occupies 94th rank with 90.8 % literacy, whereas our state concerned, Andhra Pradesh stands at 28th position with literacy of 67.66 % of the 35, states (28) and union territories (7).

India has about 574,000 primary schools (Classes I – V) and 156,000 upper primary schools (classes VI – VIII), with the number of teachers in them being 1705 million and 1082 million, respectively. The enrolment at the primary and upper primary stages is 109 million and 40 million, respectively. The Indian elementary education system is thus one of the biggest such systems in the world, providing accessibility within 1 km to over 825,000 habitations, covering 94 per cent of the country's population. During the past one decade, the enrolment rate has grown close to 100 per cent at the primary stage.

However, universalisation of elementary education (UEE) in its totality is still an elusive goal and much ground is yet to be covered. Drop-out rates continue to be high (36.3 per cent in classes I – V and 53 per cent in classes VI – VIII), with retention of children in schools being poor, achievement levels are low and wastage is considerable. Despite increased participation of girls, disparity still exists, more particularly among Scheduled Castes (SCs) and Scheduled Tribes (STs).

Despite all the efforts of the Government of India, Universalization of Elementary Education in India remains as of now a distant dream. This is because of the persistent poverty and various prejudices prevailing in the Indian society. While the female literacy is increasing at a faster rate than male literacy, the gap in the male and female literacy has been a major hindrance in the universalization of elementary education in India.

It can be seen that these differential rates of progress leave approximately 300 million illiterate adults in the country, among the largest number of illiterates in the world. By the Government estimate, out of 200 million children in the age-group of 6 to 14 in India, around 59 million do not attend school. Of the rest, who are currently in school, four out of every 10 children beginning to attend school will drop out before completing their primary school education. In addition, various studies of children's learning achievement indicate that the situation is actually grim.

That is why, so many Indian children, especially the rural poor, are out of school, as indicated by a number of recent studies, which help dispel two resilient myths that have tended to cloud official thinking and public debates on this subject, which explains the problem of educational deprivations in India.

1) Myth one is that Indian parents have little interest in education. It is the opinion of the close official circles in

rationalization of the State's failure to achieve universal elementary education. Further, to illustrate Probe Survey in which it is found that, in India's most educational backward States, the parents expressed that their children have to be educated as high as 98 per cent for boys and 89 per cent for girls. Only 3 per cent parents opposed compulsory education. And there is a consistency between parental aspirations and the constitutional goal of 8 years education for all children.

2) Myth two is that the economic dependence of poor families on child labour, is the primary reason, as so many children are still out of school. Contrary to this presumption, recent studies tell that large majority of out-of-school children do relatively little work. According to D.P. Choudary, children who are neither going to school, nor doing enough work to be counted as members of the labour force, while another recent case study of working children, they have nothing else to do, as the schools are not very attractive and teaching conditions are very poor.

The school hours in India are, in practice, quite short (about 4-6 hours a day for about half of the days in the year. If parents are interested in education, and if most children have enough spare time to attend the school, there is consistency between parental aspirations and Constitutional goal of eight-year education for all children (universal primary education).

In answering this question, the first point to note is that sending a child to a school on regular basis demands a lot of effort, time and attention, e.g., to prepare a child for school in the morning stimulates his or her interest, help him or her with home work and establishes rapport with teacher. In many respects, these efforts are much more in demand for unprivileged families, especially, when the children are first-generation-school-goers.

At a time when there is a great deal of buzz about India taking off as a "knowledge-based economy and society," Prime Minister Manmohan Singh's admission that the dropout rate in schools continues to be "high" is honest recognition that, even after Independence, the socio-political system has failed to ensure that at least a majority of children between the ages of 6 and 14 are in school, instead of making up the world's largest child labour force. If 53 per cent and 34 per cent of children enrolled in Class I do not complete Class VIII and Class X, respectively. This is powerful evidence of the inability of the Indian democratic and State system to come up with ways and means meaningfully to implement Article 21 (A) of the Constitution, which confers on the citizen the fundamental right to free and compulsory education between ages 6 and 14.

The cess introduced to fund the "Sarva Shiksha Abhiyan" programme is certainly a significant step forward. However, political India needs to move towards a deeper conceptual appreciation of the imperative of compulsory and free school education, if the goal of universal elementary education is to be reached in conceivable future, says the Prime Minister in his exhaustive work on child labour, literacy, and school education in India.

Such a far-going legal change at the national level would put tremendous pressure on the supply side, the glaring weaknesses of which the Prime Minister highlighted, when he spoke of "the lack of adequate facilities, large-scale absenteeism of teachers, and inadequate supervision by local authorities". It would require the State to put its money and other ways and means, where its mouth is. It would mean the Centre, the States, and Panchayati Raj institutions together guarantee the infrastructural and teaching facilities and the learning environment so vital to the realization of the right and duty encapsulated in Articles 21 (A) and 45.

In fact, the budget allocations belie all such expectations. To make elementary education a fundamental right, "the surest way of ensuring rapid inclusive growth", as stated by the Prime Minister, Manmohan Singh, in the 80th Annual General Body Meeting of the Federation of Indian Chambers of Commerce and Industry on February 15, 2008 and the Union Government might take on all the financial responsibility of the Bill which is estimated to be as high as Rs 12.5 billion a year.

There are two major Central Schemes in elementary education, which are the Sarva Shiksha Abhiyan (SSA), launched by the Government of India in 2000, as the single largest holistic programme addressing all aspects of elementary education and as a time-bound scheme for realizing the goals of universalisation of elementary education and the national programme of mid-day meals in schools. The two schemes together account for 97 per cent of the total allocation made for elementary education in 2008-09, which constituted 84 per cent of the Tenth Plan expenditure on elementary education.

Chapterisation

The study spread over Six chapters as follows:

Chapter-1: Introduction, profile of the study area and statement of the problem.

Chapter-2: Review of literature.

Chapter-3: Methodology and Objectives

Chapter-4: Interviews with Respondents

Chapter-5: Results & Analysis.

Chapter-6: Summary of Results, Suggestions and Conclusions.

Statement of the Problem

The bulk of Indian illiterates live in the country's rural, tribal and slum areas in big cities, where social and economic barriers play an important role in keeping the lowest strata of society illiterate. Government programmes alone, however well intentioned, may not be able to dismantle barriers built over centuries.

Since Independence so many committees and commissions were appointed and also conducted various seminars, workshops, interactions, debates have been conducted, still going on. But we have not achieved even after lapse of 65 years of Independence it has become an elusive goal for the nation in the attainment of Universalisation of Elementary Education. In this backdrop the Government of India passed a historical bill, now the education has become fundamental right to everyone. They took initiative to plan powerful, prosperous and intelligent Bharat. Though the bill is enacted late, it is right step in a right direction at a right moment. *But the bill does not make the children go to school.*

The basic education is input channel for higher education. Without a vibrant basic education system, we will not have a sound university education system. So the elementary education system is very important for higher learning and better quality of society or human resources.

The really critical aspect of the Indian public education system is its low quality. Even in educationally advanced States, an unacceptably low proportion of children who complete all grades of primary school have functional literacy. Moreover, the quality of 'literates' of the school system is very low. The actual quantity of schooling that children experience and the quality of teaching they receive are extremely insufficient to any mastery of basic literacy and numeric skills. This seems to be true of both the educationally more advanced States as well as the educationally backward ones.

India has made strides in educating its population of more than a billion people, yet a lot remains to be done. It is commonplace now that education is both intrinsically valuable and also instrumental for economic well-being, and this is true for individuals and entire nations. No country has been able to develop without the spread of mass education. An educated population is a prerequisite for take-off into a period of sustained high growth.

Here the main targets of the study are backward areas, tribal areas and weaker sections of society which have become

The researcher interacted with the children in a class room but the problem is all the children from Ist class-Vth class are in the same room and there is no teacher.

The picture shows that there is no teacher out of two (both were absent) in the class room during visit of researcher at Rama Krishna Beach, Visakhapatnam, A.P.

The researcher is interacting with the teacher while the children are sitting in the class

The students are wishing the researcher while he entered the class. The teacher is seen at the right

The school was with dilapidated railway-bungalow-tiles. It appears that at any moment, the tiles may fall on the children

However the quality of mid-day meal is not up to the mark as it is a case of low caloried food served owing to various problems

During the school hours there are neither students nor teachers at school, (Pallam Bakam mandal Vizianagaram district). But all the doors and windows that are kept open for public misuse

This is the school occupied by the local sadhus in Chinthapall Mandalam, Visakhapatnam district, A.P.

A couple of boys in a spree to plough the Land

A 11 yrs non-school going girl who is collecting groundnut in the field in scorching heat. However there is a fear that for girl's modesty to be outraged as she is half naked because of poverty

The above children dressed with Gandhi's appearance covered with dangerous silver coating which leads to skin cancer and other allied diseases as exposed to scorching heat during the day light and suffering miserably as well as shortening their life expectancy

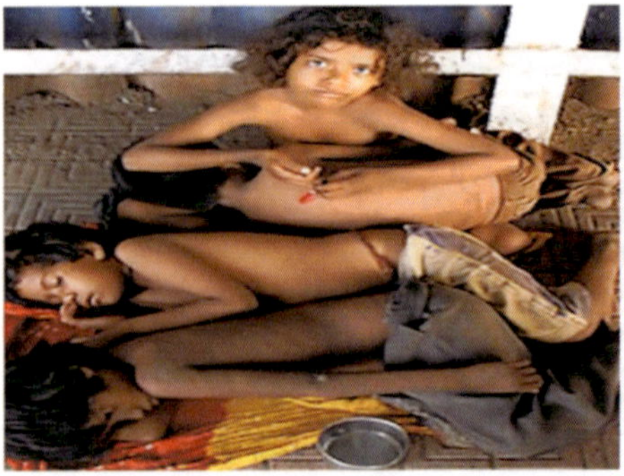

Four street children sleeping on the open road side

A group of boys sitting on the rail track, smoking narcotics, one after another. In other words they are on the death track prone to train accidents. The railway staff fails to rescue them and make efforts to admit them in the schools

Stray children on the route to begging instead of finding their way to be good citizens of the country

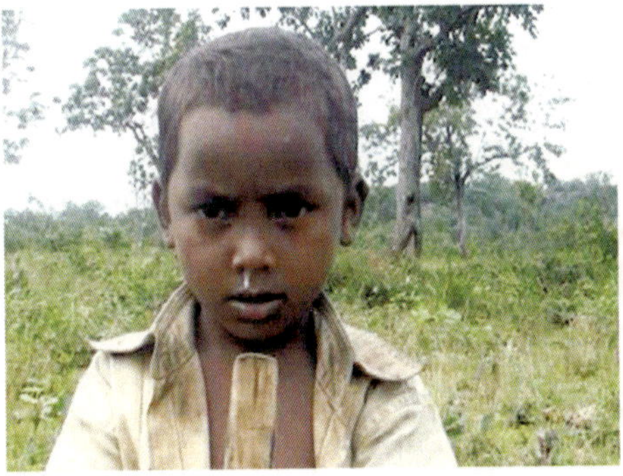

The non-enrolled tribal boy in the age-group of 4-5 years suffering from nose running, not knowing how to clean his nostrils. Researcher analyses his future that his life remains the same till his last breath

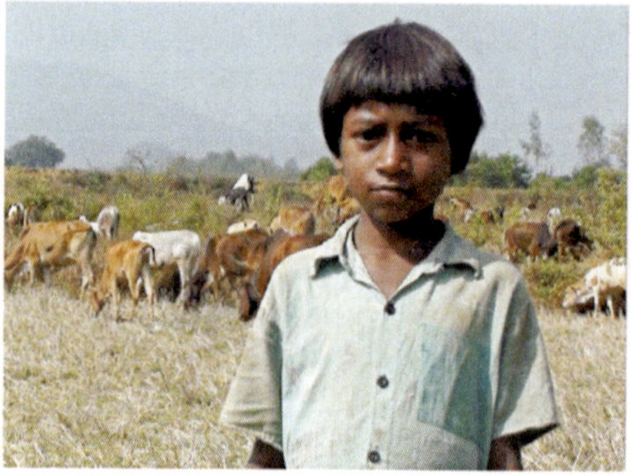

A 11 years non-enrolled rural one watching cow herd looking after a cattle who does not know basically of free education

A tribal starving boy is helplessly sitting in a melancholy condition not having food and scope to go to school

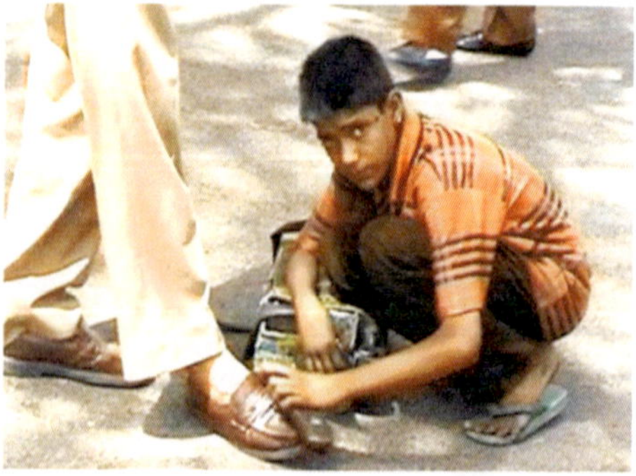

Another boy can be seen polishing shoes for livelihood

The boys are cleaning the buffaloes instead of going to school

A group of children both girls and boys are inevitably driven to work in the field due to poverty

All the above girls are daughters of a drunken father of whom two are dropped out from the school the others are absentees consequently. Besides the teachers of the concerned school are disinterested to take back them to the school. (to enroll the non en-rolled, RTE Act does not work out)

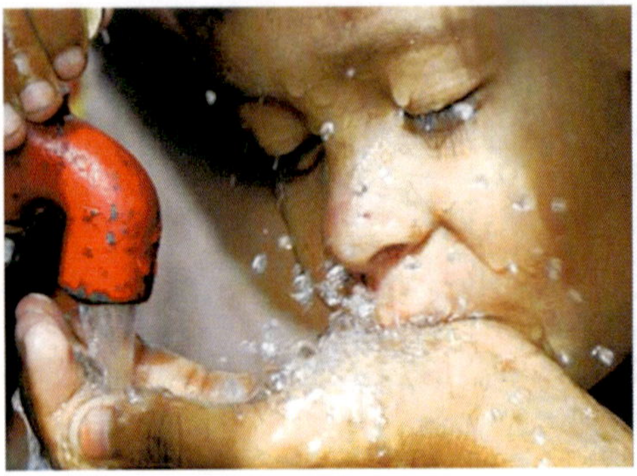

Boy sequence the tap water

Couple of girls are begging in spite of pouring heavy rain

Children are begging with monkeys

victims of illiteracy, hunger and they have become victims of exploitation and social insecurity and also they are crying for food, shelter, clothing, health and medicine. Therefore, illiteracy is the root cause of all these problems.

But there are many inequalities in educational achievement between men and women, between rural and urban and between different social segments. In 1960 the Kotari Commission recommended egalitarian system of education which is termed common schooling system to atleast reduce educational inequalities, which still remain as a dream. For unprivileged poor people government schools are the resorts ailing with low quality education.

Educational Scenario of India and Andhra Pradesh

At the outset, regarding literacy rate there has been a quantum jump from 1901 to 2011, 5.35% to 74.04% respectively. But we still have a long way to go. And we must march ahead. In this regard a brief discussion is given below.

India's effective literacy rate has recorded 9.2 per cent rise to reach 74.04 per cent in the past 10 years, according to provisional data of the 2011 census. Interestingly, literacy rate improved sharply among females as compared to males. While the effective literacy rate for males rose from 75.26 to 82.14 per cent marking a rise of 6.9 per cent, it increased by 11.8 per cent for females to go from 53.67 to 65.46 per cent. According to provisional totals of the latest census, literates constitute 74 per cent of total population aged seven and above. Presently the Indian population (2011) about 121,01,93,422 out of which 77,84,54,120 are literates with 74.04%, out of which the male population is 62,37,74,248 out of which 44,42,03,62 literates with percentage of 82.14, whereas the female population (2011) in India is 58,64,69,174 out of which 32,42,50,358 literates with percentage of 65.46. Interestingly, female literacy level saw a significant jump as compared to males 'between' 2001-2011. The gender gap of literacy, between male and female is 16.68% (2011).

As per the 2011 statistics more than one-fourth of India's population still continues to be illiterate. About one-third of our women can not still read or write. The number of illiterates in India is probably the highest among all nations of the world. Persistent illiteracy, particularly among women, scheduled castes, scheduled tribes, minorities and other disadvantaged groups, is a challenge that India must face and meet ahead on.

Number of Literates & Literacy Rate in India 2011

	India		
All	*Population*	*Literates*	*Lit. Rate*
Total	1,21,01,93,422(2011)	77,84,54,120	74.04
Male	62,37,24,248(2011)	44,42,03,762	82.14
Female	58,64,69,174(2011)	33,42,50,358	65.46
Gender Gap	37,255,074	10,99,53,404	16.68

Crude Literacy Rate in India from 1901 to 2011

Census Year	*Total (%)*	*Male (%)*	*Female (%)*
1901	5.35	9.83	0.60
1911	5.92	10.56	1.05
1921	7.16	12.21	1.81
1931	9.5	15.59	2.93
1941	16.1	24.9	7.3
1951	16.67	24.95	9.45
1961	24.02	34.44	12.95
1971	29.45	39.45	18.69
1981	36.23	46.89	24.82
1991	42.84	52.74	32.17
2001	64.83	75.26	53.67
2011	74.04	82.14	65.46

Since Independence, the literacy rate has grown from 16.67 per cent in 1951, to 28.30 per cent in 1961, 29.45 per cent in 1971, 36.23 in 1981, 42.84 per cent in 1991, 64.83 in 2001 and 74.04 per cent in 2011. During the same period, the population grew from 361 million to 1,210 million.

Ranking of States and Union Territories by Literacy Rate*

*The State of Andhra Pradesh stands at 31st Rank in Literacy out of 35 States (28) & Union Territories (7).

Rank	*State/U.T.*	*Literacy Rate*	*Male Literacy Rate*	*Female Literacy Rate*
	1	*2*	*3*	*4*
1	Kerala	93.9%	96.0%	92.0%
2	Lakshadweep	92.3%	96.1%	88.2%
3	Mizoram	91.6%	93.7%	89.4%
4	Tripura	87.8%	92.2%	83.1%
5	Goa	87.4%	92.8%	81.8%
6	Daman & Diu	87.1%	91.5%	79.6%
7	Puducherry	86.5%	92.1%	81.2%
8	Chandigarh	86.4%	90.5%	81.4%
9	NCT of Delhi	86.3%	91.0%	80.9%
10	Andaman & Nicobar Islands	86.3%	90.1%	81.8%
11	Himachal Pradesh	83.8%	90.8%	76.6%
12	Maharashtra	82.9%	89.8%	75.5%
13	Sikkim	82.2%	87.3%	76.4%
14	Tamil Nadu	80.3%	86.8%	73.9%
15	Nagaland	80.1%	83.3%	76.7%
16	Manipur	79.8%	86.5%	73.2%
17	Uttarakhand	79.6%	88.3%	70.7%
18	Gujarat	79.3%	87.2%	70.7%
19	Dadra & Nagar Haveli	77.7%	86.5%	65.9%
20	West Bengal	77.1%	82.7%	71.2%
21	Punjab	76.7%	81.5%	71.3%
22	Haryana	76.6%	85.4%	66.8%
23	Karnataka	75.6%	82.8%	68.1%
24	Meghalaya	75.5%	77.2%	73.8%

Contd...

	1	2	3	4
25	Orissa	73.5%	82.4%	64.4%
26	Assam	73.2%	78.8%	67.3%
27	Chattisgarh	71.0%	81.5%	60.6%
28	Madhya Pradesh	70.6%	80.5%	60.0%
29	Uttar Pradesh	69.7%	79.2%	59.3%
30	Jammu and Kashmir	68.7%	78.3%	58.0%
31	**Andhra Pradesh**	**67.7%**	**75.6%**	**59.7%**
32	Jharkhand	67.6%	78.5%	56.2%
33	Rajasthan	67.1%	80.5%	52.7%
34	Arunachal Pradesh	67.0%	73.7%	59.6%
35	Bihar	63.8%	73.5%	53.3%

Source: 2011 Census Government of India.

Ranking of States and Union Territories by literacy rate: 2001 & 2011

Rank	*Persons India/State/Union Territory*	*(2001 Census) Literacy Rate*
	1	*2*
1	Kerala	90.92
2	Mizoram	88.49
3	Lakshadweep (U.T.)	87.52
4	Goa	82.32
5	Delhi (U.T.)	81.82
6	Chandigarh (U.T.)	81.76
7	Pondicherry (U. T.)	81.49
8	Andaman & Nicobar (U.T.)	81.18
9	Daman & Diu (U.T.)	81.09
10	Maharashtra	77.27
11	Himachal Pradesh	77.13
12	Tripura	73.66
13	Tamil Nadu	73.47

Contd...

14	Uttaranchal	72.28
15	Gujarat	69.97
16	Punjab	69.95
17	Sikkim	69.68
18	West Bengal	69.22
19	Manipur	68.87
20	Haryana	68.59
21	Nagaland	67.11
22	Karnataka	67.04
23	Chhatisgarh	65.18
24	Assam	64.28
25	Madhya Pradesh	64.11
26	Orissa	63.61
27	Meghalaya	63.31
28	**Andhra Pradesh**	**61.11**
29	Rajasthan	61.03
30	Dadra & Nagar Haveli (U.T.)	60.03
31	Uttar Pradesh	57.36
32	Arunachal Pradesh	54.74
33	Jammu & Kashmir	54.46
34	Jharkhand	54.13
35	Bihar	47.53

Rank	*Persons 2011* *India/State/Union Territory*	*(2011 Census)* *Literacy Rate*
	1	*2*
1	Kerala	93.9%
2	Lakshadweep	92.3%
3	Mizoram	91.6%
4	Tripura	87.8%
5	Goa	87.4%
6	Daman & Diu	87.1%
7	Puducherry	86.5%
8	Chandigarh	86.4%

Contd...

	1	*2*
9	NCT of Delhi	86.3%
10	Andaman & Nicobar Islands	86.3%
11	Himachal Pradesh	83.8%
12	Maharashtra	82.9%
13	Sikkim	82.2%
14	Tamil Nadu	80.3%
15	Nagaland	80.1%
16	Manipur	79.8%
17	Uttarakhand	79.6%
18	Gujarat	79.3%
19	Dadra & Nagar Haveli	77.7%
20	West Bengal	77.1%
21	Punjab	76.7%
22	Haryana	76.6%
23	Karnataka	75.6%
24	Meghalaya	75.5%
25	Orissa	73.5%
26	Assam	73.2%
27	Chattisgarh	71.0%
28	Madhya Pradesh	70.6%
29	Uttar Pradesh	69.7%
30	Jammu and Kashmir	68.7%
31	**Andhra Pradesh**	**67.7%**
32	Jharkhand	67.6%
33	Rajasthan	67.1%
34	Arunachal Pradesh	67.0%
35	Bihar	63.8%

The literacy rate has further dropped down to Ranking from 28th in 2001 to 31st in 2011 out of 35 States and Union Territories even in RTE Act in implementation stage.

Male and Female and Rural and Urban Literacy Rate (2011 Census)

Literacy rate in India has risen dramatically from 18 per cent in 1951 to 74.04 per cent in 2011. The male literacy rate is 82.1 per cent, while the female literacy rate is 65.46 per cent. Another area of concern is to reduce the gap between the rural and urban literacy rate. While 85.0 per cent urban people are literate, only 68.9 per cent of the rural population is literate, according to 2011 census data. But, these rates are still far from expectations.

Improvement in female literacy is more than males in both rural and urban areas. The gender gap in literacy has come down from 24.6 in 2001 to 19.8 in 2011 in rural areas and from 13.4 in 2001 to 9.8 in 2011 in urban areas. The improvement in literacy rate in rural area is two times that in urban areas. The rural urban literacy gap which was 21.2 percentage points in 2001, has come down to 16.1 percentage points in 2011.

Data Highlights- Census of 2011

Literacy Rate (in %)

	2001	*2011*	*Difference*
Overall			
India	64.8	74.0	+9.2
Rural	58.7	68.9	+10.2
Urban	79.9	85.0	+5.1

Male & Female Literacy Rate (in %)

	2001	*2011*	*Difference*
Males			
India	75.3	82.1	+6.8
Rural	70.7	78.6	+7.9
Urban	86.3	89.7	+3.4
Females			
India	53.7	65.5	+11.8
Rural	46.1	58.8	+12.7
Urban	72.9	79.9	+7.0

World Scenario of World Literacy Rate by Ranking

As per the UNDP report 2009 of 179 countries India stands 134th Rank

Many high-income countries, having attained high levels of literacy, no longer collect basic literacy statistics and thus are not included in the United Institute for Statistics (UIS) data.

#	Rank	Country	Literacy rate	
1	1	Georgia	100.0	
2	2	Cuba	99.9	
3	3	Estonia	99.8	
4	4	Latvia	99.8	
5	5	Barbados	99.7	[j]
6	6	Slovenia	99.7	[l]
7	7	Belarus	99.7	
8	8	Lithuania	99.7	
9	9	Ukraine	99.7	
10	10	Armenia	99.7	
11	11	Kazakhstan	99.6	
12	12	Tajikistan	99.6	
13	13	Azerbaijan	99.5	
14	14	Turkmenistan	99.5	
15	15	Russia	99.5	
16	16	Hungary	99.4	[j]
17	17	Kyrgyzstan	99.3	
18	17	Poland	99.5	[j]
19	19	Tonga	99.2	
20	20	Albania	99.1	
21	20	Antigua and Barbuda	99.0	[q]
22	20	Australia	99.0	[d]
23	20	Austria	99.0	[d]
24	20	Belgium	99.0	[d]

Contd...

#	*Rank*	*Country*	*Literacy rate*	
25	20	Canada	99.0	[d]
26	20	Czech Republic	99.0	[d]
27	20	North Korea	99.0	[d]
28	20	Denmark	99.0	[d]
29	20	Finland	99.0	[d]
30	20	France	99.0	[d]
31	20	Germany	99.0	[d]
32	20	Guyana	99.0	[j]
33	20	Iceland	99.0	[d]
34	20	Ireland	99.0	[d]
35	20	Japan	99.0	[d]
36	20	South Korea	99.0	[d]
37	20	Luxembourg	99.0	[d]
38	20	Netherlands	99.0	[d]
39	20	New Zealand	99.0	[d]
40	20	Norway	99.0	[d]
41	20	Slovakia	99.0	[d]
42	20	Sweden	99.0	[d]
43	20	Switzerland	99.0	[d]
44	20	United Kingdom	99.0	[d]
45	20	United States See also: Literacy in the United States	99.0	[d]
46	46	Italy	98.9	
47	47	Samoa	98.8	[l]
48	48	Croatia	98.8	
49	49	Trinidad and Tobago	98.7	[l]
50	50	Uruguay	98.3	
51	51	Bulgaria	98.3	
52	52	Spain	97.9	[d]
53	53	Cyprus	97.9	
54	54	Bosnia and Herzegovina	97.8	
55	55	Serbia	97.8	

Contd...

#	*Rank*	*Country*	*Literacy rate*	
56	56	Saint Kitts and Nevis	97.8	[k]
57	57	Romania	97.7	
58	58	Argentina	97.7	
59	59	Mongolia	97.5	
60	60	Greece	97.2	
61	61	Israel	97.1	[k]
62	62	Macedonia	97.1	
63	63	Maldives	97.0	
64	64	Uzbekistan	96.9	[j]
65	65	Chile	96.5	
66	66	Costa Rica	96.1	
67	67	Grenada	96.0	[q]
68	68	China	95.9	[k]
69	69	Bahamas	95.8	[j]
70	70	Venezuela	95.2	
71	71	Brunei Darussalam	95.3	
72	72	Portugal	94.9	[l]
73	73	Saint Lucia	94.8	[q]
74	74	Qatar	94.7	
75	75	Singapore	94.7	
76	76	Hong Kong	94.6	[j]
77	77	Palestinian Authority	94.6	[p]
78	78	Paraguay	94.6	[l]
79	79	Kuwait	94.5	
80	80	Fiji	94.4	[j]
81	81	Sri Lanka	94.2	[w]
82	82	Thailand	94.1	
83	83	Panama	93.6	
84	84	Philippines	93.4	
85	85	Mexico	93.4	
86	86	Equatorial Guinea	93.3	
87	87	Colombia	93.2	

Contd...

#	*Rank*	*Country*	*Literacy rate*	
88	88	Vietnam	92.8	
89	89	Malaysia	92.5	
90	90	Malta	92.4	
91	91	Indonesia	92.0	
92	92	Myanmar	92.0	
93	93	Zimbabwe	91.9	[l]
94	94	Seychelles	91.8	
95	95	Bahrain	91.4	
96	96	Jordan	91.1	
97	97	Ecuador	91.0	
98	98	Turkey	90.8	
99	99	Bolivia	90.7	
100	100	Suriname	90.4	
101	101	United Arab Emirates	90.0	[l]
102	102	Brazil	90.0	
103	103	Lesotho	89.7	
104	104	Peru	89.6	
105	105	Lebanon	89.6	[j]
106	106	Dominican Republic	89.1	
107	107	Libya	88.9	
108	108	Sao Tome and Principe	88.8	
109	109	Namibia	88.5	
110	110	Saint Vincent and the Grenadines	88.1	[q]
111	111	Dominica	88.0	[q]
112	112	South Africa	88.0	
113	113	Mauritius	87.9	
114	114	Gabon	87.7	
115	115	Kenya	87.0	
116	116	Swaziland	86.9	
117	117	Jamaica	86.4	
118	118	Saudi Arabia	86.1	

Contd...

#	Rank	Country	Literacy rate	
119	119	Cape Verde	84.8	[l]
120	120	Syria	84.2	
121	121	Ecuador	84.2	
122	122	Botswana	84.1	
123	123	El Salvador	84.1	
124	124	Honduras	83.6	
125	125	Iran	82.3	
126	126	Oman	81.4	
127	127	Republic of the Congo	81.1	[l]
128	128	Vanuatu	80.2	
129	129	Iraq	78.1	
130	130	Nicaragua	78.0	
131	131	Tunisia	77.7	
132	132	Solomon Islands	76.6	[k]
133	133	Cambodia	76.3	
134	134	Algeria	75.4	
135	135	Belize	75.1	[q]
136	136	Guatemala	74.5	
*137	137	India	74.04	[2]
138	138	Comoros	74.2	
139	139	Malawi	73.7	
140	140	Uganda	73.3	
141	141	Tanzania	72.9	
142	142	Nigeria	72.0*	[l]
143	143	Zambia	70.9	
144	144	Madagascar	70.7	
145	145	Rwanda	70.7	
146	146	Djibouti	70.3	[j]
147	147	Sudan	70.2	[aa]
148	148	Angola	70.0	
149	149	Laos	68.7	
150	150	Nepal	68.2	

Contd...

#	Rank	Country	Literacy rate	
151	151	Cameroon	67.9	
152	152	Democratic Republic of the Congo	66.8	
153	153	Eritrea	66.6	
154	154	Ghana	66.6	
155	155	Burundi	66.6	
156	156	Egypt	66.4	
157	157	Yemen	62.4	[l]
158	158	Haiti	62.1	[j]
159	159	Papua New Guinea	60.1	
160	160	Pakistan	58.2	
161	161	Mauritania	57.5	
162	162	Morocco	56.1	
163	163	Bangladesh	55.9	
164	164	Côte d'Ivoire	55.3	
165	165	Central African Republic	55.2	
166	166	Mozambique	55.1	
167	167	Togo	53.2	
168	168	Bhutan	52.8	[v]
169	169	Guinea-Bissau	52.2	
170	170	Timor-Leste	50.1	[ab]
171	171	Senegal	49.7	
172	172	Gambia	46.5	[j]
173	173	Benin	41.7	
174	174	Sierra Leone	40.9	
175	175	Guinea	39.5	
176	176	Ethiopia	35.9	
177	177	Chad	33.6	
178	178	Burkina Faso	28.7	
179	179	Niger	28.7	
180	180	Afghanistan	28.0	
181	181	South Sudan	27.0	
182	182	Mali	26.2	

Source: United Nations Development Programme Report, 2009.

District-wise Literacy Rate of Andhra Pradesh - 2011 census

District	*Persons*	*Males*	*Females*	*Literacy %*	*Male %*	*Female %*
1	*2*	*3*	*4*	*5*	*6*	*7*
Total	*51438510*	*28759782*	*22678728*	*67.66%*	*75.56%*	*59.74%*
Adilabad	1503106	864990	638116	61.55%	71.22%	51.99%
Nizamabad	1421759	809721	612038	62.25%	72.66%	52.33%
Karimnagar	2263247	1292858	970389	64.87%	74.72%	55.18%
Medak	1677732	975710	702022	62.53%	72.50%	52.49%
Hyderabad	2906923	1540195	1366728	80.96%	83.35%	78.42%
Rangareddy	3669033	2018557	1650476	78.05%	84.00%	71.82%
Mahbubnagar	1984586	1183860	800726	56.06%	66.27%	45.65%
Nalgonda	2035177	1178956	856221	65.05%	74.93%	55.05%
Warangal	2116037	1211953	904084	66.16%	75.91%	56.45%
Khammam	1656686	918880	737806	65.46%	73.20%	57.85%
*Srikakulam	1516425	870196	646229	62.30%	72.25%	52.56%
*Vizianagaram	1256342	720623	535719	59.49%	69.04%	50.16%
*Visakhapatnam	2612624	1450555	1162069	67.70%	75.47%	60.00%
East Godavari	3324111	1737357	1586754	71.35%	74.91%	67.82%
West Godavari	2654267	1380713	1273554	74.32%	77.63%	71.05%
Krishna	3065669	1630049	1435620	74.37%	79.13%	69.62%
Guntur	3006999	1660019	1346980	67.99%	75.40%	60.64%
Prakasam	1926495	1122249	804246	63.53%	73.53%	53.40%
Sri Potti Sriramulu Nellore	1852239	1021639	830600	69.15%	75.93%	62.30%
Y.S.R.	1745178	1012105	733073	67.88%	78.41%	57.26%
Kurnool	2182149	1279938	902211	61.13%	71.36%	50.81%
Anantapur	2350294	1365701	984593	64.28%	74.09%	54.31%
Chittoor	2711432	1512958	1198474	72.36%	81.15%	63.65%

Source: 2011 Census Government of India. *Study Area of North coastal Andhra Pradesh.

Educational Scenario of Andhra Pradesh

As far as the Andhra Pradesh is concerned which stands at 28th Rank when compared to other states and Union Terrioties. In this backdrop, there is no doubt moderate increase in literacy rate between 2001 to 2011 from 60.47% to 67.66% respectively, out of which the males are 23,444,788 with the percentage of 70.32 whereas in 2011 the total male literates population is 28,759,782 with the percentage 75.56. At the same time the female literates are 16,489,535 with the percentage of 50.43 in 2001 and whereas as per the 2011 statistics the female literates are 22,678,728 with the percentage of 59.74. The gender gap between the male and females is 19.89 in the year of 2011, whereas the same gender gap is 15.82 in 2011 census. However the gender gap is dramatically reduced or minimized between male to female literacy rate.

Some of the Keywords, the Right of Children to Free and Compulsory Education Act, 2009

1. *Child:* A male or female child of the age of six to fourteen years.
2. *Teacher:* A person who teaches in a school. The teacher is a dynamic force of the school. There is no greater need for the cause of education today than the need for strong manly men and motherly women as teachers for the young. As social engineers, the teachers can socialize and humanize the young by their man-like qualities.
3. *School:* An institution for educating children. Any recognized school imparting elementary education and includes
   i) A school established, owned or controlled by the appropriate Government or a local authority
   ii) An aided school receiving aid or grants to meet whole or part of its expenses from the appropriate government or the local authority

iii) A school belonging to specified category; and An unaided school not receiving any kind of aid or grants to meet its expenses from the appropriate Government or the local authority.

4. *Parent:* Either the natural or step or adoptive father or mother of a child.

5. *Guardian:* In relation to a child, means a person having the care and custody of that child and includes a natural guardian or guardian appointed or declared by a court or a statute.

6. *Literacy:* Literacy as the "ability to identify, understand, interpret, create, communicate, compute and use printed and written materials associated with varying contexts. Literacy involves a continuum of learning in enabling individuals to achieve their goals, to develop their knowledge and potential, and to participate fully in their community and wider society." (UNESCO). Literacy as acquiring the skills of reading, writing and arithmetic and the ability to apply them to one's day-to-day life. The achievement of functional literacy implies (i) self-reliance in 3 R's, (ii) awareness of the causes of deprivation and the ability to move towards amelioration of their condition by participating in the process of development, (iii) acquiring skills to improve economic status and general well-being, and (iv) imbibing values such as national integration, conservation of environment, women's equality, observance of small family norms (National Literacy Mission).

7. *Crude literacy rate:* The total percentage of the people of an area at a particular time aged seven years or above who can read and write with understanding, taking the total population of the area (including below seven years of age) as the denominator.

8. *Elementary education :* The education from first class to eighth class.

9. *Universalisation of elementary Education (UEE):* The term univeralisation includes universal enrolment, universal retention and universal achievement and equity, acceptable level of reading, writing and arithmetic.

10. *Compulsory Education:* Obligation of the appropriate Government to provide free elementary education to every child of the age of six to fourteen years; and ensure compulsory admission, attendance and completion of elementary education by every child of the age of six to fourteen years.

11. *Inclusive Education:* the objective of inclusiveness will be achieved through the following: reduction of regional imbalances; support to institutions located in border, hilly remote , small towns and educationally backward areas; support to institutions with larger student population of SCs, STc, OBCs, minorities, and physically challenged; support to the SCs, STc, OBCs minorities physically challenged, and girl students with special scholarship, hostel fecilities, remedial coaching, and other measures; setting up of an Equal Opportunity office'in all universities to bring all schemes relation to this group underone umbrella for effective implementation.

12. *Free "Elementary education:* The education from first class to eighth class.

13. *Provision for admission above six years child:* Where a child above six years of age has not been admitted in any school or though admitted, could not complete his or her elementary education, then, he or she shall be admitted in a class appropriate to his or her age.

14. *Provision for Completion of Elementary Education:* Where in a school, there is no provision for completion of elementary education, a child shall have a right to seek transfer to any other school, excluding the school specified in sub-clauses (iii) and (iv) of clause (n) of section 2, for completing his or her elementary education.

15. *Neighbourhood School:* The neighbourhood has been given a wide definition in the Model Rules of the Act. Ordinarily it is 1 km walking distance from the habitation of a child at the primary level and 3 km for upper primary level. However, in areas with sparse populations, or those prone to natural disasters or with difficult terrain or civil unrest, this limitation may be changed and transportation or residential facilities provided to children so that their education is not interrupted or disrupted.

16. *School Infrastructure:* A building with proper ventilation and lighting, a roof made of material that is poor conductor of heat, partition facility between classes, adequate furniture and required electrical fittings, drinking water facility, sanitation facility separately for boys, girls, and teachers, and a compound wall to ensure that common people do not misuse the school infrastructure for illegitimate purposes.

17. *Local Authority:* a Municipal Corporation or Municipal Council or Zilla Parishad or Nagar Panchayat or Panchayat, by whatever name called, and includes such other authority or body having administrative control over the school or empowered by or under any law for the time being in force to function as a local authority in any city, town or village.

18. *Child Labor:* "Child labor" is, generally speaking, work for children that harms them or exploits them in some way (physically, mentally, morally, or by blocking access to education).

19. *Street Children:* A street child is a child who lives on the streets of a city, deprived of family care and protection. Most children on the streets are between the ages of about 5 and 17 years old.

20. *Disadvantaged Group:* "Child belonging to disadvantaged group" means a child belonging to the Scheduled Caste, the Scheduled Tribe, the socially and educationally backward class or such other group having disadvantage owing to social, cultural, economical, geographical, linguistic, gender or such other factor, as may be specified by the appropriate Government, by notification.

21. *National Commission for Protection of Child Rights (NCPCR):* means the National Commission for Protection of Child Rights constituted under section 3 of the Commission for Protection of Child Right Act, 2005.

Some of the Government Progressive Programmes and Institutes in Making India Literate

In this backdrop the Government of India as well as State Government(s) are also working towards achieving total literacy in the next 10 years period. As the part of the commitment, Government has started a number of progressive programmes and legislations for the empowerment and welfare of the common person, the aam aadmi. The National Rural Employment Guarantee Scheme, the Right to Information Act, the Rural Health Mission, the Sarva Siksha Abhiyan and the National Mid-day Meal Programme are all efforts in that direction. Literacy is central to the success of all these programmes and initiatives. Therefore some of the progrmmes are being discussed.

1. The government is effectively implementing *Midday Meal Scheme* up to tenth to motivate the students to attend the school regularly.

2. Implementing *Sarva Siksha Abhiyan (SSA)* with aim of providing useful and relevant elementary education and

to improve infrastructure facilities in primary schools with constructions of school buildings, additional class rooms, recruitment of teachers etc.

3. *District Primary Education Programme (DPEP)* is centrally sponsored project aiming at improving the quality of primary education in the country. The project draws inspiration from the National Education Policy (NEP).
4. *Kendriya Vidyalaya Sangathan.*
5. *Navodaya Vidyalaya Samiti.*
6. *Kasturba Gandhi Balika Vidyalaya (KGBV).*
7. *Model schools* are being established to achieve qualitative change in primary schools.
8. To strengthen existing secondary schools new scheme called *Rastriya Madhyamika Siksha Abhiyan* is providing computers to schools to meet the growing demand for man power with the computer skills
9. NVEQF Schools.
10. Gurukula Patasala.
11. A new scheme called *Saakshar Bharat Mission 2012* is proposed to be implemented as a central sponsored scheme. The main focus of the programme is to eradicate illiteracy among women.

Midday Meal Scheme

The mid-day meals is the world's largest school feeding programme reaching out to about 12 crore children in 2.65 lakh schools across the country. Mid day meal in schools has had a long history in India. Tamil Nadu state was the pioneer of this scheme providing cooked meals to children. In 1923 a mid-day meal programme was introduced for disadvantaged children in Madras Municipal Corporation. By the mid 1980s three states, viz. Gujarat, Kerala and Tamil Nadu and the UT of Pondichery had universalised a cooked mid-day meal programme with a view to enhancing enrolment, retention and improve attendance and simultaneously improving nutritional levels to children. The national programme of nutritional support to Primary education (NP-NSPE) was launched as a Centre sponsored scheme on 25th August, 1995 with the twin objectives of increasing enrolment, retention and attendance rates in primary education and simultaneously improving the nutritional status of school going children. In 1995, it covered just 3.34 crore children in 3.22 lakh schools. In 2006-07, the number of children receiving meals was 12 crore in 9.5 lakh schools. *This is regarded as the world's largest school lunch programme.* The programme was extended to upper primary classes (VI-VIII) in 3,479 educationally backward blocks in October 2007. This was estimated to increase the coverage of children by 1.7 crore. One might expect this to have resulted in an increase in the actual (revised) budget expenditure over and above the budget allocation made for 2007-08. But, surprisingly, the revised budget expenditure (Rs. 6,678 crore) for the mid day meal scheme was less than the budget provision (Rs. 7,324 crore). In the current budget proposal, it is to be extended to cover all blocks in the country, i.e., to benefit additionally 2.5 crore children, in all, to cover 13.9 crore children. Will the small increase in allocation of resources to the scheme be adequate to meet the increasing numbers of children to be covered? On the whole, does the stagnation or even the likely real decline in the allocations to elementary education signal the end of the special priority accorded to elementary education in recent years in allocation of resources?

Implementation of Mid-day Meal Programme

The Mid-day meal programme is really boon for daily searching bread winner for all the parents of the children.

However, this scheme is implemented in only some areas like, in cities and plain areas, in some areas it is being periphery whereas it is not being properly and effectively implemented in tribal as well as remote rural areas. Therefore, the Mid-day meal scheme tends to be evaluated positively in terms of child growth. Most of the Indian children are struggling and suffering from (who are BPL), Malnutrition, and under nutrition. Though India has emerged as one of the most important rising global powers it also has one third of the world's under nourished children and one of the highest rate of child's under nutrition in the world. Therefore, it is needed a national nutrition strategy and further strengthen the programme of Mid-day meal. Besides, some financial support may be provided to the parents. Under BPL the right to food campaigns, a national food security acts makes important demands, but even if some of them are met they will need transparent monitoring of resources, and provide accountability of all stakeholders. However, the parents of the school children who are BPL shall be provided the following:

1) To further implementation of MGNREGP effectively and also funds may be further enhanced or increased for 100 days to 200 days employment. Now there has been a big debate is going on misuse of MGNREGP.

2) Make agriculture more pro-nutritional by focusing it more to people living in poverty.

3) Experiment with cash based alternatives to the parents.

4) Report community led approaches, sanitation and increase coverage of essential nutrition intervention in context of a stronger public health system.

5) Further strengthen adult continuing education for quality-wise.

While implementing the mid day meal programme various problems, evil kinds of practices are being taken such as corruption and mismanagement. The positive effects of mid day meals scheme are to arrest class room hunger and reducing social discrimination. Further the mid day meal programme has many benefits such as increasing involvement and attendance in schools especially of girl children. It has also large socialization and educational benefits. Accordingly to the observation of the study relating to mid-day meals scheme, in many places especially in rural and tribal areas not adequately serving mid day meals. During the serving of mid day meal the researcher found the quality of meal is under nutritious and low quality of calories, whereas in other schools the scheme is not at all being implemented. In some cases school authorities openly accepted showing higher attendance because of shortage of funds. It is also observed that the mid day meal programme is not properly monitoring about utilization of rice, stock register, which were filled at the end of the month without checking the actual number of children eating or the actual amount of rice cooked. Therefore the over all observation is that there is a mismatch between school attendance (supply of meals to the children) and actual physical presence of the children. Apart from the quality of food it is also not properly served to the children.

Sarva Siksha Abhiyan

Sarva Shiksha Abhiyan (SSA) forms the cornerstone of government interventions in basic education for all children. SSA, launched in November 2000 was to support and build on primary education in the country. The Sarva Siksha Abhiyan scheme is a boon to the rural, tribal and slum school children.

Sarva Siksha Abhiyan (SSA) is a Government of India's flagship programme for achievement of hundred percent in a time bound manner, as literacy mandated by 86th

Amendment in the constitution of India making free and Compulsory Education to the children of 6-14 years age group, a Fundamental Right. The programme seeks to open new schools in those habitations which do not have schooling facilities and strengthen existing school infrastructure, provision of additional class rooms, toilets, drinking water, maintenance grant of school improvement grants. SSA seeks to provide quality elementary education including life skills. SSA has a special focus on girl's education and children with special needs. SSA also seeks to provide computer education (to bridge the digital divide).

The Goals of SSA

1) A programme with a clear time frame for UEE.

2) A response to the demand for quality basic education with emphasis on education for life.

3) An opportunity for promoting social justice through basic education.

4) Effort at effectively involving the Panchayat Raj institution, School Management Committees, Village and Urban Slum level Education committees, Parents Teachers Association, *Mother Teacher* Universal retention by 2015 *Association.* Tribal Autonomous Councils etc.

5) An expression of political will for UEE.

6) A partnership between Central, State and Local Self Government.

7) An opportunity for states to develop their own vision of elementary education.

8) To provide useful and relevant elementary education for all the children in the age group of 6-14 and to improve infrastructure facilities in elementary schools

with construction of school building, additional class rooms, compound wall, toilets, specially for girls etc.

9) Bridge all gender and social category gaps at the primary stage.

District Primary Education Programme (DPEP)

District Primary Education Programme (DPEP) is centrally sponsored project aiming at improving the quality of primary education in the country. The project draws inspiration from the National Education Policy (NEP), which reaffirms national commitment to Universalisation of Elementary Education (UEE). The programme is implemented in 110 districts in the country, chosen on the criteria of low female literacy, high drop out rate, and low enrolment of socially disadvantaged groups. The estimated cost of the project, which is implemented in two phases, is Rs. 1,950 crore, out of which Rs. 1,720 crore will be external aid. The contribution of the Central Government will be 85 per cent, with the respective States pooling in the rest 15 per cent.

Kendriya Vidyalaya Sangathan

The Vidyalaya is strivings hard to achieve excellence under the able leadership of the Principal and a team of highly experienced, qualified and educated teachers. Excellence in Education and Good Character are the hall-marks of the Model Temple of Learning. This Model School stands second to none in the field of discipline, cleanliness, academics and co-curricular activities. This vidyalaya is running a fast race to reach its goal of perfection.

The Kendriya Vidyalaya has a four-fold mission, viz.,

- To cater to the educational needs of children of transferable Central Government employee including-Defence and Para-military personnel by providing a common programme of education;

- To pursue excellence and set the pace in the field of school education;
- To initiate and promote experimentation and innovations in education in collaboration with other bodies like the Central Board of Secondary Education (CBSE) and the National Council of Education Research and Training (NCERT) etc; and
- To develop the spririt of national integration and create a sense of 'Indianness' among children.

NAVODAYA VIDYALAYA SAMITI: "Jawahar Navodaya Vidyalayas"

First established in 1985 at Amravati, Maharashtra, they are the brain child of P.V. Narasimha Rao. They were started during the Prime Ministership of Rajiv Gandhi to find and foster talented children from the rural parts of India. In accordance with the National Policy of Education (1986) Government of India started Jawahar Navodaya Vidyalayas (JNVs). Presently the JNVs are spread in 27 States and 7 Union Territories. These are co-educational residential schools fully financed and administered by Government of India through an autonomous organization, Navodaya Vidyalaya Samiti. Admissions in JNVs are made through the Jawahar Novodaya Selection Test (JNVST) at Class VI. The medium of instruction in JNVs is the mother tongue or regional language up to class VIII and English thereafter for Maths and Science and Hindi for Social Science. Students of the JNVs appear for X and XII class examinations of the Central Board of Secondary Education. While education in the schools is free including boarding, lodging, uniforms and textbooks, a nominal fee of Rs.200/- per month will have to be paid by the children from IX to XII class. However, children belonging to SC/ST, Girls and Physically Handicapped and from the families whose income is below poverty line are exempted from payment of fees.

Objectives

1. To impart good quality modern education to talented children (selected on the basis of a written merit test) predominantly from rural areas, without regard to their family's socio-economic condition.

2. To ensure that all students of Jawahar Navodaya Vidyalayas attain a reasonable level of competence in three languages as envisaged in the Three Language Formula.

3. To serve, in each district, as focal points for improvements in quality of school education in general through sharing of experiences and facilities.

4. The motto of these schools is to come in to learn and go out to serve.

5. To provide good quality modern education including a strong component of culture, inculcation of values, awareness of the environment, adventure activities and physical education to the talented children predominantly from rural areas.

6. To ensure that students attain a reasonable level of competency in three languages.

7. To promote national integration through migration of students from Hindi to non-Hindi speaking State and vice-versa.

Kasturba Gandhi Balika Vidyalaya (KGBV)

The Government of India has approved a new scheme called Kasturba Gandhi Balika Vidyalaya (KGBV) for setting up upto 750 residential schools with boarding facilities at elementary level for girls belonging predominantly to the SC, ST, OBC and minorities in difficult areas. The scheme will be coordinated with the existing schemes of Department of Elementary Education and Literacy viz. Sarva Shiksha Abhiyan (SSA), National Programme for Education of Girls at Elementary Level (NPEGEL) and Mahila Samakhya (MS).

Model Schools in Backward Mandals

With an intention to provide quality education to girl students and others in the rural areas, the State Government will start 355 model schools in the educationally backward mandals from the year for which 412.09 crores were already released by the Central government. These schools will be run as a model of Kasturba Gandhi girls schools.

To be established as a joint venture of Central Government and State Government the schools will be open to students from 5th and (+) two std class and the medium of instruction will be English.

These schools will not clash with the existing system and they will function independently. Teachers and non-teaching staff will also be recruited separately while the structures would also come up at separate lands giving it a unique identity.

Staff pattern and admission mode are likely to be on the Kendriya Vidyalaya model and to formulate the guidelines for these schools. These schools will be different from the Success schools launched by the State Government a few years back with focus on attracting students through English medium of instruction. Success schools will be open to every student across the State while admissions in these model schools will be through a different selection process. They will be run on the lines of A.P. Residential Schools, popular in the 70s and 80s in the State, and that were replicated at the national level as Navodaya Vidyalayas.

Rashtriya Madhyamika Siksha Abhiyan

This programme is proposed to be implemented from 2010-11, with Central Assistance of 75%. Our government is providing computers to schools to meet the growing demands for manpower with computer skills for 9th and 10th classes from 65% to 100% and to strengthen existing secondary schools. The outlay was Rs. 9824 Crores provided for school education department for the financial year 2010-11.

National Vocational Education Qualifications Framework (NVEQF)

It envisages strengthening of the 1,000 existing vocational schools and establishment of 100 new vocational schools by the State governments. The government will provide assistance to 500 vocational schools being run under the private-public partnership mode and in-service training of existing and fresh teachers. The focus will be on development of 250 competency based modules for each individual vocational courses and assistance to 150 reputed non-governmental organisations to run short duration innovative vocational education programmes.

The unique part of the vocational framework is that it will be integrated with mainstream education and thus provide students multi-level entry and exit options, to enable them to seek employment after class XII.

Earlier this year, the government set up a GoM consisting of state Education Ministers to suggest developing NVEQF.

Further it imparts the new skills required in the agriculture sector should also be included under the purview of NVEQF and that courses in this field to be launched by 2013.

Gurukula Pathasala

The 21st century Gurukulam (21CG) is a new educational program designed to provide enhanced opportunities for gifted rural youth of Andhra Pradesh. A 21CG is envisioned as a self-sustaining, and self-supporting community, modeled after the ancient Gurukulam and the modern-day Kibbutz. Its primary purpose is to provide remedial education and IT training leading to a postgraduate degree in IT for the current top 1% of the rural youth.

The entrance test is state-wide but the selection is based among the best in each mandal. The rural mandal residency will be determined based on the location of the high school graduation of the candidate.

The 21st Century Gurukulam (21 CG), Andhra University centre is one of the educational institutions set up by the government of Andhra Pradesh, with an aim to empower rural youth. The 21st Century Gurukulam functions under the aegis of Andhra Pradesh State Council of Higher Education (APSCHE). Recently a newly owned building is opened beside Sivaji Park, M.V.P. Colony, Visakhapatnam. However the 21st Century Gurukulum has failed to fulfill the targets and majority of the students remain unemployed.

Saakshar Bharat Mission 2012

It is a new scheme proposed from 2012, to be implemented, as a centrally sponsored scheme. The main objective of the programme is to eradicate illiteracy among adult women and to achieve 80% literacy rate by decreasing gender gap in literacy to 10%. The districts with 50% and below female literacy are going to be covered in this programme.

The project was launched across the country on September 8, 2009-covering 167 districts in the first phase. The two adult education programmes of the Centre – Total Literacy Mission and Continuing Education Mission – were scrapped and the Saakshar Bharat Mission was launched. The mission, which aims at making women literate by 2012, targets districts where the literacy level is less than 50 per cent. The programme will focus on women from backward, Dalit and minority communities.

Literacy is central to the success of all these programmes and initiatives. Female literacy is especially so. Female literacy is a force multiplier for all action for social development. This is self-evident and does not require any elaboration. In fact, many observers have seen infrastructure development in the economic sector and female literacy in the social sector as two very critical factors that impede India's steady climb to a higher and sustainable level of growth and development. Female literacy is also absolutely necessary to empower the Indian woman in her every day struggle in dealing with multiple deprivations on the basis of class, caste and gender. Persistent illiteracy, particularly among women, Scheduled Castes, Scheduled Tribes, Minorities and other disadvantaged groups, is a challenge that we must face and meet head on. We must make our nation fully literate, if we want to empower the average citizen and make rapid progress.

Why Parents in A.P. are Opting for Private Schools?

Many more parents are opting out of free government schools to pay for a private education for their children, even if it means making sacrifices, he said.

Researchers believe that this is the result of "the very poorest parents making hard choices about which of their children they can afford to send to fee-paying private schools".

A preference for English-medium teaching and growing dissatisfaction with government schools have led to a "dramatic" rise in the number of parents in Andhra Pradesh, including those on low-incomes, opting for private schools over state schools, according to new research by Oxford University.

The University said that the study, which randomly selected from different social and economic backgrounds, found that the number of children attending private schools had almost doubled in seven years—from 24 per cent in 2002 to 44 per cent in 2009.

"The study suggests that the trend is fuelled by the availability of low fee-paying private schools, and the perception among parents that children will make better educational progress in private schools. Parents said that they valued English-medium teaching offered by private schools. whereas government schools mostly teach in the regional language, Telugu," it said.

Prof. Woodhead said that there was need for reforming government schools to make sure they "deliver quality education".

"Regulation of private schools is also essential including increasing access to the most underprivileged," he said.

The Role of Teacher, Parent, Community and Government

Teacher's Active Plan, The role and Importance of the Teacher

Teachers are no doubt the corner stone to mould children in a right path. The teacher is the yard stick that measures the achievements and aspiration of the nation. The worth and potentialities of a country get evaluated in and through the work of the teacher. They are the real nation builders.

Further, the teacher is the dynamic force of the school. As social engineers, the teacher can socialize and humanize young by their man like qualities.

Since beginning the system of education, the teacher receives more respect from the children, parents and from the society. A good teacher always commands respect in all social situations.

Tender children always observe the actions, movements and the behavior and character of teacher and imbibe all this from the teacher so that teacher role is very crucial regarding lives of children as otherwise the same lives will be deviated and they would be injurious to himself, family, and society at large being delinquents. Further a teacher who has to feel teaching as social service as he directs the child and ultimately mould the child like nursing, he contributes to the well behavior of children. It is a moral binding, that every teacher should strive with heart and soul to raise children upto highest perfection of mankind with humility, and love.

Gone are the days when staff common-rooms were filled with small talks on saris or the latest films in the town. Now-a-days, teachers talk about their activity plan, share experiences and ideas and exchange notes. With no extra allowance of perk, the sole inspiration for majority of teachers is the positive change they notice in their students. The multi-grade approach wherein teachers can attend to both the above and below average students in the same classroom also instills confidence in the children.

The programme provides for monthly cluster level meetings of teachers of 5 – 6 nearby schools, where the teaching programme for the next month is planned. The Block and District level Committees help sort out problems faced by the cluster level teachers. This two-way communication instills confidence in the teachers, gives them more flexibility in planning and implementation.

Interaction with Parents

Researcher interacted with above parents in connection with their children education under RTE Act

Interaction with Teachers

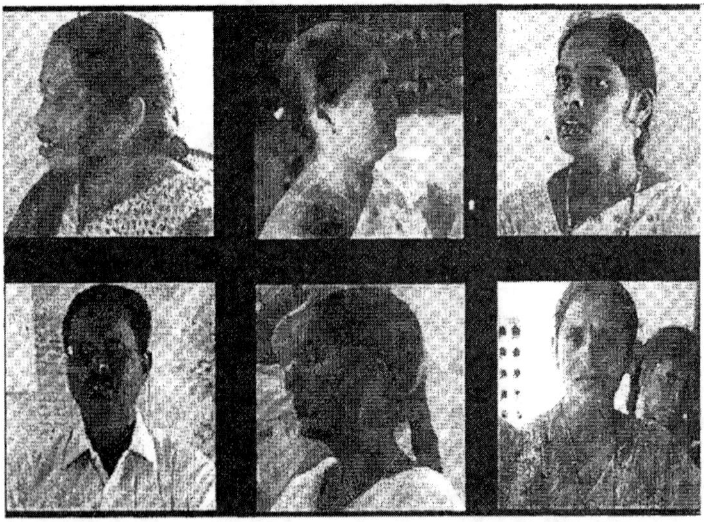

Researcher interacted with above teachers from various schools of the study area regarding mid-day meal scheme, quality of education, dropouts, and as to enroll the non-enrolled children

A teacher who came regularly, stayed in the school for the stipulated time, did not use excessive force (beating, using abusive language, shouting and punishment) and taught with interest was, known as a motivated teacher. The ability of their children to learn to read and write and pass examinations was another important indicator.

Teachers and the Local Body Administration

"A 'motivated' teacher comes to school every day, does what he is told and provides information to the higher-ups want!" Almost all teachers believed that daily attendance and complying with orders and requests for information were reasonable indicators of motivation. Administrators at the district level described a motivated teacher as one who was regular, did what she or he was told and was, by and large, complaint free. Children were no where in the picture, nor were the teaching and learning processes. Learning was incidental to the maintenance of data they gathered and fed into the system. Enrolment, attendance, midday meal distribution and participation in training programme and workshops – cold figures – had become the indices of education. Administrators at higher levels associated motivation with low absenteeism, maintaining discipline, proper-record keeping, collection and reporting of data, utilization of funds allocated for teaching and learning material and giving exercises in the classroom and correcting them.

Increases in enrolment rates, attendance figures and midday meal distribution do not convey the true picture of the state of the education system in our country. Equally disturbing is the high dropout rate from primary to upper-primary levels, the blame for which lies partly with educators, especially teachers, who in Government schools and in more rural areas, appear demotivated and disheartened.

Reviewing the progress in the elementary education sector on February 21, 2005, the Prime Minister of India said that he was pained to note that "only 47 out of 100 children enrolled in class I reach class VIII, putting the dropout rate at 52.79 per cent". This, he said was 'unacceptably high" and attributed the high dropout rate to "lack of adequate facilities, large-scale absenteeism of teachers and inadequate supervision by local authorities" (*The Hindu,* New Delhi, February 22, 2005). This is not the first time that teachers and local authorities have been blamed for India's poor performance in elementary education, civil society organizations and the media have highlighted the issue of accountability for over 20 years. Yet, it is only in the last three to four years that political leaders and administrators have begun to openly admit that motivation and accountability among teachers and local administrators is a big problem and that while data on enrolment is impressive, many children leave primary school without learning the basic skills of reading and writing.

The political scientist Myron Weiner asserted the virtue of the State enforcing compulsory schooling by law and in a framework that rejects societal biases and hierarchical factors, which deprive large sections of classes and castes, of the right to be educated.

In their path-breaking work on development and social opportunity, Nobel laureate Amartya Sen and his collaborator Jean Dreze frame basic education as a mass political issue and emphasise the intrinsic as well as the instrumental role of education in the development process as a whole. Such an expansion of social opportunity by providing decent, quality education to all must go hand in hand with a scheme that compels school attendance. Given the long history of failed attempts at 'universalising' elementary education, the Prime Minister needs to evolve a concrete proposal that goes beyond voluntarism and schemes such as the Sarva Shiksha Abhiyan, and enthuses and obliges truant authorities to fall in line with his "iron law of development" – "there is not one modern economy in the world today that does not have a literacy rate of at least 80 per cent." A pupil who stays away from school without permission or explanation, wandering.

Rapport among Teachers, Parents and the Community

An effort at effectively involving the Panchayat Raj Institutions, School Management Committees, Village and Urban Slum level Education Committees, Parents' Teachers' Associations, Mother Teacher Associations, Tribal Autonomous Councils and other grass root level structures in the management of elementary schools.

Educationists, on the other hand, argued that a motivated teacher was one who could communicate with children. He / she drew energy from his / her interaction with children, was concerned about what and how much they were learning and his / her ability to attract and retain children in the school. They also believed that only a motivated teacher could build a rapport with the parents and the community and go beyond the call of duty to ensure that every single child attended regularly, even if it meant visiting their homes and persuading the parents to send their children to school. They admitted the irregular attendance of teachers was uncommon in private (aided and unaided) schools and that teachers taught for the stipulated hours / periods. It is possible that the gap between the educationist's perception of motivation and that of teachers, administrators and the larger community may be lower in educationally advanced states like Kerala, Tamil Nadu and Himachal Pradesh.

Interaction with the cross-section of the society regarding eradication of illiteracy

Mr. Viswajethu   Ms. L .Satya Vathi   Ms . Nissa

Miss. Prasanna   Miss. Padam vathi   Miss. Varalakshmi

Mr.Sasibhushan   Miss. B. Janaki   Miss.Llakshmi

Mr. Satyanarayana   Miss. Krishnavani   Miss. Santhosi

Miss. Prabavathi   Miss. Padma   Mr. Yadagari

Miss. Sai   Miss. Gowri   Miss. Varalakshmi

The Role of State Government(s)

It is a fact that the State had been negligent to educational reforms as it was basking in the glory of excellent human development indices like longevity, low infant mortality, health care and literacy for all. But the dismal performance at school leaving examinations for quite some time was hinting at some serious flaws in the system. Already into the third year, DPEP has started showing results. Its fiercest critics have turned out to be its admirers. Agrees O.M.Shankaran, the programme office in charge of Pedagogy, "When these children grow up, they will definitely excel in their chosen field of profession, be it medicine, engineering, agriculture or carpentry, as a lot of care is being taken at the beginning to draw out the innate ability within each of them". The State will surely reap rich dividend, as the effect of the project will begin to show in all walks of life.

Dropout-prevention or dropout recovery is one of their primary objectives. The intervention reviewed provides a mix of services, such as counseling, monitoring school restructuring, curriculum redesign, financial incentives and community services to mitigate factors impeding academic success.

The Andhra Pradesh government has also designed schemes such as for accessing the school under various literacy schemes and programmes. (i) Maa badi – Our school; (ii) Chaduvukundam – Back to school; (iii) Akshara Sankranthi – Akshra Jyothi – Chaduvula Pandaga; (iv) Residential schools; (v) Anganvadi centers; (vi) pre-primary schools (supply of dry ration, text books, uniform etc.). (vii) The government also adopted the "Bridge-school" to improve access to children, women and disadvantaged communities such as Scheduled Castes and Scheduled Tribes children; (viii) "Vidya volunteer" scheme was started to support single teacher schools.

Main Features of the RTE Act

Features of RTE Act

The framers of the Constitution in their wisdom chose to include education in the Directive Principles of State Policy and not in the section on fundamental rights and correspondingly Article 45 stated that: "The State shall endeavour to provide, within a period of ten years from the commencement of the Constitution, for free and compulsory education for all children until they complete the age of fourteen years." However education remained a neglected area of state policy with universalization of elementary education continuing to be a distant goal. Efforts from educationists, academics and civil society groups that focused on a rights based approach finally yielded results in 2002, when the 86th Constitutional Amendment was passed by Parliament and Article 21A, which makes right to education a fundamental right, was included in the Constitution. In so doing it put the Right to Education on par with the Right to Life stated in Article 21. Article 21 A states: "the state shall provide free and compulsory education to all children of the age of 6 to 14 years as the state may, by law determine".

Following from this a Right to Free and Compulsory Education Act (RTE)_was drafted and passed in Parliament on August 27, 2009 (notified on February 16, 2010 to come into effect from April 1, 2010).

1. Makes Elementary Education Free
2. Makes Elementary Education Compulsory for the State to provide
3. Mandates education of children along their peer age group ("age-appropriate"); provides for "special training" to facilitate age appropriate education
4. Sets quality norms for all schools

5. Sets qualification and working norms for Teachers in all schools
6. Mandates curriculum in all schools to be in consonance with Constitutional Values
7. Mandates a system of evaluation that is free of the oppression of annual exams
8. Enhances role of PRIs in implementation as well as grievance redressal.
9. Mandates participation of civil society in the management of schools; makes teachers accountable to parents and the community
10. Democratizes education delivery in the country by mandating 25% reservation for children from weaker sections in private schools.
11. Protects children from labour, marriage, exploitation, discrimination, abuse, violence and neglect.
12. Separates agency for implementation of Act (Education Department) from agency charged with monitoring the implementation of the Act (NCPCR).

Compulsory Elementary Education: The word compulsory has implications for the government alone. In other words while it is the duty of the parent to send their children to school (Article 15k) it is the obligation of the government to ensure not just enrolment but attendance and completion of elementary education. This implies that the government

a. Must identify all children that are out of school or dropped out.

b. Make sure that they are enrolled in school.

c. Make sure they attend school on a regular basis.

d. Make sure they complete the elementary cycle of education.

e. If parents are reluctant to send their children it is the responsibility of the government to find a way of convincing the parents, without use of force/ violence/ pressure to send their children to school.

Age Appropriate Education

a. This means that children will be enrolled in the class that corresponds to their age. In other words, if a 10 year old has not been to school or dropped out earlier, she will be enrolled in class 5.

b. To enable the 10 year to cope in class 5 "special training" will be provided on the premises to bring the child up to the age appropriate level.

Quality Norms for ALL schools. The Act lays out some basic norms for all schools (government and private):

a. Pupil-Teacher Ratio (cannot exceed 1:30)

b. Minimum days of school functioning in a year (200 and 250 for Primary and Upper Primary, respectively)

c. Minimum hours of instruction in school (4 and 5 hours a day for primary and UP)

d. Minimum working hours for the teacher (45 hours a week)

e. Separate subject teachers and head-teacher.

f. One room for every teacher.

g. Separate and functional toilets; clean and adequate drinking water.

h. Playground, boundary wall, library, kitchen.

Qualifications for Teachers

- Para Teachers banned

- All teachers must subscribe to minimum qualifications and training norms laid out by Academic Authority within 5 years.
- Teacher education and teacher training institutes to be upgraded to enable fulfillment of quality and qualification norms for teachers.

Curriculum in line with Constitution

a. This means that curriculum, syllabus and books must conform to Constitutional values. It implies that communal and harmful agendas cannot be part of the materials used and taught in ANY school of the country.

b. Syllabus and Books must also take into account age and learning levels of children.

Evaluation System to be based on Principle of Continuous and Comprehensive Evaluation (CCE)

a. No failure till completion of elementary cycle.

b. Evaluation to be done throughout the year and not be based on an annual exam.

c. Teachers to maintain Pupil Cumulative Record (PCR) for every child.

d. Evaluation to be on "comprehensive" performance of child, reflecting all facets, talents of the child and not be based on just a few subject areas. The PCR to include music, theatre, leadership skills, social skills etc., as well.

Role of Panchayati Raj Institutions

The PRIs have been given a wide range of functions related to the implementation of the provisions of the RTE, such as identification of out of school children; neighbourhood-wise school mapping; maintenance of child records (child-tracking) public display of information; education of children from migrant families; participation in School Management Committees (SMCs).

PRIs have also been made responsible for grievance redressal in matters related to violations of the rights of the child under RTE.

Participation of Civil Society

a. School Management Committees consisting largely of parents (75%) and of PRIs officials and civil society partners have been given a wide range of functions under the Act, including the preparation of the School Development Plan

b. Teachers have been made accountable to the SMCs.

Reservation in Private Schools

a. All private schools are required to admit in their incoming class 25% children from weaker sections and socially disadvantaged groups from their neighbourhood.

b. Limits of definition to be extended if 25% seats are not being filled within the standard limits of neighbourhood.

c. Private schools to be reimbursed for these children by the government at the rate of per learner costs of government schools in the state.

Separation of Implementation and Monitoring Agency

a. Implementation responsibilities lie with the education departments in conjunction with the PRIs.

b. Monitoring role has been given to the National Commission for Protection of Child Rights (NCPCR) and the corresponding State Commissions.

c. This separation is very important and a first in the history of such legislations and allows for independent monitoring of the implementation of the Act.

d. NCPCR/ SCPCR have quasi-judicial powers and can function as a civil court. Complaints and grievances can be addressed to them as well.

The researcher conducted a study on Right to Education Act 2009, Its Implementation and Social Development in India. Apart from the study we organized National seminar on the above said theme for getting further information by calling for Research papers to explore new vistas.

Though the bill is enacted late, it is a right step in the right direction at the moment. But Laws and Bills do not make children go to school. Therefore the National conference was conducted on the following sub-themes on 22nd -23rd March 2011 in Andhra University, Visakhapatnam, Andhra Pradesh to understand the multifaceted out-come from the Right to Education Act. Academicians, scientists, administrators, planners, social activists intellectual communities and research scholars attended and presented their research papers at the conference on the following sub themes.

Sub-themes

- To study socio-economic background of the family
- To study level of education of the family/guardian
- To assess supervision of school management committee/ local education body
- To study parents interaction with school teachers for their children education (teacher-parent meet)
- To study impact of mid-day meal programme and other incentives
- To study infrastructural facilities in the schools
- To study the extent of dropouts and non-enrolled children
- To study changes in the attitude and motivation of parents after Right to Education Act 2009
- To study attitudes, efficiency and commitment of teacher after Right to Education Act 2009.

National Conference of Right to Education Act 2009 and its Themes Held on 22nd-23rd March 2011

- To study the overall impact of Right to Education Act 2009
- To study the impact of private schools with government schools.

Basing on the above said sub-themes, a brief report of some of the important papers submitted by researchers are given below.

National Conference on Right to Education Act 2009 held 'between' 22nd - 23rd March 2011 to explore other vistas:

A brief report: Prof. Bilmoria Rani and Ch. Jagan Mohan Rao in their papers observed that society and education are inseparable. Every society develops a system of education suitable to its own structure. Man without education would be living just like an animal. Any country's socio-economic development depends mainly on its human resources development for successful implementation of Right to Education Act. The multi-dimensional and systematic approach needs that the human resources can be developed qualitatively by imparting quality of education at all levels of education.

Prof. V. Krishna Murthy, Dr. R.V.L.N. Ratnakara Rao and Dr. P. Kishore Kumar and others examined the right to education in the context of LPG that is liberalization, privatization and globalization. He distinguished between holistic education and education in the narrow sense of the term. He pleaded for man-making education and value oriented education. Gandhi advocated education of head, heart and hand. The well to do population of the society should adopt individuals, groups or villages and contribute for the education of the society and thereby achieve the dream of education for all.

Dr. M. Swarnalatha and Mrs. Harsha Vardhini tried to focus on the issues concerning the policy implementation and also tried to assess the awareness among the implementing agencies at district level.

Nalla Sushma and P. Nalini pointed out that education serves as the main catalytic agent in the developmental process of a nation. Illiteracy on the other hand is the greatest ingredient to any improvement in the socio-economic status of the people.

Dr. T. Nirmala Jyothi, N. Sujatha and V. Syamala suggested that the National Commission for Elementary Education shall be constituted to monitor all aspects of elementary education including quality education.

Dr. C. Gayatri Devi discussed the practical problems in the implementation of the Act. She pointed out that even after a long time of passing this legislation, there are no guidelines and proper discussion from the Education Department regarding norms for recognition of private schools.

K. Sudharani observed the enactment of revolutionary step taken by the government. Mahatma Gandhi advocated universalisation of education way back in 1937.

K. Mahendra Rao, Nandika Sujata K.V. and Amar Nath and others viewed that human rights and education are two faces of the same coin. Right to education is a basic human right which has been recognized by the Indian Constitution as a fundamental right.

Dr. J.K.L. Sujatha, in her paper mentioned that education is one of the basic necessities of life. Unless the people in this country are not educated, the objectives of the preamble cannot be achieved.

I. Veerendrandha Kasyap observed that socialist theory recognized that individuals had claims to basic welfare services against the state and education was viewed as one of these welfare entitlements.

Dr. P. Usha and Dr. S. Pulla Rao observed that as a result of the continuous effort of the government for the improvement of socio-economic status of women especially in education, the girls enrolment in primary and secondary education is significantly increased.

E. Ashok Kumar and B.S.S. Mrutunjaya attempt to analyse the plausible ingredients in the implementation of Right to Education Act 2009 in Visakhapatnam in tribal areas.

M. Uma Sivan examined that despite several well designed plans and programmes over six decades, India still has one of the lowest female literacy rates in Asia.

Prof. P. Vijaya Prakash, P. Vasanthi and K. Srinivasu conducted study of Lampthempadu, a tribal village which revealed the major aspects of development, one benign the education and the other communication, the former triggered by a school teacher who was working during 1991 – 2000 and the latter electrification of the village during 1998 – 99.

Dr. Dharmana Rama Rao and Dr. Gulipilli Rajeswari suggested that as per the implementation of Right to Education Act 2009, the state government has to take up an action plan in Visakhapatnam district to make the district out of the school children (DSC) after the year 2011 – 2012. The details of the action plan are discussed in the paper.

Dr. J. Ramu Naidu suggested the qualities of the ideal teacher. It is necessary for an ideal teacher to be loving and caring, then only he in turn infuses the finer quality of generating love in the children in his charge.

Dr. L. Manjula Davidson emphasized that India has to play a socially responsible role contributing to the upliftment of the underprivileged section of the society.

Prof. M. Lakshmipathi Raju and K. Srinivasa Rao pointed out that the Act has been criticized for being hastily drafted, not considering the quality of Education and including children under 6 years of age.

Dr. T. Sharon Raju and Dr. D. Nagaraja Kumari observed that over the years there has been significant spatial and numerical expansion of elementary schools in the country, yet the goal of universal elementary education continues to elude us.

Prof. S. Bhaskar and S. Babu Praveen Kumar suggested that community members should be involved in the planning of the primary education programme and for providing voluntary support for the quality improvement in the school.

N. Kedareswarim, N. Sushma and Prof. D. Syamala Devi observed that the teacher is a dynamic force of the school. A school without teacher is just like a body without soul, a skeleton without flesh and blood, a shadow without substance.

N. Solomon Benny quoted among others Dr. S. Radhakrishnan, "the teacher's place in society is of vital importance. He acts as the pivot for the transmission of intellectual traditions and technical skills from generation to generation and helps to keep the lamp of civilization burning".

Dr. G. Jaya Lakshmi mentioned that Education is important among other social indicators, which is directly linked with socio-economic development.

S. Madhuri Paradesi observed that parents have a vital role in their children's education. They can help them enjoy school more, improve their studying and homework skills.

Dr. P. Kishore Kumar and Mr. Venkatesh discussed media initiatives related to education and poverty reduction.

Mr. Murthy P.V.N., Ms. Prasanna Laxmi, Ms. M. Swapna said that a teaching job is equally challenging and rewarding as that of any other profession.

Y. Narasimham and Varahalu Dora discussed the significant information communication technology (ICT) policy issues in education.

M. Manikya Rao discussed the impact of television on young children.

K. Joseph Stephen explained the role and responsibilities of local governments in effectively implementing "Right to Education Act, 2009".

Mr. Koteswara Rao and Dr. Israel Raju said that some of the qualities of a good teacher are confidence, understanding, patience, creativity and passion etc.

Koti Ravi Kumar, Ch. Ramakrishna and P. Kishore Kumar lays emphasis on the importance of teacher's role in shifting students from a passive role to an active participation in teaching and learning process.

Prof. D.S. Prakash Rao observed that especially the minority institutions demand more money in the form of fee, donations in an uncontrolled and irregular manner. The government in the name of public interest wants to put a control in one way or other on those private institutions.

Dr. A.B.S.V. Ranga Rao, Dr. P. Kishore Kumar and B. Chennaiah examined that as Gandhian philosophy for basic education was based upon the goal of freeing India from colonial domination.

P.D. Satya Pal argues that the most important change needed in India is in the mindset of our educationist, government and society.

Dr. S. Pulla Rao and Dr. P. Usha attempted to evaluate the mid-day meal programme which is implemented in Greater Visakhapatnam Municipal Corporation (GVMC) schools in Visakhapatnam city.

P. Vijaya Ratnam observed in his study that despite Government programme India's literacy rate increased only sluggishly.

Dr. T.J.M.S. Raju, Dr. N.V.S. Suryanarayana, Mr. J. Ramesh dealt with the governmental policies for the development of education in minority groups.

S. Sunila Jawahar pointed out many deficiencies in elementary education, such as lack of infrastructure, lack of quality teachers, lack of proper environment and multiple regulatory mechanisms.

Dr. K. Venkata Naidu attempted in his paper to know about the impact of mid-day meals programme on educational development.

Y. Yadla Ramana, Dr. P. Kishore Kumar and Ramakrishna said that Education plays a significant role in facilitating access to better level of life, eradicating poverty, reducing child labour and promoting gender equality.

T.J.M.S. Raju, S.N. Rao and T. Sharon Raju mentioned that the traditions, customs, false beliefs, dowry system, poverty, male dominance cause backwardness of women.

Mrs. S. Prasanthi Sri and Dr. T.V. Ramana in their paper attempted to analyse the implementation and impact of mid-day meal programmes in the state of Andhra Pradesh.

M. Madan Mohan and P. Mahendra in their paper dealt with various weaknesses of our education system, especially elementary education.

Supreme Court upheld Validity of RTE Act

The Hon'ble Supreme Court of India upheld validity of RTE Act 2009 the judgement is reproduced below.

The Supreme Court on 12.04.2012 (Thursday) by a majority of 2:1 upheld the constitutional validity of the Right of Children to Free and Compulsory Education Act, 2009, which provides for free and compulsory education to children between the age of 6 and 14 years and mandates government/adied/and non-minority unaided schools to reserve 25 per cent of the seats for these children.

In its 174-pages verdict, the court rejected the contentions of several private unaided schools contending that the Act had violated their fundamental rights guaranteed under Article 19(1)(g) which provided autonomy to private managements to run their institutions without any interference from government.

A Bench of Chief Justice S.H. Kapadia and Justice Swatanter Kumar while upholding the law, however, held that it would not be applicable to unaided minority schools. Justice K.S. Radhakrishnan, gave a dissenting judgment.

The majority judgment said: "We hold that the Right of Children to Free and Compulsory Education Act, 2009 is constitutionally valid and shall apply to a school established, owned or controlled by the appropriate Government or a local authority; an aided school including aided minority school(s) receiving aid or grants to meet whole or part of its expenses from the appropriate Government or the local authority; a school belonging to specified category; and an unaided non-minority school not receiving any kind of aid or grants to meet its expenses from the appropriate government or the local authority."

The CJI who wrote the judgment said: "It will operate from today. In other words, this will apply from the academic year 2012-13. However, admissions given by unaided minority schools prior to the pronouncement of this judgment shall not be reopened.

"By judicial decisions, right to education has been read into right to life in Article 21. A child who is denied right to access education is not only deprived of his right to live with dignity, he is also deprived of his right to freedom of speech and expression enshrined in Article 19(1) (a). The 2009 Act seeks to remove all those barriers including financial and psychological barriers which a child belonging to the weaker section and disadvantaged group has to face while seeking admission".

The Bench said: "It is true that, as held in the T.M.A. Pai Foundation as well as the P.A. Inamdar judgement, the right to establish and administer an educational institution is a fundamental right, as long as the activity remains charitable under Article 19(1) (g). However, in the said two decisions the correlation between Articles 21 and 21A, on the one hand, and Article 19(1) (g), on the other, was not under consideration.

Further, the content of Article 21 A flows from Article 45 (as it then stood). The 2009 Act has been enacted to give effect to Article 21A. For the above reasons, since the Article 19(1) (g) right is not an absolute right as Article 30(!), the 2009 Act cannot be termed as unreasonable".

The Bench said: "To put an obligation on the unaided non-minority schools to admit 25 per cent children in class I under section 12(1) © cannot be termed as an unreasonable restriction. Such as law cannot be said to transgress any constitutional limitation. The object of the 2009 Act is to remove the barriers faced by a child who seeks admission to class I and not to restrict the freedom under Article 19(1) (g).

"From the scheme of Article 21A and the 2009 Act, it is clear that the primary obligation is of the State to provide for free and compulsory education to children between the age of 6 and 14 years and, particularly, to children who are likely to be prevented from pursuing and completing the elementary education due to inability to afford fees or charges."

How to "Right to Education" was born

Anyway, in 2002 the then government amended the constitution and made education as a fundamental right. The next logical step would be to determine the manner in which this right will be implemented. A new government came to power in 2004 and took about 5 years to determine the manner. The result was *The Right of Children to Free and Compulsory Education Act, 2009* released on the 27th of August, 2009. One of the most important rule reads:

- On reserving 25 per cent seats, the bench said: "Earmarking of seats for children belonging to specified category who face financial barrier in the matter of accessing education satisfies the test of classification in Article 14. Further, section 12(1) (c) provides for level playing field in the matter of right to education to children who are prevented from accessing education because they do not have the means or their parents do not have the means to pay for their fees. Such a condition would come within the principle of reasonableness in Article 19(6).

"Poor" really benefited?

The act specifies that 25 per cent of seats during admission have to be reserved for disadvantaged and weaker sections of the society. The act defines:

- "Child belonging to disadvantaged group" means a child belonging to the scheduled caste, the scheduled tribe, the socially and educationally backward class or such other group having disadvantage owing to social, cultural, economical, geographical, linguistic, gender or such other factor, as may be specified by the appropriate government, by notification;
- "Child belonging to weaker section" means a child belonging to such parent or guardian whose annual income is lower than the minimum limit specified by the appropriate government, by notification

Laying down the rules

- All schools must reserve seats for 25 per cent students from economically weaker sections in neighborhood for admission to class I
- Unaided minority institutions kept outside the purview of the Act
- SC Verdict on the Act to come into force from academic year 2012-13
- No retrospective effect on admissions already undertaken
- Centre and states to share the burden of compensation incurred on schools admitting poor students.

Real Issues of RTE Act

The RTE Act provides a strong legal framework for addressing most of the challenges that confront the elementary education sector, but unless it is backed by political will and commitment translated into institutional capacities with adequate resources, it will remain a wasted opportunity.

The Supreme Court in its verdict on the constitutionality of the Right to Education Act in relation to the reservation of seats for Economically Weaker Section [EWS] and socially disadvantaged [SD] children has rightly upheld the principle of integration. It is hard to see how it could have been any other way. In fact, the arguments against segregation and in favour of diversity in schools have long been settled in international debates on education. In India, where disparities are wide and reflected in the increasing gap between private and public schools, the need to make schools inclusive is perhaps even greater. This is not to deny that there will be challenges faced by all concerned—school managements, teachers, parents and children—in enforcing the law both in letter and in spirit. But given that children from the EWS and SD backgrounds are being inducted in the "incoming" class of a school, the anxiety being expressed seems somewhat exaggerated. It is another matter that it is being expressed almost exclusively by the "elite" sections of society. No EWS parent or child, for whom the "trauma" is likely to be greater, is complaining or wanting to do ways with the quota.

For all the efforts of government programmes in the last decade, and especially through the Sarva Shiksha Abhiyan [SSA], basic education in this country is still a far city from being universal or of satisfactory quality. It could even be argued that the RTE may not have been needed were this the case. There is a growing realisation that education, particularly but not exclusively, in the public sector has been a downside, and that nothing, short of radical change was required to turn the tide. This is reflected in the provisions of the RTE Act. The Act establishes for the first time standards for not just infrastructure such as classrooms, toilets and drinking water, but also for quality by stipulating that teaching—teachers' education and training, their recruitment rules, their professionalisation, their accountability—be redesigned. It also addresses teaching methods, curriculum formation and evaluation procedures, as well as corporal punishment and discrimination, all of which are intrinsic to quality and all of which are in need of reform.

But the task ahead is clear. Less than 20 per cent of children in this country go to some form of private school; the rest are either enrolled in a government school or not in any school at all. It is these children who need to be addressed and towards whom the RTE Act is largely directed. Quality education for close to 80 per cent of the children in this country still needs to be guaranteed within the framework of RTE. Herein lies the real challenge.

These are all children who have fallen out of the loop of mainstream education, but the system has no means of accounting for them. They include the urban homeless, the stigmatised, the migrant, but also the many, many children who, while enrolled, attend school at best sporadically. In an exercise conducted by the National Commission for the Protection of Child Rights (which is mandated to monitor the RTE), a house-to-house survey was conducted in 12 districts across the country to assess the situation of out-of-school children [OOSC]. The gap between the official figures of OOSC and what the NCPCR found was startlingly large. While the data are yet to be fully analysed, a preliminary look shows the gap to be as much as 40-50 per cent in some areas. And this is only the tip of the iceberg. Identifying all the children, bringing them to school, providing adequate physical infrastructure and qualified teachers and then ensuring they attend regularly and learn all they are meant to learn in an atmosphere free of fear and trauma–all this is a very tall order. What it means is that many more resources and far greater efforts will be required, especially within the ambit of the RTE Act.

It also means that the institutional structures of the state will need to be geared towards meeting these goals. Within the education sector itself, the National Council for Teacher Education (NCTE)—the body responsible for overseeing teacher education—will need to be overhauled; teacher training institutes—the District Institutes of Education and Training—will need to be reformed; the Block Education Office—the administrative unit closest to the people—will need to be revitalised. The NCPCR and SCPCRs, mandated to monitor RTE, will need resources, structures and staff. At the current allocation of Rs. 50 per cent school/year and no sanctioned posts, it is hard to see how the huge task of monitoring across the country can be optimally achieved.

No rules have been framed and no resources allocated to the PRIs to undertake any form of grievance redress. In other words, the understanding that elementary education is now to be enforced as a fundamental right and not implemented as yet another schemes is still to be given institutional shape and form. For this, the Education Departments and the Panchayati Raj Departments will need to develop a framework for how grievances related to RTE will be addressed. The pace of implementation needs to be accelerated before people start to lose faith in the enforcement of this fundamental right.

2

Review of Literature

Ancient History of Education

The history of education in India is very interesting to go through the ancient Indian education beginning with the 3rd century BC through the sayings of sages and scholars imparted education orally. But after the development of letters, it took the form of writing on Palm leaves and barks of trees which in turn, helped spread of written literature. Temples and community centers often took the role of schools from those days.

These were recited by priests of a pre-Hindu tradition. They taught correct recitation and pronunciation of the Vedas. Which comprised of hymns and prayers. They also taught grammar and derivation, composition, the rules of sacrifice, versification, understanding secrets of nature, reasoning including logic, science, knowledge of herbal medicines and skills necessary for an occupation. Although education was free in the Vedic society over a time it became discriminatory as the caste system began.

500 BC saw the birth of the Hindu texts and scriptures called Upanishads, these texts provided an exploratory learning process for both teachers and students, the teaching methods used reasoning and questioning. Two epic poems namely the *Mahabharata* and *Ramayana* explore themes of human existence and the concept of karma and dharma.

India has a long tradition of education both through formally organized institutions (such as institutes of higher learning at Takshashila and Nalanda) as well as less formal ones like hermitages or 'ashrams' where pupils were under the complete custodial care of their gurus.

The Vedas, Puranas, Ayurveda, Yoga, Kautilya's *Arthashastra* are only some of the milestones that the traditional Indian knowledge system boasts of. There are evidences of imparting formal education in ancient India under the Gurukul system.

Gurukul System of Education

Gurukul schools were traditional Hindu residential schools of learning which taught in the teacher's house or a monastery. The subjects taught were philosophy, literature, history, religion, scriptures, warfare, medicine and astrology. Sanskrit literature consists of poetry, drama science, philosophy and other Hindu religious texts. Education was free, but students from affluent families paid a voluntary contribution called gurudakshina. The gurudakshina could also be monitoring of a special task the teacher would want the student to accomplish.

Only students belonging to Brahmin and Kshatriya communities were taught in these gurukuls.

The teacher and the student resided together as equals irrespective of their social standing, learning and helping the guru in his day to day life, including doing mundane chores such as cooking, cleaning and washing clothes, they strongly believed in the guru-shishya parampara (tradition)

The Vedic school of thought prescribes an initiation called upanayanam to all individuals, including women before the age of 8 or latest by 12. From initiation until the age of 25 all individuals were prescribed to be students and to remain unmarried.

By the colonial era, the gurukul system declined in India except in a few regions, such as Kerala, where the warrior Nair clan and their own military gurukulas called Kalaris, still maintained the tradition.

The 5th century BC saw the birth of Takshashila. Buddhism and Jainism because of their democratic character made access to education easier, the early high school centers of education were at Nalanda, Ujjain and Vikramshila Universities.

Each university had its specialization in a subject.

Ujjain specialized in astronomy

Takshashila specialized in the study of medicine.

Nalanda was the biggest centre hence it handled all branches of knowledge.

Takshashila

Situated in Rawalpindi District of Punjab province of Pakistan, Takshashila (Taxila) is an important archaeological site considered as an early centre of learning dating back to at least the 5th century BC. It is considered as a place of religious and historical sacredness by Jain and Buddhists. Takshashila has been described in details in later Jataka tales which were written in Sri Lanka. Generally a student entered Takshashila at the age of sixteen. The vedas and the eighteen arts that were taught included skills such as Elephant Lore, Archery, Hunting, Medical School, Law School and School of Military Science. It attracted students from around the old world until the destruction of the city in the 5th century BC.

Here are some existing gurukulas in India:

Andanda marga gurukula

Vivekananda College near Madurai

Sree Swaminarayan Gurukul Hyderabad

ISKCION gurukulas are several. The Bhaktivedanta gurukula and international school in Vrindavan and one in Mayapur (West Bengal) are the oldest institutions.

Nalanda

Nalanda Mahavira was regarded as one of the first greatest universities in the recorded history; it was founded in 413-455 AD during the time of the great Gupta dynasty. The history of Nalanda goes back to the days of Mahavira and Buddha in 6th century BC. As a great monastic-cum educational institution for oriental art and literature in the whole Buddhist world, it attracted students and scholars from korea, Japan, China, Tibet, Indonesia, Persia and Turkey. Chinese travelers Huen Tsang and I-Tsing also studied here in the university. Conferred academic degree titles to its graduates and also offered post-graduate courses.

Nalanda had dormitories for students that could accommodate over 10,000 students and 2,000 teachers. The university was considered an architectural masterpiece, and was marked by a lofty wall and one gate. The subjects taught at the university covered every field of learning like theology, grammar, logic, astronomy philosophy, metaphysics and medicine.

Vikramasila

Vikramasila University is another important centre of learning. It was established by king Dharmapala; the university was located in Bhagalpur district of Bihar.

Subjects like philosophy, grammar, metaphysics, Indian logic were taught here, but the most important branch of learning was tantrism. Vikramasila employed tantric preceptors.

Madrasahs

It is the Arabic word for any type of educational institution, whether secular or religious. Madrasah means academy in Persian and usually refers to Islamic school. These universities in Persia offered training in medicine, philosophy, theology and science. The faculties were versed not only in the Zoroastrian and Persian traditions, but in Greek and Indian learning as well. They were the most important medical centers of the ancient world.

Today the school teaches two courses of study: a course teaching memoristion of the Quran and course leading the candidate to become an accepted scholar in the community. A regular curriculum includes courses in Arabic, Quranic interpretation, Islamic law, recorded sayings and deeds of Prophet Muhammad, Logic and Muslim history.

Some schools also offer additional advanced course in Arabic literature, English, other foreign languages, science and world history. Ottoman madrasaha also taught styles of writing, grammar, syntax, poetry, composition, natural sciences, political sciences and etiquette.

An important function of the madrasah is to admit orphans and poor children in order to provide them with education and training. Madrasah enroll female students but they study separately from the men.

Although the ancient system of education has produced many geniuses and still a major area of research, it was hardly egalitarian. Women and people of lower castes gradually lost their right to educate themselves. The spread of Jainism, Buddhism, Bhhakti and Sufi movements did have some liberating effects on the condition of the women, Shudras and Atisudras.

When Buddhism spread in India, education became available to one and all, which led to the establishment of some world famous educational institutions like Nalanda, Vikramshila and Takshashila. These educational institutes in fact arose from the monasteries. In particular, history has taken special care to give Nalanda University, full credit for its excellence. This university used to have around 10,000 resident students and teachers on its roll at one time. These students including Chinese, Sri Lankan, Korean and other international scholars.

It was in the 11th century A. D. that Muslims established elementary and secondary schools, which led to the forming of few universities too at cities like Delhi, Lucknow and Allahabad. Medieval period saw excellent interaction between Indian and Islamic traditions in all fields of knowledge like theology, religion, philosophy, fine arts, painting, architecture, mathematics, medicine and astronomy.

Later, when the British arrived in India, English education came into being with the help of European missionaries. Since then, Western education has made steady advances in the country. With hundreds of universities and thousands of colleges affiliated to them, scores of colleges in every discipline, India has positioned itself comfortably as a country that provides quality education to its people in specific areas and to the world, in general.

The Decline of Traditional Education

Education had spread in India during 18th century. There was a school for every temple, mosque or village in most parts of the country. The subjects taught were reading, writing, arithmetic, ethics, medical science, religion, theology, astronomy, laws and metaphysics. Students from all classes of society attended the schools.

Mahatma Gandhi claimed that the traditional educational system was destroyed during the British rule.

The current system of education with its western style and content was introduced and founded by the British during the British Raj following recommendations by Lord Macaulay.

Traditional structures were not recognized by the British government, hence they declined. Some British colleges like St.Xavier's College, Sydenham College, Wilson College, and Elphinstone College in Mumbai, India were established.

History of World Education

China

Education in China goes back to the Zhou dynasty in 1045 BC to 256 BC. There were five national schools. One being Pi Yong (an imperial school) and four other schools for the aristocrats and nobility. The subjects taught were 6 type of arts like rites, archery, charioteering, music, mathematics and calligraphy, at the age of twelve boys were taught arts related to ritual (music and dance) and when older, archery and chariot driving. Girls learned ritual, good mannerisms. silk production and weaving. This was the time when native Chinese philosophy also developed.

During Han Dynasty in 206 BC- 221 AD, boys at the age of seven started learning basic skills in reading, writing and calculation, education during this period was a luxury.

Greek and Roman Empires

In ancient Greece, education was mostly private except in Sparta where children were taught to become warriors with complete obedience, courage and physical perfection. In Athens, apart from two years of military training, anyone could open a school and decide the curriculum. Parents could choose any subject they wanted their child to learn at a monthly fee they could afford. Girls rarely received formal education. They were taught gymnastics, athletics, sports, wrestling, music, poetry, drama history and academics. The youngest students learnt alphabets through songs. Further they copied the shapes of letters with a stylus on a waxed wooden tablet.

In 350 BC, children could also study drawing, painting and sculpture, the affluent continued education by studying with sophists, from whom they could learn subjects such as rhetoric, natural history, geography, mathematics, logic and politics.

Greek was the primary language of science. Boys and girls were educated, only the elite would get complete formal education. Higher education in Rome was more of a status symbol than practical concern.

Europe

The monasteries of the Catholic Church were the centers of education and literacy. The first medieval universities were established in Italy, France and England for the study of theology, arts, law and medicine. Classes were taught by nuns and monks. Monasteries were built all over Ireland and these became centers of great learning.

There was an open air primary school in Bucharest, Romania in 1842. Later Cambridge and many other universities were founded; education was made available to a wider class of people. Art and architecture were vital educational mediums through which religion, philosophy and history were taught to people.

Russia

The abolition of illiteracy became the primary task in the Russian SFSR in 1919. A new system of universal compulsory education was established for children. Millions of illiterate adult people all over the country, including residents of small towns and villages were enrolled in special literacy schools.

They believed that studying in native languages was the quickest way to increase educational levels of future generations.

Challenges in Ensuring Elementary Education For All

While Rustagi outlines the importance of elementary education and the progress made to universalize elementary education, Jandhyala Tilak critically analyses various educational policies and the underlying problems in the elementary education.

A review of the achievements in enrolment, retention and attainment of a given level of learning highlights both the improvements and conspicuous failures. The gross enrolment ratio (GER) for the schooling-aged children in 2004 – 05 for the country as a whole was 93.5, which has risen from 32 in 1950 – 51 and 86 in 1990 – 91. Thus, between 1990 – 91, 2004 – 05, the GER improved only by 7.3 per cent points. The rate of dropouts from elementary schools in the same year remains as high as 50.84 per cent. Even at the primary level in 2003–04, the dropout rate was 31 per cent.

The State-wise data between 1990 – 1991 and 2000 – 2001 and 2004 – 2005 show no significant improvement in access to primary schools. In fact, there was decline in access between 1990 – 1991 and 2000 – 2001. There were 66 primary schools, on an average, for every one lakh population in 1990 – 1991, and this declined to 62 in 2000 – 2001. Access to public (government schools and government-aided) schools is highly limited in the case of primary education. Only three-fourths of the villages on an average have a Government school or Government-aided primary school and 42 per cent of the households in urban areas have access to such a school. Further, against the current norm for pupil-teacher ratio (PTR) of 40 in primary schools, the real ratio stands at 46 at all India level in the year 2004 – 2005. This ratio varied across States; 1:104 in Bihar and 1:50 in Uttar Pradesh.

Most of the State Governments have shunned the recruitment of full-time qualified and trained teachers and appoint part-time, contractual and part-time teachers. Tilak points out that the 'barefoot teacher and barefoot schools" may finally produce a barefoot system of education.

In the National Policy on Education, 1986, the government allocated 6 per cent of the national income to education from the public exchequer by 1986. However, currently, only 3.7 per cent of the gross national product (GNP) is being invested in education. Although expenditure on elementary education has increased modestly, it lies far below the desired level of 3 per cent of the GNP and at least 6 per cent for the total education sector.

Disparities

Dhir Jhingran and Deepa Sankar in their articles measure the spatial disparity in the universalisation of education. They unravel the significant variation across the districts within a State and the country. Elementary education needs a major shift to target districts, blocks and panchayats and specific social groups that are lagging behind.

Sunil Datra elaborates different forms of inequities, quantitative and qualitative prevailing in the current system. As against, the national literacy rate of 64.84 per cent in 2001, 47.1 per cent of scheduled tribes and 54.7 per cent of scheduled castes were literate.

The difference in the quality of education arises due to different forms of schools – public schools versus private schools, different types of private schools and different forms of government schools. Divided by class, education of parents, degree of wealth and region, private schools cater to different sections of the fee-paying population. Between 1986 and 1993, 60 per cent of the urban enrolment growth in primary education occurred in private unaided schools, only 16 per cent of the total enrolment growth was accommodated by private unaided schools. Such different private schools generate a systematic inequity among different economic strata. Instead of working towards reform in schools that under-perform, government schemes rely on creating new schools to address "excellence" and, in turn, breed new kinds of inequities in the Indian school system.

Nowhere Children

The dropout of children from the primary and upper primary level remains a serious concern. It varies significantly across different regions, social, economic and gender groups. For example, 57 per cent of the SC children and 66 per cent of the ST children who enter Grade 1, dropout before reaching Grade VIII. About 80 per cent of the ST girl children dropout before reaching Grade VIII in Andhra Pradesh, Orissa, Tripura and West Bengal (2004 – 05). Even among ST boys, the corresponding rates are above 75 per cent in their States. The dropout rates are also consistently higher among girls than boys.

Tilak points out that the reasons for never attending schools and dropping out are broadly similar: the most important reason is the high cost of schooling (including the opportunity costs). Moreover, mere provision of a school faculties is inadequate to attract and retain students in the schools rather than schools should have reasonably good physical infrastructure, committed teachers and should provide an attractive learning environment. The 52nd round of National Sample Survey shows that lack of interest in education accounts for 30 per cent of non-enrolment.

Vimala Ramachandran and Afke De Groot provide evidence from their field visit and interviews of various stakeholders of the education system in Andhra Pradesh and Rajasthan. While official data claims near universal enrolment, 24 per cent of the children in the survey sample were reported as being never re-enrolled. Groot cites the number of 'nowhere children' around 100 million. The children who are neither in school, nor reported to be participating in the labour force have been termed as 'a nowhere children' by D.P. Chaudhri. Apart from the economic condition of family, socio-cultural factors, quality of education, inaccessibility of schools and their improper functioning act as the major factor keeping children out of school.

Questions have been raised on the number of out of school children and their whereabouts. L. Rustagi, Balwant Singh Mehta and Sunil Kumar Mishra provide a detailed account on this. As per the Census 2001, more than 87 million children are still out of school which constitutes 34 per cent of all children in the age group of 5 to 14 years. Although, all States have registered a decline from 1991 to 2001 in the proportion of children outside of school cover, a high degree of disparity persists among States. While Bihar records the highest 57 per cent of children out-of-school, in Kerala this figure is as low as 11 per cent. Moreover, many of them work as labourers. The Census 2001 data reveals that around 11 per cent of the out-of-school children work as child labourers. The decade between 1991 and 2001 shows a downward trend in the child work participation. Around 96 per cent of child workers were out-of-school. This figure fell into 74 per cent in 2001 reflecting that the proportion of school going children among the child workers is increasing.

Quality Concerns

The quality of elementary education, particularly in government primary schools remains a matter of serious concern. Shaik Galab, Moestue, Antony McCoy, Ravi and Prudhvikar Reddy demonstrate from a field study in Andhra Pradesh that, firstly, children in private schools have better literacy and numeracy skills regardless of wealth or caste than children in public schools; Secondly, children with uneducated parents (especially, mothers) are at a disadvantage; Thirdly, this disadvantage is greater in public schools than in private schools, and, finally, girls have lower learning scores than boys.

Krishna Kumar in his article discusses the conceptual issues pertaining to the quality of education and the failure of two innovative schemes – Basic Education (BE) or Nai Talim and Hoshangabad Science Teaching Programme (HSTP). The two programmes were designed to change the social character of school learning and thereby improving the quality of education available to rural children. Krishan Kumar stresses that while evaluating the quality of education, we should depart from the 'outcome' approach and the conditions shaping the school's everyday reality. In this context, the chapter by Rahul Mukhopadhyay argues that the assessment of the quality based only on the parameters like "total admission in school', "total attendance", "percentage of retention of these throughout the year and marks / grades scored by them", "promotion to next class", and "percentage of passes" would fail to account for the socio-economic contingencies that actually shape the domain of learning.

Curriculum, Pedagogy and Learning

Debates surrounding the National Curriculum Framework (NCF) 2005 have been discussed by Padma M. Sarangapani with insights from Popper's philosophy. It is pointed out that although the goal of education should be to navigate social reform, it should not subdue the local identities, history and knowledge for establishing a singular national identity and a universal knowledge system. Education system should rather facilitate for multi-curriculum and plurality. Sadhana Saxena points that although greater progress has been made on raising the female literacy and in higher education, patriarchal values pervade the school pedagogy. Although substantial contributions have been made by the feminist scholars to the so called mainstream discipline, this knowledge generally does not become part of school curriculum. Saxena, thus, calls education as a political process, where the interests of women have been sidelined.

Sudesh Mukhopadhyay reflects upon the inadequacy of measures to address the needs of the children with disabilities in spite of the rhetoric made in several international forums. A very high level of illiteracy prevails among persons with disabilities, especially in rural areas and except for the persons with locomotor disability. About three-fourths of the disabled persons in rural areas are illiterate. In urban areas, the position is slightly better and except in the case of mentally retarded persons, about half the disabled are literate, while among people with locomotor disability, the proportion of illiterates is about 32 per cent.

Regarding the presence of over-aged children in all the classes, Usha Menon points out that one-third of these over-aged students are older by four years or more than the expected age for entry into schooling. With bivariate analysis, she argues that, the presence of over-aged students negatively affects the overall performance of the class. To get rid of this negative effect she suggests exploring alternative enrolment schemes.

Since Independence the Government of India as well as concerned state governments including Government of Andhra Pradesh introduced various types of educational programmes and schools introduced for eradication of illiteracy as follows:

The Vision 2020 document rightly identifies the problems ailing the education system in the state. The document identified low literacy levels of parents, poverty, lack of access to school and poor infrastructure facilities as the main causes of low literacy rates.

The important programmes initiated in tune with new education policy (1986) are Operation Black Board (OBB), Andhra Pradesh Primary Education Project (APPEP) and

District Primary Education Project (DPEP). The OBB programme, supported by the Government of India, focuses on supportive infrastructure such as construction of school buildings, providing teaching aids, playground and creation of additional teacher posts. The APPE was assisted by the Overseas Development Authority (ODA) with the objective of improving the quality of schooling, construction of additional class rooms and teacher training centres. This programme was merged with the DPEP after 1995. DPEP in Andhra Pradesh was launched initially in five backward districts in 1996 and later extended to 14 districts with an objective of involving local community and NGOs in designing, implementation and participation in the education programmes through education committees. This programme has many incentive schemes such as midday meal/supply of dry rations to enhance enrolment, regular attendance of the students and to reduce dropout and also to maintain the nutritional status of the students. The Andhra Pradesh government has also designed schemes such as 'Mabadi" (our School) 'Chaduvkundam' (Back to School) and 'akshara sankranti' to improve access to children, women and of disadvantaged communities in tiny habitations. The 'Vidya volunteer' scheme was started to support single teacher schools.

AP School Programme: The state of Andhra Pradesh has also initiated various programmes such as Maa badi – Our school, Chaduvukundam – Back to school, Akshara Sankranthi – Akshra Jyothi – Chaduvula Pandaga, Residential schools, Anganvadi centers, pre-primary schools (supply of dry ration, text books, uniform etc.) and also adopted the "Bridge-school" to improve access to, women and disadvantaged communities such as Scheduled Castes and Scheduled Tribes children; "Vidya volunteer" scheme was started to support single teacher schools.

Independence and Recent Scenario

After Independence, education became the responsibility

of the states in 1976, education was made a joint responsibility of the states and the center through a constitutional states that education is a fundamental right for all children aged 6-14 years, the Indian education system became marks-based. However, recently some states have introduced a grades–based system in order to help curb the cutthroat competition and rote learning, and focus on creative aspects and personality development.

India, after 66 years as a republic; continues to demonstrate the strength of its political instutions and economic growth and brought significant improvement in material conditions and opportunities in most parts of the country. Education and instutions learning are crucial both to creation of individual capabilities and social development. Therefore the government of India as well as concerned state govts. envisaged various programmes and schemes apart from various models of educational institutions started viz. Mid-day meal programme (MMD), Sarva Siksha Abhiyan (SSA), Rashtriya Madhyamika Siksha Abhiyan, Gurukula Pathasala, Model Schools, Navodaya Vidyalaya Samiti: Jawahar Navodaya Vidyalayas, National Vocational Education Qualifications Framework (NVEQF), Sakshar Bharat Mission 2012.

The target of universalising elementary education was put into action; this made education accessible to children and made sure that they continued the government launched Sarva Shiksha Abhiyan , that monitors drop-out rate, creates parental awareness, community mobilization, economic incentives, minimum levels of learning, district primary education programme, and national programme of nutritional support of primary education (Mid-Day Meals Scheme).

India has been a major seat of learning for centuries, currently, the country has some of the best universities (IITs, IIMs, AIIMS, IISc) in the world; let us continue this tradition with each one teach one.

3

Methodology of the Study

Introduction

This study was conducted in three coastal districts of Andhra Pradesh is known as Uttar Andhra viz. Srikakulam, Vizianagaram and Visakhapatnam which are backward districts of Andhra Pradesh. The study deals with Primary/ Elementary Education only and it is limited to govt. run primary schools of tribal and remote rural areas of North Coastal Andhra. The study has made use of both primary as well as secondary data. The primary data were collected from parents/guardians, teachers, members of school Education committee and cross section of the society. Secondary data were collected from government records, both State and Central government and from the website and from daily newspapers. Experts in primary education have been interviewed to make sure that the study covers all aspects, a study of this kind should cover.

The total sample was 270 from the field area from the three districts.

Significance of the Study

The Education sector has been of vital importance to the Indian Government which has been regularly formulating rules and schemes for promoting elementary education. Since 1950 several steps have been taken for universalization of elementary education (UEE).

The Right to Education has also been enshrined as a Fundamental Right by the Constitution of India. It reads that "The State shall provide free and compulsory education to all children of the age of six to fourteen years in such a manner as the State may, by law, determine." With all the efforts in this direction, India could make vast development with regard to increase in number of institutions, teachers and students in elementary education.

Education is the most powerful input in the process of empowerment as well as creating human capital. Since 1950 efforts were made towards achievement of this goal. In this regard the Govt. of India passed a legislation as a fundamental right as Free and Compulsory Education to all the children upto 14 years of age. Apart from, the Government of India is sincerely committed for eradication of illiteracy for which they started mid-day meal programme, and the programes of Navodaya Vidyalaya Samiti, Sarvasiksha Abhiyan, District Primary Education Programme (DPEP), Sakshar Bharat Mission (2012), Rashtriya Madhyamika Siksha Abhiyan, Gurukula Patha sala, Model schools in backward mandals. In spite of all these efforts, India has not yet achieved universalisation of elementary education even after lapse of 64 years of Independence. It is estimated that 140 million children enrolled in the 6 to 14 age group in primary schools. Of these, 30 million cannot read. 40 million can recognize only a few alphabets, 40 million can read some words, 30 million can read few paragraphs. Over 55 million of the children will not complete 4 years of schooling, eventually adding to India's vast illiterate population. If the same trend continues, we cannot achieve the desired literacy in the near future. In this backdrop, the researcher has given below information based on secondary data, as such. Out of 187 countries in the world, India stands 147th Rank with 66% as per the United Nations Development Programme Report 2009. As per the 2011 Census, India's literacy was 74.04%. Out of all the 35 States & Union Territories, Andhra Pradesh stands 28th Rank with 67.66%. The average literacy rate of study area is (63.16%) (Uttarandhra viz. Srikakulam (62.30%), Vizianagaram (59.49%), Visakhapatnam (67.70%) for 2011. In this scenario, the researcher aimed to study to achieve effective implementation of Right to Education Act and attainment of the Universalisation of Literacy in a specific period of time as a part of national endeavor of development.

In spite of the above said impressive achievements there are certain draw backs in the program. Out of the 200 million children in the age group of 6 - 14 years, 59 million children are not attending school. Of this, 35 million are girls and 24 million are boys. There are problems relating to drop - out rate, low levels of learning achievement and low participation of girls, tribals and other disadvantaged groups. There are still at least one lakh habitations in the country without schooling facility within a kilometre. Coupled with it are various issues like inadequate school infrastructure, poorly functioning schools, high teacher absenteeism, large number of teacher vacancies, poor quality of education and inadequate funds.

Precisely India is yet to achieve the goal of Universal Elementary Education (UEE) i.e. 100% enrollment and retention and to fill this gap Government of India has launched Sarva Siksha Abhiyan (SSA).

As mentioned in the aims of Sarva Shiksha Abhiyan, useful and relevant education signifies a quest for education system that does not alienate and draw on community solidarity. Its aim is to allow children to learn about and master their natural environment in a manner that allows the fullest harnessing of their human potential both spiritually and materially.

The *Sarva Shiksha Abhiyaan* is also known as the *"Education for All"* a movement of 'Each One Teach One'. It was introduced in 2000-2001 as the flagship programme run by the Government of India. This scheme is framed to provide useful and relevant elementary education for all children in the age group of six to fourteen by 2010.The Sarva Shiksha Abhiyan aims to bridge social, regional and gender gaps, with the active participation of the community in the management of schools.

To make elementary education a fundamental right, "the surest way of ensuring rapid inclusive growth", as stated by the Prime Minister, Manmohan Singh, in the 80th Annual General Body Meeting of the Federation of Indian Chambers of Commerce and Industry on February 15, 2008 and the Union Government might take up all the financial responsibility of the Bill which is estimated to be as high as Rs 12.5 billion a year.

Keeping all the above said concerns in view the researcher has undertaken the research with the main aim to find out the impact of educational programs in three districts and nine mandals of the state of Andhra Pradesh with the following objectives.

Objectives of the Study

1. To assess the financial conditions of the sampled respondents from rural area (the three districts).
2. To know the educational qualifications of the respondents (parents / guardians).
3. To assess parents opinion of children's primary education standards / quality of education.
4. To assess the opinion of teachers for effective implementation of Right to Education Act 2009.
5. To study parents opinion about the regularity, punctuality and sincerity of teachers.

6. To know parents and teachers opinion about infrastructural and other facilities available for students in the schools besides the inspecting officers.
7. To study the parents opinion about School management committee on the day to day functioning, monitoring and to avoid pitfalls in school education programme.
8. To study the strategies adopted by the Government for increasing literacy in the country.
9. To suggest professionals and academicians opinion about the plans, if any for effective implementation of Right to Education Act in toto.

Profile of Andhra Pradesh

Andhra Pradesh is considered to be the fifth largest state of India by its land area and population. Total area of Andhra Pradesh is 275,068 sq. km. The state lies between 12N & 22 N latitude and 77E & 84 E longitude. Andhra Pradesh is also the largest and most populous state in South India.

The state of Andhra Pradesh is surrounded by Chhattisgarh, Maharashtra and Orissa in the North, Tamil Nadu in the South and Karnataka in the West. The Bay of Bengal borders the state in the East.

The total Andhra Pradesh Area is divided into 23 districts. The name of the districts are–Adilabad, Anantapur, Chittoor, East Godavari, Guntoor, Hyderabad, Kadapa, Karimnagar, Khammam, Krishna, Kurnool, Mahbubnagar, Medak, Nalgonda, Nellore, Nizamabad, Prakasam, Rangareddi, *Srikakulam, Vizianagaram, Vishakhapatanam,* Warangal and West Godavari.

The state of Andhra Pradesh is also divided into four Governance Regions. They are- Telangana, Rayalaseema, Coastal Andhra and *North Coastal Andhra.*

The uneven ratio of Teacher-Student in the Elementary schools of Andhra Pradesh

Indication of No. of Teachers in Schools in the year of 2010 Academic year

	No. of Students	*0 teachers*	*1 teachers*	*2 teachers*	*3 teachers*	*4 teachers*	*5 teachers*	*More than teachers*	*Total schools*
No. of students in various schools	0-5	365	883	251	36	7	5	15	1562
	6-10	273	1092	252	11	2	0	1	1631
	11-20	930	3171	1519	49	4	2	4	5679
	21-30	1282	4649	4999	165	18	12	6	11131
	31-40	970	2204	6145	408	47	10	5	9789
	41-50	697	1297	4629	684	103	24	20	7454
	51-60	333	508	1948	569	138	28	9	3533
	61-70	212	317	1182	736	167	45	20	2669
	71-80	132	198	574	522	197	56	21	1710
	81-90	108	151	415	529	196	63	31	1493
	91-100	73	104	217	370	188	76	33	1061
	100 and more	399	596	1275	2198	2040	1429	1314	9251
	Total	5774	15170	23416	6267	3107	1750	1479	56963

Therefore it is essential to have rational distribution of teachers basing on the student strength.

In 5774 schools out of 59,963 Elementary schools, there is not even a single teacher in each: 15170 schools, are run by a single teacher in each school, whereas in 23,460 schools there are two teachers in each school, in 6267 schools there are 3 teachers in each , 4 teachers each in 3107 schools, similarly there are five (5) teachers each in 1429 schools and more than 5 teachers working in each of the 1479 schools.

The above table indicates that there is no rational distribution of teachers basing on the student strength as even there is single student in a particular school where more than 5 teachers are working. Further it indicates that the table where there are more than 100 students, inversely there is no single teacher even in 399 schools. Further it also shows that the teacher-student ratio Viz, 5:1, 5:4, 5:6, 5:9, and so for more or less other 1470 schools like this in A.P.

Profile of the Study Area (North Coastal Andhra Pradesh)

North Coastal Andhra Pradesh is situated between 17° 10′ to 19° 10′ N latitudes and 81°53′ to 84° 50′ E longitudes. It is bounded on the North by Orissa state, on the South by East Godavari district, on the eastern part bordering with Bay of Bengal and on the West by East Godavari district and part of Orissa comprising Srikakulam, Vizianagaram and Visakhapatnam districts (Fig-1). The irrigated and rain fed areas of North Coastal Andhra Pradesh with a total area of about 85,2700 hectares is under cultivation from the total geographical area of 23,48,612 hectares of the three districts. The major river systems are Vamsadhara, Nagavali, Janjavathi, Champavathi, Vegavathi, Vattigadda, Gosthani, Sarada, Varaha and Thandava. The soils are red loamy and alluvial. The area is divided into coastal, plain and hilly land areas. The main crops are rice, sugarcane, groundnut, fingermillet, sesamum, jowar, bajra and mesta etc. The cultivated fields of the region are infested with a large number of weeds causing heavy losses to crop yield. It is pertinent to note that the presence of weeds in herbaceous crops like rice, sugarcane, groundnut, sesamum, fingermillet, sesamum, jowar, bajra and legume implicit major losses.

Demograhphic Profile of North Coastal Andhra: Srikakulam, Vizianagaram & Visakhapatnam Districts. 9 mandals comprising 3 districts survey conducted in 27 villages, taking samples from each village. The total sample is 270.

Srikakulam: Palakonda, Polaki and Seethemmapeta Mandals.

Vizianagaram: Gummalakshmipuram, Kurupam and Pachipenta Mandals.

Visakhapatnam: Chintapalli, Madugula and Paderu Mandals.

Scenario of the Study Area

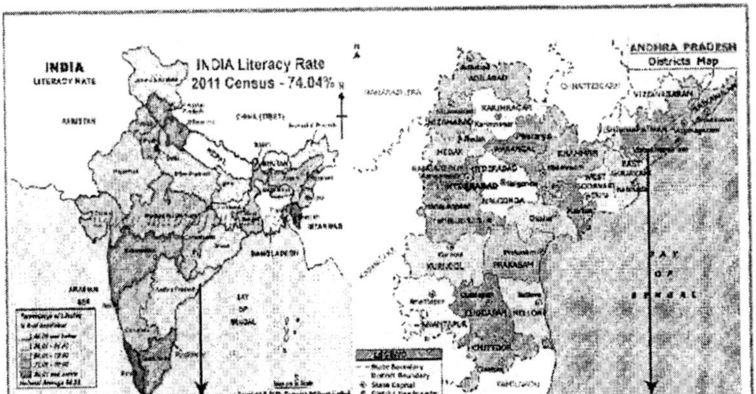

Andhra Pradesh Stands at 31th Position with 67.66% (2011 Census) of 28 States and 7 UTs

North Coastal AP(SKLM, VZM,VSKP) Districts Average Literacy rate as per the 2011 Census 63.16%

The study is undertaken in nine mandals of three districts of the state of North coastal Andhra Pradesh they are Srikakulam Vizianagaram and Visakhapatnam to be listed 9 mandals (Palakonda, Seethampeta, Polaki, Gummalakshmipuram, Kurupam, Pachipenta, Madugula, Paderu and Chintapalli Mandals). Detailed description of the study area is given in chapter III. The study area has been carried out in three districts of the state of Andhra Pradesh. The state on account of its diverse and pluralistic socio economic and physical characteristics offers a unique form of miniature India. Further the inter district classification of these four regions show that the following districts have attained a high level of social development, viz. East Godavari, West Godavari, Krishna, Guntur in South Coast area, Hyderabad and Ranga Reddy and some of other districts except Mahaboob Nagar in Telangana region whereas in Rayalaseema is almost all the districts are one and the same in social development. The state on account of its diverse and pluralistic socioeconomic and physical characteristics, the pattern of social development in the state has been highly skewed as some districts have marched ahead, while others have lagged behind. This uneven growth in social sectors across various regions of this state has unduly affected the pace of development, accentuating the problem of rural-urban and inter-district migration, plight of capital and incidence of poverty. The state has been divided into four geographical regions such as North Coastal Andhra, Coastal Andhra, Rayalaseema and Telangana. If these regions are selected on the basis of their level of social development as high, medium and low. Out of these four regions North Coastal Andhra has lower level of social development in all aspects.

On account of time constraint the study selected only three districts is known as North Coastal Andhra viz. Srikakulam, Vizianagaram and Visakhapatnam. Therefore study selected only North Coastal Andhra region as being the low developed one. Hence the sample survey in 9 mandals form these three districts. These three districts were selected with the help of a three stage stratified sampling techniques.

District-wise Literacy Rate in India - 2011 Census

District	*Persons*	*Males*	*Females*	*Literacy %*	*Male %*	*Female %*
Total	51438510	28759782	22678728	67.66%	75.56%	59.74%
Adilabad	1503106	864990	638116	61.55%	71.22%	51.99%
Nizamabad	1421759	809721	612038	62.25%	72.66%	52.33%
Karimnagar	2263247	1292858	970389	64.87%	74.72%	55.18%
Medak	1677732	975710	702022	62.53%	72.50%	52.49%
Hyderabad	2906923	1540195	1366728	80.96%	83.35%	78.42%
Rangareddy	3669033	2018557	1650476	78.05%	84.00%	71.82%
Mahbubnagar	1984586	1183860	800726	56.06%	66.27%	45.65%
Nalgonda	2035177	1178956	856221	65.05%	74.93%	55.05%
Warangal	2116037	1211953	904084	66.16%	75.91%	56.45%
Khammam	1656686	918880	737806	65.46%	73.20%	57.85%
*Srikakulam	1516425	870196	646229	62.30%	72.25%	52.56%

Contd...

District	*Persons*	*Males*	*Females*	*Literacy %*	*Male %*	*Female %*
*Vizianagaram	1256342	720623	535719	59.49%	69.04%	50.16%
*Visakhapatnam	2612624	1450555	1162069	67.70%	75.47%	60.00%
East Godavari	3324111	1737357	1586754	71.35%	74.91%	67.82%
West Godavari	2654267	1380713	1273554	74.32%	77.63%	71.05%
Krishna	3065669	1630049	1435620	74.37%	79.13%	69.62%
Guntur	3006999	1660019	1346980	67.99%	75.40%	60.64%
Prakasam	1926495	1122249	804246	63.53%	73.53%	53.40%
Sri Potti Sriramulu Nellore	1852239	1021639	830600	69.15%	75.93%	62.30%
Y.S.R.	1745178	1012105	733073	67.88%	78.41%	57.26%
Kurnool	2182149	1279938	902211	61.13%	71.36%	50.81%
Anantapur	2350294	1365701	984593	64.28%	74.09%	54.31%
Chittoor	2711432	1512958	1198474	72.36%	81.15%	63.65%

Source: 2011 Census Government of India.

Study area known as North Coast Andhra Pradesh viz. Srikakulam, Vizianagaram, Visakhapatnam Districts.

As per the 2011 census the latest scenario of most backward districts of Andhra Pradesh, Srikakulam, Vizianagaram and Visakhapatnam is as follows:

Since 1951, the literacy rate of these districts (North Coastal Andhra region) is below the average level of other regions of Andhra Pradesh as a whole and also below average the national literacy. As per the 2011 census in this region average literacy rate is 63.16% whereas the AP average literacy rate is 67.66% and the Indian average literacy rate is 74.04%. It is one of the important social indicators to assess backwardness. Further it is analyzed district-wise of the region (Srikakulam, Vizianagaram & Visakhapatnam) North Coastal Andhra known as Uttarandhra is discussed as below.

In Srikakulam (SKL) district the literacy rate is below average literacy of A.P. as well as India. The total literacy rate of SKL is 55.31% in 2001 and 62.30% in 2011 out of which the male literacy rate 67.19% in 2001 and 72.25% in 2011 whereas the female literacy is 43.68% in 2001 and 52.56% in 2011. The value is 23.50% in 2001 and 19.69% in 2011 in SKLM dist if it is also below the average literacy of the state as well as the nation. The literacy rate of Vizianagaram (VZM) distt. is 51.07%in 2001 and 59.49% in 2011 out of which 62.37% in 2001 and 69.04% in 2011 is male literacy and 39.91% in 2001 and 50.16% in 2011 female literacy. The value of male and female is 22.46% in 2001 and 18.88% in 2011 in VZM dist. It is also below the average literacy of national as well as state. Whereas the literacy rate of Visakhapatnam (VSKP) is 59.96% in 2001 and 67.70% in 2011 out of which 69.98% in 2001 and 75.47% in 2011 is male literacy and 50.12% in 2001 and 60.00% in 2011 is female literacy. The value between male and female rate is 19.56% in 2001 and 15.47% in 2011 in VSKP district. These

All	*Andhra Pradesh*	*Visakhapatnam*			*Vizianagaram*			*Srikakulam*		
	Lit. Rate	*Population*	*Literates*	*Lit. Rate*	*Population*	*Literates*	*Lit. Rate*	*Population*	*Literates*	*Lit. Rate*
Total	(2001) 60.47	3,832,336	2,002,316	59.96	2,249,254	997,482	51.07	2,537,593	1,217,659	55.31
	(2011) 67.66	4,288.113	2,612,624	67.70	2,342,868	1,256,342	59.49	2,699,471	1,516,425	62.30
Male	(2001) 70.32	1,930,197	1,171,082	69.68	1,119,541	605,038	62.37	1,260,020	731,778	67.19
	(2011) 75.56	2,140,872	1,450,555	75.47	1,161,913	720,623	69.04	1,340,430	870,196	72.25
Female	(2001) 50.43	1,902,139	831,234	50.12	1,129,713	392,444	39.91	1,277,573	485,881	43.68
	(2011) 59.74	2,147,241	1,162,069	60.00	1,180,955	535,719	50.16	1,359,041	646,229	52.56
Gender Gap	(2001)19.89 (2011)15.82			(2001)19.56 (2011)15.47			(2001)22.46 (2011)18.88			(2001)23.50 (2011)19.69

figures indicate that this region known as north coastal Andhra Pradesh is literally backward. Therefore this region is selected as the study area. Our sample targeted only three sets of households that were almost all living below the poverty line. The classification of the villages is made on the basis of their geographical, population, infrastructure facility of the village.

During the participant observation the researcher found some of the difficulties, that the performance of this region in attaining literacy has been very low. Most of the rural, tribal population are living below poverty line, suffering from unemployment and illiteracy. Further this area mostly drought haunt area. As per the official source nearly about - 40 percent not only paddy and other crops are being damaged every year due to various reasons including, untimely rains, scanty rains sometimes heavy rains and floods whatever the reason may be. Further this region considered to be socially, culturally, economically and historically backward.

Infact parents are interested to pursue their children's education but they are unable to attend due to poverty, hunger, unemployment, illiteracy and ill health, Apart from this there has been lack of motivation to the parents from various corners. For example, sending a child to school on a regular basis demands a great deal of effort, to start with schooling is expensive. Though the government schools collect zero fee, slates, pencils, free uniform and other stationery, transportation etc, but the main problem is maintaining livelihood of the family (earning of daily bread). In addition to that, sending a child to school demands a good deal of time and attention, eg. to prepare a child for school early hours in the morning, stimulating his/her interest, help them with home work and establish support with teacher. In many respects, these efforts are much more in demand for unprivileged families, especially when the children are first generation school goers. Therefore, the researcher found non-enrolled as well as dropout children during the middle of the academic year; prevalence is very high in the region of North Coastal Andhra which is taken as study area.

Methodology

The Study has used mixed methodology meaning both qualitative and quantitative methods. A sample questionnaire was used consisting of 52 simple way of questions covered with respondents/parents age, family profile including economic status, (especially for expenditure on education) size of the family, community, teacher's attitude of the school committee as well of the cross section of the society. While collecting the data in the field area the discussions from all sections are depicted and interviewed respondents (parents), teachers, school management committee(SMC) and cross sections of the society (see interview schedule look at page from 15 to 25 page) .

Data: This study is mainly based on the primary source of data which has been collected through:

1. Survey of the study area
2. Survey of the selected area
3. Survey of sampled parents' respondents' households

The survey was conducted on the basis of questionnaire interview (Appendix-1). The field work was done during the year 2009-2011 for getting accurate information the sampled villages and the house holds of the sampled parents were frequently visited. The data from secondary sources have been collected from various Government offices, journals, bulletins, websites and given in the bibliography.

Sampling Procedure

For the purpose of selecting the sample, multi-stage stratified sampling design was adopted. 90 samples were collected from and total sample was 270. The first stage consisted of selection of villages from the 9 mandals of three districts of North Coastal Andhra Pradesh. While selecting the villages accessibility factor was kept in mind since some villages are not having even path route/katcha route even today. All the villages selected were categorized into the three heads on the basis of geographical educational and socio–economic background. The total sample size consisted of 270 parents. A total of 15 villages were thus purposely selected because of the above mentioned reasons.

Interview Schedule

During the field work the researcher interviewed and opened the discussions with the educational experts, social scientists of various universities and also school teachers from both Corporate and Government schools as well as parents and cross section of the society. A draft schedule was then prepared consisting of parts. The first part was focused on parents, seeking information about their age, sex, religion and caste, education, marital status, family type, size, housing conditions, family and their occupation. The second part sought information on quality of education of their children, dropouts, no-enrollment and alcoholism, teacher's attitude, infrastructure facilities, school committee and teacher student ratio etc.

A team of researchers consisting of the coordinator, deputy coordinator, department staff, research fellows, field assistants / workers conducted the village and household survey. They developed close contacts with the parents, teachers and village educational committee. The parents were interviewed by this team of researchers on the basis of schedule developed. Direct observation, with photographs, video film were also made.

Collection of Data

Nearly about one year was taken for the collection of data. The selected parent(s)/respondents were interviewed personally by the researchers on the basis of the schedule. Some of the household respondent(s) were visited atleast thrice to cross-check the information provided. First they were hesitant but gradually they opened up and gave all the relevant information. The data was collected from all the villages, it was then tabulated and entered by using computer basically Microsoft excel package. Later analysis was done.

Application of Tools and Techniques

Interview schedule was adopted to collect the data from respondents viz., children studying in these schools, parents of these children, teachers working in these schools and local leaders along with members of school education committee in all the nine mandals comprising three districts.

For all the variables, the data are presented district-wise and mandal-wise. Parents, teachers and cross section of people at local level were the respondents. The interview schedule was covered with socio-economic and education background. Statistical techniques like percentages, mean values, standard deviation and chi-square values are used for socio-economic and educational variables of the respondents.

Limitations of the Study

1. Non-responsive behavior and relutance on the part of the parents noticed while collecting the data is major limitation of the study.

2. Some of the schools situated in remote rural and tribal areas do not have access as there are no Katcha Road or foot path.

3. There are few schools which remain closed during the school hours. Therefore teachers are not available.

4. The mid-day meal which is provided to the children is vague and uncertain. As some schools remain closed, we could not assess the mid day meal programme.

5. Information from the teachers regarding their schools in respect of their duty and imparting education to the students is reluctant and scarce.
6. During the field work most of the parents were not available as they are going to get their daily bread or on some other work.
7. In remote Rural Tribal areas the response of parents was very poor as they cannot understand the main regional language as they only know their Vernacular language.

4

Gloom to Bloom Through Education

All of these students who belong to poor family have been awarded as state toppers in intermediate examination through Government institutions. The other physically handicapped people of whom some completely blind and some of them are suffering from lack of upper limbs as well as lower limbs. In spite of that, they acquired higher qualifications and also have been striving to reach further better positions.

In this backdrop, the researcher interviewed the above respondents viz. Mrs. Ramanamma, Mr. Srinivas, Ms. Ayesha, and Mr. Venkat and others that there are people who live in precarious conditions and people do not have sense organs but can occupy better positions owing to their hard work. As such, every one who deserves should be given a helping hand to prove their mettle, and utilize human resources, so that they can be of great service to the society at large.

Education is the most important ingredient to every one. As it paves the way for better future and makes man eligible and thrive. It reaches man in the pursuit of realization of various abilities and capacities. Finally, it gives the capacity to succeed in the struggle for survival. As such, in the circumstances, we are bringing some episodes from gloom to bloom through education, as a catalyst.

From Gloom to Bloom Through Education

Discourse on the Subject

As a catalyst the researcher conducted interviews with various respondents including physically challenged persons, students studied from government schools and parents of the children.

Question 1: what is your name?

Answer: **Mohana Rao, K.** (Mr. K. Mohan Rao: is a 25-year old innocent young blind boy, who appears teeming with full of joy and is in a happy mood. With him, there is not any kind of ill feeling owing to his blindness. He feels himself very normal. When the researcher saw him, he was found immersed in pursuit of his study. He recites his lessons in the college premises, before the commencement of regular classes)

Question 2: What are you studying?

Answer: M. A. [Political Science]

Question 3: Where are you studying?

Ans: In Andhra University.

Question 4: Though you are physically challenged person with blindness, how are you pursuing your higher education?

Ans: Sir, there is no bar for learning or acquiring higher qualifications, as I am from a poor family. Apart from that, I am physically handicapped. But I never neglect my education, as education not only covers knowledge, it also covers morals, ethics and religion among other skills and as such ignorance can be mitigated.

Question 5: What is your life's pursuit?

Ans: My life's pursuit is to become a good teacher and impart knowledge to children.

Question 6: Can you say anything more?

Ans: Yes, I don't like others showing any sympathy and pity for any handicap. But instead, one can admire our hard work.

Finally, he expresses his strong views on education, saying that with education, one can overcome any kind of trouble and problem. And ultimately, he believes that he can achieve his life's goal. Let us hear about it in his own words.

Question 7: Will you tell us your name?

Ans: My name is **Ramanamma Chitrada**

Researcher interacted with Ramanamma, a physically handicapped of Andhra University

Question 8: What are your qualifications?

Ans: I studied M.Com.

Question 9: Where did you complete your M.Com.?

Ans: I completed my M.Com. in Andhra University.

Question 10: What is your advice to make education reach the unreached?

Ans: Sir, I come from scheduled caste, apart from suffering from poverty, being physically handicapped. I have overcome all these problems and had successfully completed my post-graduation, while doing my job.

I believe that there can be no bar for learning and attaining education with poverty, caste, colour or even physical handicap, which are all irrelevant.

Of this, I am aware from my personal experience and it is my sincere opinion that if any one is really interested in pursuing education, nothing can be any hurdle or obstruction for learning. However with motivation, infrastructure facilities are very essential to those who are unable to pursue their educational career.

Interview with Srinivas Rao

Question 11: Dear Srinivas Rao, could you tell your opinion about importance of education especially elementary education?

Ans: Sir, I am born blind. I come from a remote rural background and I belong to a poor family and my parents are also illiterates.

During my childhood I had been feeling some kind of helplessness as I am completely blind. My parents and my kith and kin and also my villagers have dissuaded me to go outside for education in view of my blindness. But my conscience has not permitted me to burden my parents or even anyone. Hence, I took certain steps on my own and requested my parents to join me in a blind school. During course of time, I worked hard in my studies and finally, I have built up my confidence myself that I can be able to lead my life on my own without burdening any one. Education also gave me certain confidence that can't be stolen by any one. That is the importance of education sir.

Interview with Siva Krishnan's Parents

Question 12: You are running a pan-shop. Did you expect that your son could get 19th rank (922 / 1000) in intermediate course in the State?

Ans: **Father:** (He replied with shedding of happy tears) Sir, I myself am a semi literate, running a small pan-shop and my wife is illiterate. However, right from the beginning, my son is working hard. Apart from this, there are good teachers who take lot of interest in imparting education.

PARENTS (Sivakrishna)

Mother: (His mother joined in the discussion and said:) "My boy always pursues his studies day-and-night without taking any rest, though we are illiterates and poor".

Question 13: Will you expect any support from the Government?

Ans: Yes, the Government is supporting. They also further support and encourage the poor meritorious children.

Interview with Yedukondalu

Question 14: What is your good name, please?

Ans: My name is Yedukondalu.

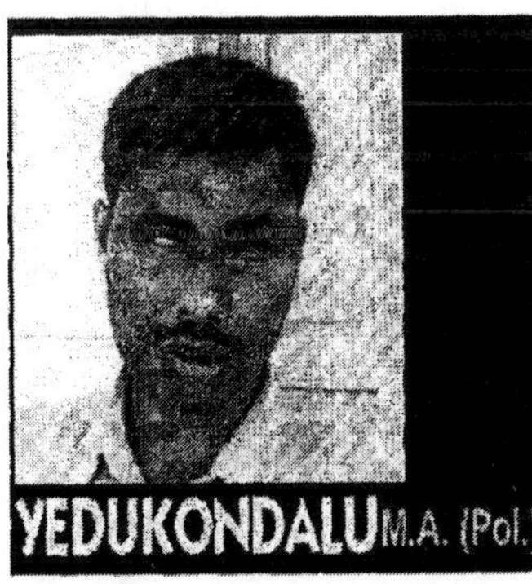
YEDUKONDALU M.A. (Pol.)

Question 15: What are you studying?

Ans: I am studying M. A. (Political Science) in Andhra University.

Question 16: Mr. Yedukondalu, though you are a blind person, you are seriously pursuing higher education with commitment. What is your viewpoint as a blind person regarding individuals, who are neglecting education as a pursuit?

Ans: Frankly telling, we should not be burdensome to even our parents. In fact, we should not beg or borrow anyone. As such, education is very essential for individual's empowerment to overcome all the problems and hurdles, for which education is the only instrument for making survival of right persons.

First of all, my suggestion is that the Government should identify problems and rectify pitfalls and loopholes, wherever located, by which proper action can be taken up for the benefit of society, in the attainment of the goal of Right to Education.

Interview with Rank-holder – Lakshmi

Question 17: What is your good name?

Ans: Lakshmi.

Question 18: Which rank you secured in intermediate in the State?

Ans: 42nd Rank – 907 / 1000

Question 19: Kum. Lakshmi, how could you get that rank as you are from a complete rural background?

Ans: I worked very hard with teachers and parents support.

Teachers

A. There are very good teachers who have worked in rural area from primary to inter and degree. They are not at all in favour of any private managed corporate institutions. If Government teachers are further dedicated to their profession all the corporate / private schools, will be closed in near future.

Question 20: What is your view point about government educational institutions?

Ans: (i) First of all, Government should provide infrastructure facilities.

(ii) Secondly, there are efficient teachers who could dedicate their services exclusively to impart knowledge to students.

(iii) Thirdly, parents also should show interest and motivate their children.

Interview with Miss. Koyajakshi

Question 21: Miss Koyajakshi, what do you want to tell about yourself?

KOYAJAKSHI M.A. Socio.

Ans: I belong to a tribal community and we live in very remote tribal area, where there are scarce facilities. However, I am pursuing my post-graduation course in Sociology in Andhra University.

I wish all children like me should get educated, especially all tribal children. I request the government to take up further steps for the development of tribal communities to join the main stream.

Discourse on the Subject

Question 1: Could you tell your name?

Ans: My name is **Kandari Lakshmana Rao** (Fisher Man).

When asked about their children's education Mr. Lakshamana Rao

Impact of Adult's Consuming of Alcohol on Childern's Education

expressed his anguish over children's education. Further he expressed categorically:

- No teacher would take any interest to educate children.
- The child doesn't know alphabets at all even after seven years schooling. For example, age-wise, this boy should be studying seventh standard. But presently he is in 2nd standard and he doesn't know alphabets as such.

Question 2: Could you say anything else Lakshmana Rao?

Ans: He replied that:

- Due to absence of teachers, children completely do not like to go to school, as there is no use of going there.
- Coming to absence and apathetic attitudes of teachers, this is what children tell their parents.

Question 3: Mr. Kadimudili Bullaiah. Is there any impact on children's education due to consumption of alcohol?

Ans:

- There is no impact, even our children studied upto 5th standard in the Government school, they cannot read or write at least their name in Telugu (cinema poster). In our school.
- No government teacher will take any positive interest.
- Salaries given to them, go waste. It is better to close the schools. This is a reply with a sense of anguish.

Question 4: When asked **Mrs. M. Dhana** about her children's education

Ans: she said that

- The Government school teachers never bother about children's education.
- Some parents ask the teacher, whenever he physically punishes their children in the name of not studying well.
- As such, our children were not willing to go to school and they want to discontinue their studies.

Question 5: Mrs. Korlamma Yedula. Is there any impact on your children's education due to consumption of alcohol by your husband?

Ans: She replied her view, in this manner:

- We have no money to send our children to private schools. Therefore we send our children to Government school only.
- Even then, there is no progress in Government schools as those schools are meant for poor people like us.
- Due to sending children to school, we lose both children's education as well as their help at home and it makes them roaming on the streets.

Ans: Another fisherwoman, **Mrs. Lakshmi** interacted herself during the interview and said, that every day her husband does not have daily-work,

- On that day, he gets drunk and harasses the entire family using abusive language and physically harass the family members.
- He does not even spare his elderly daughter and old parents and as such, it becomes a routine life.
- Mentally, we prepare ourselves for such a worst contingency and troublesome life.

- In such a background, we cannot prepare our children to go to school. Even if we send them, there is no use at all.
- As the Government school teachers will not take care of children's education, owing to our poverty.

Question 5: Mrs. Yellayamma, Is there any impact on your children's education due to consumption of alcohol by your husband?

Ans:

- Certainly, there is. When my husband was drunk, children were afraid to see him and mentally they become upset and will be having fear-complex of a worst kind.
- He shouts and terrorizes the whole family.
- And, sometimes, due to fear, they run away from home, as they cannot concentrate on their studies.
- He will not even spare children and old parents.
- My husband never bothers about children's education.
- As such, alcohol is a root-cause of all problems like illiteracy, poverty, ill-health and early death, etc.

When researcher asked a couple of women (Sarswathi and Yellayyamma), they jointly replied that their husbands are always in a drunken state.

- When the husband does not have money for drink, he shouts and physically batters all of the family members.
- He will not spare his old parents either. Sometimes he ransacks the entire home on some pretext or other and cannot concentrate on children's education.

- Because of this, we fail to send our five children to school.

During the interview, another lady (**Ramanamma**) joined the issue and said that:

- Recently due to consumption of alcohol, 8 members died in their colony.
- As they started to drink at the age of 12 years, instead of going to school and they are habituated to take alcohol regularly.
- When father is a drunkard, naturally children also start to drink alcohol and naturally their education and career will get affected.

Later Mr. Yedla Krishna joined in the discussion and he confessed himself and said that:

- Due to his faulty behaviour, his children are also affected, in that they are out of control from discipline.
- He further tells, that he is unable to stop drinking alcohol.
- But we are optimistic about prevalence of better education for children, which could be realized at school, where it is presently abysmal.

The general voices of working class women about alcohol

- It is the general voice of public especially working class women/vulnerable class women who expressed their opinion as respondents.
- Most of their husbands / family members are addicted for consumption of alcohol.

- It is the evil of them as it reduces health and finally takes the life. It also pushes the family into poverty.
- Further expressed not only destroying their families but their children's education also.
- Alcohol is one of most important aspect for prevalence of high illiteracy in lower class.
- Alcohol is the root cause of all social evils like crime, illiteracy, broken marriage and family system and laxity of social values.

Finally labour and vulnerable working women pray the Government to impose strict ban on alcohol to improve the quality of society in all respects otherwise no use of providing welfare and developmental activities to them what they said.

Interaction with Sr. Advocates

The researcher interacted with Vizag-bar members about the pros and-cons in its letter and spirit implementation of the RTE Act.

1. Shri. D.V. Subbarao, Fomer Chairman Bar Council of India, Ex. Mayor, Visakhapatnam
2. Shr. K.A. Prakash, President, Bar Asson, VSP.
3. Shri. K. Krishna Mohan, Advocate and Journalist
4. Shri. V. Deveswararao, Sr. Advocate

Some of the Suggestions Made by the Academicians, Professors and Senior Advocates

Sri D. V. Subba Rao

Former Chairman, Bar Council of India
& Former Mayor of Visakhapatnam

Q: Sir, what do you suggest for implementation of the provision of the RTE ACT 2009?

1) RTE Act is brought by the central government for free and compulsory education to children between 6 to 14 years is a boon to the deprived sections of the society.
2) I am happy at least now at the belated stage the Government has brought out this piece of legislation.
3) It should be state policy as it is in the constitutional ambit and gravity to speed up with gust and determination.
4) Till now it remained unimplemented comparatively with other developed countries.
5) Illiteracy, poverty are the pains of the nations to declare holy hopes of constitutional declaration. Therefore illiteracy to be removed for the progress of the nation in all respects.
6) Child labour can be eliminated if they go to schools. For them primary education is a goal to schools and colleges basing on their economic position. They can pursue higher education and be able to participate in the national progress. The implementation of RTE Act must be sped up with determination.

Prof. P. Hrushikesava Rao

Former Director, School of Distance Education, Andhra University, Visakhapatnam

Some concrete remedial measures have to be taken to help realize the dreams of the Authors of the Legislation:

1) Provision of adequate infrastructure facilities in the Government schools with the combined efforts of both the Central and State Governments.

2) Provision of compensatory stipends for poor children to reduce dropout rates, thereby avoiding problems of child labour.

3) Provision of budgetary allocations towards primary education should be enhanced.

4) Funds should be released at least during the second quarter of the financial year from out of the fourth quarter.

5) Recruitment of quality teachers is a must to impart quality education.

Prof. N.L. Narasimha Rao

Director, School of Distance Education, Andhra University, Visakhapatnam

1) Children particularly girl children are dropping from schools due to lack of infrastructure facilities.

2) Steps to be taken to improve the quality of education which is poor in government schools.

3) Teachers and parents and Vidya committee should be made totally responsible for the strict and effective implementation of the Act.

4) At rural level, many a teachers are reluctant to go to smaller and remote areas and perform their duties with utmost sincerity and an element of sacrifice. They should also be provided with some incentives.

Master Vinaesh

IVth Standard

Etasy Timpany School, Visakhapatnam

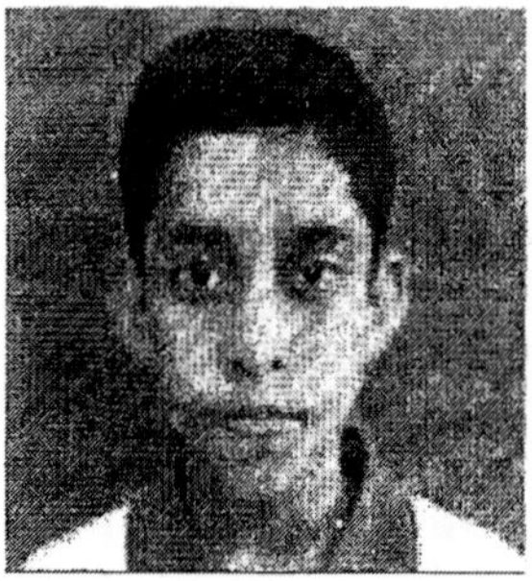

1) The development of health and medicine, science and technology, research, agriculture, defence, general knowledge and religion, which are all covered by the field of education, is very broad and vital for human society.

2) I, therefore, request both Central Government and State Government to allocate more funds to make complete educated society as the present pumping money is not sufficient for attainment of 100 % literacy.

3) I request all the teachers, who are respected next to the parents, to make their full efforts with dedication to impart knowledge to the children.

4) Finally, I pray to all the parents to send their children to the school without fail as illiteracy is the root cause of all problems.

Sr. Valasamma Joseph
Head Mistress, R.C.M.,
St. Peter's Primary School, Visakhapatnam

1) Number of schools have to be opened to fulfill the objective of UEE..
2) All the major festivals and events are being celebrated in the school, throughout the year.
3) Children's educational awareness programme has to be taken up among parents by locals, NGOs and mass media.
4) Teaching methods have to be made attractive to create wholesome atmosphere like that of home.
5) Teachers will have to further dedicate their services with sincere commitment and love for learning.

Prof. A. Rajendra Prasad
Principal, College of Law
Andhra University, Visakhapatnam

1) Now it is high time to remind the responsibility of parents, especially in the rural areas, to send the children to the schools and not to the odd jobs.
2) The environment of school should also be attractive.
3) The system should be strengthened.
4) A single teacher cannot devote his energies to motivate the students to continue their education and prevent drop-outs from the schools.

Prof. T. Viswanadha Rao
Professor of English
Andhra University, Visakhapatnam

1) We may have infrastructure, we may have electronic devices and we may have other gadgets. Yet, it is ultimately the living voice of a dedicated teacher that makes all the difference.
2) We, as teachers, have to rededicate ourselves to the task of promoting literacy and education among the millions that badly need it.
3) The first step therefore in promoting literacy is to create more and more awareness among the masses.
4) Practice, not precept, is the need of the hour. Practice that was dear to great people like Mahatma Gandhi, must be dear to us all.

Dr. U.V.N. Das
General & Family Physician
Consultant Hospital Administration

1) Many Acts and Laws have been made on many subjects since our Independence, but many failed to reach the goals.
2) However, the crux falls on the executive and administrative authorities at the grassroots level of implementation, particularly at the rural and semi-urban levels.
3) At the rural level, many teachers are reluctant to go to remote areas and perform their duties with utmost sincerity and sense of sacrifice.

4) The teachers are expected to be the builders of society in the growth of a new generation of citizens.

Prof. B. Sambireddy
Professor of Chemical Engineering,
Andhra University, Visakhapatnam

1) This Act is a culminating tribute to the late Prime Minister Sri Rajiv Gandhi, who had visualized the importance of human resource and renamed the education at Central level as "MHRD".
2) Universalisation of Primary Education in India is a right step in the right direction at the right moment
3) Along with "NREGS" and 'Midday Meal Scheme' strict implementation of 'Child Labour Act' is a must and three-pronged approach for making right to education Act practicable without allowing it to remain as mere legislation.

Prof. A.V.V. Narasimha Swamy
Professor of English,
Andhra University, Visakhapatnam

In this context, a few suggestions are made to make this Act successfully implemented with more zeal and application:

(a) Involve service organizations like R.K. Mission, Rotary Club and Lions Club and like minded ones.

(b) Recruit experienced retired teachers and give them supervisory posts, along with conducting training classes for raw recruits.

(c) Take a firm line during recruitment of concerned teachers so that they will have to serve a minimum period of time at the least.

If these fundamentals are taken are, there is no reason why this dream of universal education and social development would not be a success.

Prof. D. Harinarayana
Pro Vice-Chancellor
GITAM, Visakhapatnam

1) Modern education starts from age 4. It includes children above 6 also which gap should also be filled.

2) Sending poor children to schools should be made obligatory, by providing to them some incentives.

3) Bureaucracy in this context should be proactive in the implementation.

4) Private schools are faring better, when compared to the government schools as seen from their performance, Access to good private schools is limited.

Dr. J. Chandra Prasad
Professor of Commerce and Management Studies,
DNR College, Bhimavaram
Adkikavi Nannayya University, AP

1) Right to Free and Compulsory Education Act 2009 is a fitting strategy for the promotion of literacy and education development.

2) At the ground level, necessary re-engineering is needed for achieving the desired direction.

3) There is also a need of face-lift of Government schools which are in dilapidated condition.

4) The Village Surpanches (as envisaged by 73rd, 74th Constitutional Amendment) should be shouldering the responsibility of checking child labour and sending them to schools.

Prof. E. Udaya Bhaskara Reddi
Dept. of Environmental Science,
Andhra University, Visakhapatnam

1) The Concept of Neighbourhood Schools with free, compulsory, quality and even education will make society homogeneous.

2) Prevent destabilization of both rural and urban ecosystems by preventing migration from rural to urban.

Prof. N. Ramulu
Kakatiya University, Warangal

1) There must be redesigned as economic provision for tribal, rural and weaker sections.

2) At all levels loopholes must be plugged.

3) Though education is the main ingredient to empowerment, it cannot be tackled in isolation.

4) Poverty-reduction / poverty alleviation programme, asset building, production building network must be integrated to achieve right to education.

Dr. D. Rama Rao
Prof of Sociology
Andhra University, Visakhapatnam

1) By educating the parent about the importance of the primary education. Implementation of innovative techniques in teaching. Prohibition of child labor.

2) Teacher should show love affection and care towards the pupil.

Prof. M. Lakshmipathi Raju
Professor of Social Work

The quality of education varies from the government to the corporate private educational institutions that will overcome by the following:

1) The government educational institutions, as they are functioning today suffer from certain limitations, i.e., inadequate staff, lack of minimum facilities, lack of proper monitoring and lack of motivation on the part of the teachers.

2) There is need for appointment of school social workers to motivate the students and their parents for fulfilling the objectives of the Right to Education Act and its implementation.

3) The students and their parents need counselling services by trained professional counselors.

Prof. M.P. Narasimha Raju
Department of Sociology
SV University, Tirupati

To come out of this, recently our Government made Primary Education as Fundamental Right.

Causes for the widespread illiteracy should be erased in our society and also to see the proper implementation of the Act.

To motivate the parents concerned to send their children to schools rather than to fields.

The provision for pre-school (6 – 14 years) education in Government schools should be provided in the Act.

Prof. S. Bhaskar
Department of Sociology
UGC Emeritus Fellow
SV University, Tirupati

1) To correct the defective administration of the Government relating to education, as otherwise, the Act will be an ornament to the Indian society.

2) Provision of proper transportation facilities to the teachers to reach the schools which are located in remote areas.

3) Stringent action be taken over teachers and defective administrators who are involved in matters other than teaching and other affairs like business and politics.

4) Insistence over teachers to stay at working place should be there.

5) Let there be strict supervision by the concerned authorities over the teachers.

6) Let only the teachers coming from village background have to be appointed in schools located in villages.

V. Deveswara Rao
Senior Advocate
Visakhapatnam

1) School should have a pucca building, library, playground including equipment. The teachers to be trained to ensure values and targets.

2) Newly developed technologies have to be taken close to the villages.

3) To impart freedom struggle, national integrity, sovereignty and national progress are at the beginning stage.

4) In adult education, revolution should be taking plea for eradicating illiteracy among the adults.

Prof. Seshagiri Rao
Professor in Nuclear Physics
Andhra University, Visakhapatnam

1) The Government, should compensate the loss of income to the families of these children, who are bread-earners of their families in utter poverty and whose fathers have already left the family for their own good or who are drunkards offering no help to the family.

2) Regarding living accommodation to teachers posted in far-flung villages, where even a hut is not available for rent, such teachers should also be paid extra incentive salaries substantially.

Dr. M. Venkata Rao
Head Master
Primary School, Srikakulam

1) Teacher absenteeism is one of the important factors for the dropout situation along with the socio-economic factors.
2) Government should provide proper in-service training to develop commitment among the teachers working under Government and Zilla Parishad / Mandal Parishad.
3) A systematic monitoring should be made in the schools to track their levels.

Prof. V. Reddeppa Naidu
Department of Sociology
SV University, Tirupati

1) Create awareness among parents motivation by
   - mass-media
   - community workers
   - the caste leaders and
   - the NGOs.
2) Each one to educate one
   - Compulsory stay for the PG and Degree students in villages and slums to encourage the parents and the children in summer before the children are admitted in schools.
3) A school should be a *day care centre.*
   - Breakfast, lunch and dinner should be provided to the poorest students, instead of providing mid-day meal.
   - The student after completion of evening meal and home work has to go back to home without burdening the parents.

Prof. P. Krishna Prasad
Professor of Pol.& Pub. Adm.,
Andhra University, Visakhapatnam

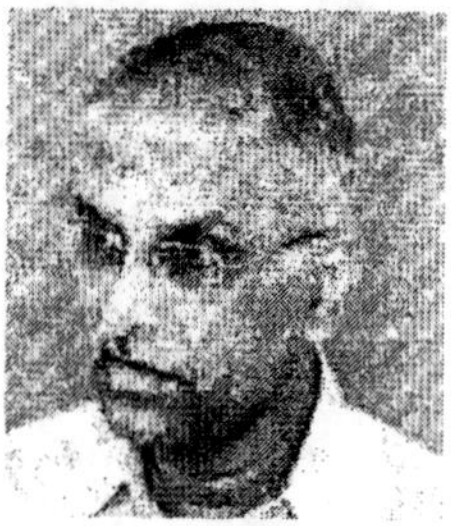

Right to free and compulsory education as a fundamental right indicates the spirit of our national movement and our constitution. By this Act we have formally set right to education as an important goal.

Realization of any such goal demands commitment on the part of those who are entrusted with the task of implementation of this act. There is a need for augmentation of non-governmental efforts which can supplement government efforts. Public participation is very important to achieve this type of goal.

Prof. M. Bilmoria Rani
Professor of Sociology,
Andhra University, Visakhapatnam

1) To fulfill objective of UEE number of schools to be opened.
2) There is a great need of strict supervision over some schools those who do not function well.
3) Enrolment drive to be started to enroll the non-enrolled children as at present 22 per cent of children are not enrolling in schools at all.
4) 40 per cent of teachers are abstaining from teaching activity – Amartya Sen Study.
5) Strict measures to be taken to solve these problems of teacher absenteeism, infrastructure and quality expanding school education.

Prof. Bhoopathi Rao
Professor of Politics & Public Administration
Osmania University
Hyderabad

I would like to suggest the following for implementation of Right to Education Act 2009.

1) School should have a pucca building, library, playground including equipment. The teachers to be trained to ensure values and targets.

2) Newly developed technologies have to be taken close to the villages.

3) To impart freedom struggle, national integrity, sovereignty and national progress are at the beginning stage.

4) Let only the teachers coming from village background have to be appointed in schools located in villages.

Prof. E. Viswanatha Reddy
Dean of Examinations (PG & Professional)
Andhra University, Visakhapatnam

1) Concerned DEOs and other officers should give surprise visits to schools frequently and take necessary steps to streamline the education system.

2) Teachers should attend regularly to classes. As most of the teachers are residing in towns and cities and they fail to attend to school in time. From urban areas they are going to rural areas where they are working.

3) This is one of the causes of increase in dropout rate.

At village level it is the mother of the child who can prevail upon the child to go to school. Hence, the mother should be made to understand the importance of education and the accruing benefits in the long run.

Prof. Uma Mohana Rao
Professor of Sociology,
S.K.D. University, Ananthapur

In the village teachers to be kept for a short period of only 2 years. They must be made to work with sincerity while they should live in the area of work and be in touch with their family members. The parents are not sincere for their children's education. Particularly there is no scope of interaction between the teachers and the children and their parents. In the first 5 years or newly appointed teachers should compulsorily work in the rural areas and such teachers only are eligible for promotions and any other privileges. That should be the rule and failing which although the government may make any mandates and schemes they will not yield any results and education to all will be a empty promise.

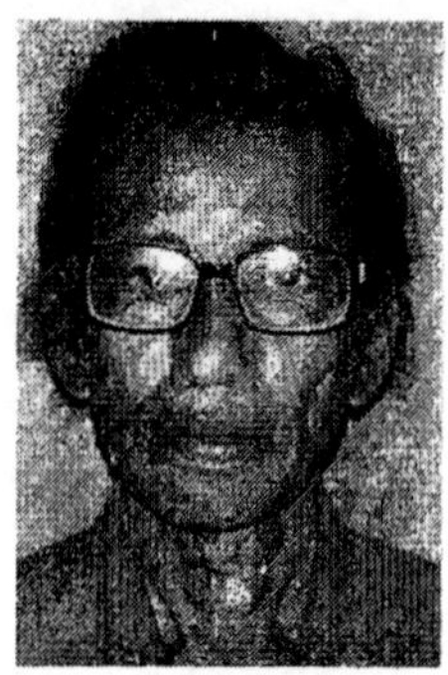

Prof. V. Krishna Murthy
Educationist
Andhra University, Visakhapatnam

I appreciate the Government of India, especially UPA Government having made a law as Right to Education and free and compulsory education. To the children between 6 to 14 years effective implementation huge funds have been sanctioned for filling up of new posts, construction of buildings and for infrastructure facilities, which are being misused even from the beginning stage as per different sources from all corners. Therefore, it is suggested that such misappropriation of funds at various levels shall at least be evaded or otherwise the spirit could be defeated.

5

Analysis and Interpretation

A. Analysis

Education Tables

S. No.	Item	Srikakulam											
		Palakonda				Polaki				Seethampeta			
		Yes	%	No	%	Yes	%	No	%	Yes	%	No	%
14 (a)	Are you taking special interest in the education of your children?	85	94.4	5	5.6	89	98.9	1	1.1	78	86.7	12	13.3

S. No.	Item	Vizianagaram											
		GLP				Kurupam				Pachipenta			
		Yes	%	No	%	Yes	%	No	%	Yes	%	No	%
14 (b)	Are you taking special interest in the education of your children?	87	96.7	3	3.3	12	42.9	16	57.1	77	85.6	13	14.4

S. No.	Item	Visakhapatnam											
		Chintapalli				Madugula				Paderu			
		Yes	%	No	%	Yes	%	No	%	Yes	%	No	%
14 (c)	Are you taking special interest in the education of your children?	86	95.6	4	4.4	80	88.9	10	11.1	47	52.2	43	47.8

Are you taking special interest in the education of your children?

14 (a): The Table analyses the responses of the sample respondents of Palakonda mandal of Srikakulam district on special interest towards their children. Out of the total sample, majority group (94.4 per cent) responded that they are taking special interest regarding their children's education and the remaining few (5.6 per cent) were not. From the total sample of Polaki mandal, majority group (98.9 per cent) responded that they are taking special interest regarding their children's education and the remaining few (1.1 per cent) were not. And from the total sample from Seethampeta mandal, a significant group (86.7 per cent) responded that they are taking special interest regarding their children's education and the remaining few (13.3 per cent) were not.

14 (b): The Table indicates the responses of the sample respondents of GLP mandal of Vizianagaram district on special interest taken towards their children's education. Out of the total sample, majority group (96.7 per cent) responded that they are taking special interest regarding their children's education and the remaining few (3.3 per cent) were not. From the total sample of Kurupam Mandal, more than fifty per cent (57.1 per cent) responded that they are not taking special interest regarding their children's education and the remaining (42.9 per cent) were taking special interest regarding their children's education. And from the total sample from Pachipenta mandal, a significant group (85.6 per cent) responded that they are taking special interest regarding their children's education and the remaining (14.4 per cent) were not.

14 (c): The Table explains the responses of the sample respondents of Chintapalli mandal of Visakhapatnam district on special interest taken towards education of their children. Out of the total sample, majority group (95.6 per cent)

responded that they are taking special interest regarding their children's education and the remaining few (4.4 per cent) were not. From the total sample of Madugula Mandal, majority group (88.9 per cent) responded that they are taking special interest regarding their children's education and the remaining (11.1 per cent) were not. And from the total sample of Paderu mandal, a significant group (52.2 per cent) responded that they are taking special interest regarding their children's education and the remaining (47.8 per cent) were not.

S. No.	*Item*	*Srikakulam*											
		Palakonda				*Polaki*				*Seethampeta*			
		Yes	*%*	*No*	*%*	*Yes*	*%*	*No*	*%*	*Yes*	*%*	*No*	*%*
15 (a)	Is there a school in your village?	85	94.4	5	5.6	89	98.9	1	1.1	68	75.6	22	24.4

S. No.	*Item*	*Vizianagaram*											
		GLP				*Kurupam*				*Pachipenta*			
		Yes	*%*	*No*	*%*	*Yes*	*%*	*No*	*%*	*Yes*	*%*	*No*	*%*
15 (b)	Is there a school in your village?	87	96.7	3	3.3	24	85.7	4	14.3	89	98.9	1	1.1

S. No.	*Item*	*Visakhapatnam*											
		Chintapalli				*Madugula*				*Paderu*			
		Yes	*%*	*No*	*%*	*Yes*	*%*	*No*	*%*	*Yes*	*%*	*No*	*%*
15 (c)	Is there a school in your village?	86	95.6	4	4.4	68	75.6	22	24.4	35	38.9	55	61.1

Is there a school in your village?

15 (a): The Table analyses the responses of the sample respondents of Palakonda mandal of Srikakulam district regarding the situation of school in their village. Out of the

total sample majority group (94.4 per cent) responded that there is a School in their village and the remaining few (5.6 per cent) said that there is no school in their village. From the total sample of Polaki mandal, majority group (98.9 per cent) responded that there is a school in their village and a negligible number (1.1 per cent) said no. And from the total sample from Seethampeta mandal, a significant group (75.6 per cent) responded that there is a school in their village and the remaining (24.4 per cent) said their is no.

15 (b): The Table analyses the responses of the sample respondents of GLP Mandal of Vizianagaram district about availability of school in the village. Out of the total sample, majority group (96.7 per cent) responded that they have a school in the village regarding their children's education and the remaining few (3.3 per cent) did not respond. From the total sample of Kurupam mandal, majority group (85.7 per cent) responded that they have a school in the village for their children's education and the remaining few (14.3 per cent) did not respond. And from the total sample from Pachipenta mandal, a significant group (98.9 per cent) responded that they have a school for their children's education and the remaining few (1.1 per cent) did not respond.

15 (c): The Table explains the responses of the sample respondents of Chintapalli Mandal of Visakhapatnam district about the availability of school in the village. Out of the total sample, majority group (95.6 per cent) responded that there is a School in the village for their children's education and the remaining few (4.4 per cent) did not respond. From the total sample of Madugula mandal, majority group (75.6 per cent) responded that they have a school in the village for children's education and the remaining few (24.4 per cent) did not respond. And in the total sample from Paderu mandal, a significant group (61.1 per cent) responded that they have no school regarding their children's education and the remaining few (38.9 per cent) responded that there is a school.

What kind of school is available?

S. No		Srikakulam		
		Palakonda	Polaki	Seethampeta
1	Primary	81 (90.0)	87 (96.7)	80 (88.9)
2	Secondary education	7 (7.8)	3 (3.3)	10 (11.1)
3	Higher education	2 (2.2)		
	Chi-square value		**8.04**	

What kind of school is available?

S. No.		Vizianagaram		
		GLP	Kurupam	Pachipenta
1	Primary	69 (76.7)	26 (92.9)	76 (84.4)
2	Secondary education	18 (20.0)	2 (7.1)	14 (15.6)
3	Higher education	3 (3.3)		
	Chi-square value		**6.92**	

What kind of school is available?

S. No.		Visakhapatnam		
		Chintapalli	Madugula	Paderu
1	Primary	69 (76.7)	84 (93.3)	68 (75.6)
2	Secondary education	20 (22.2)	5 (5.6)	20 (22.2)
3	Higher education	1 (1.1)	1 (1.1)	2 (2.2)
	Chi-square value		**12.68***	

What kind of school is available?

Srikakulam

The Table infers the responses of the sample respondents of Srikakulam district regarding the kind of school available in their village. Regarding primary education, there are 90.0 per cent in Palakonda mandal while 96.7 per cent are in Polaki mandal, with 88.9 per cent in Seethampeta mandal.

As regards secondary education, 7.8 per cent are in Palakonda mandal, 3.3 per cent are in Polaki mandal and 11.1 per cent in Seethampeta mandal. Regarding higher education 2.2 per cent in Palakonda mandal are positive. The obtained chi-square value is 8.04 which is not significant because it is less than the Table value (9.49).

Vizianagaram

The Table analyses the responses of the sample respondents of Vizianagaram district regarding the kind of school available in their village. Regarding primary education, 76.7 per cent respond in GLP mandal, 92.9 per cent in Kurupam mandal and 84.4 per cent in Pachipenta mandal. Regarding secondary education, 20.0 per cent respond in GLP mandal, 7.1 per cent in Kurupam mandal and 15.6 per cent in Pachipenta mandal. Regarding higher education, 3.3 per cent respond in GLP mandal. The obtained chi-square value is 6.92 which is not significant because it is less than the Table value (9.49).

Visakhapatnam

The Table explains the responses of the sample respondents of Visakhapatnam district regarding the kind of school available in their village. Regarding schools on primary education, 76.7 per cent respond in Chintapalli mandal, 93.3 per cent respond in Madugula mandal and 75.6 per cent respond in Paderu mandal. Regarding secondary education, 22.2 per cent respond in Chintapalli mandal, with 5.6 per cent in Madugula mandal and 22.2 per cent in Paderu mandal. Regarding higher education, 1.1 per cent respond in Chintapalli mandal, 1.1 per cent in Madugula mandal and 2.2 per cent in Paderu mandal. The obtained chi-square value is 12.68 which is significant at 0.05 level, because it is more than the Table value (9.49).

What are the physical facilities available in the school for children?

S. No.		*Srikakulam*		
		Palakonda	*Polaki*	*Seethampeta*
1	Class-rooms	90 (100.0)	84 (93.3)	83 (92.2)
2	Drinking water facilities		3 (3.3)	7 (7.8)
3	Playground		3 (3.3)	
4	Lavatories			
5	Compound wall			
6	Electricity			
	Chi-square value		**13.72****	

S. No.		*Vizianagaram*		
		GLP	*Kurupam*	*Pachipenta*
1	Class-rooms	69 (76.7)	16 (57.1)	83 (92.2)
2	Drinking water facilities	7 (7.8)	11 (39.3)	4 (4.4)
3	Playground	10 (11.1)	1 (3.6)	3 (3.3)
4	Lavatories	2 (2.2)		
5	Compound wall	2 (2.2)		
6	Electricity			
	Chi-square value		**39.02****	

S. No.		*Visakhapatnam*		
		Chintapalli	*Madugula*	*Paderu*
1	Class-rooms	76 (84.4)	83 (92.2)	71 (78.9)
2	Drinking water facilities	7 (7.8)	4 (4.4)	19 (21.1)
3	Playground	7 (7.8)	3 (3.3)	
4	Lavatories			
5	Compound wall			
6	Electricity			
	Chi-square value	**20.95****		

What are the physical facilities available in the school for children?

Srikakulam

The Table explains the responses of the sample respondents of Srikakulam district regarding physical facilities available in the school for children in their village. Availability of class-rooms, total (100.0 per cent) respond in Palakonda mandal, 93.3 per cent in Polaki mandal and 92.2 per cent in Seethampeta mandal. As about Drinking water facilities, 3.3 per cent respond in Polaki mandal and 7.8 per cent in Seethampeta mandal. Regarding availability of Playground, 3.3 per cent respond in Polaki mandal. The obtained chi-square value is 13.72 which is significant at 0.01 level as it is more than the Table value (13.3).

Vizianagaram

The above Table analyses response of the sample respondents of Vizianagaram district, regarding physical facilities available in the school for children in their village. The total class-rooms, (76.7 per cent) are in GLP mandal, with 57.1 per cent in Kurupam mandal and 92.2 per cent in Pachipenta mandal. Among Drinking water facilities, 7.8 per cent are in GLP mandal, 39.3 per cent are Kurupam mandal, with 92.2 per cent in Pachipenta mandal. For provision of Playground, 11.1 per cent in GLP mandal, 3.6 per cent in Kurupam mandal and 3.3 per cent in Pachipenta mandal. Regarding availability of Lavatories 2.2 per cent are in GLP mandal, as about availability of compound wall (2.2 per cent) are in GLP mandal. The obtained chi-square value is 39.02 which is significant at 0.01 level, as it is more than the Table value (20.1).

Visakhapatnam

The Table infers the responses of the sample respondents of Visakhapatnam district regarding physical facilities available in the school for children in their village. Our availability of class-rooms, (84.4 per cent) respond in Chintapalli mandal, 92.2 per cent in Madugula mandal and 78.9 per cent in Paderu mandal. As regards Drinking water facilities, (7.8 per cent) respond in Chintapalli mandal, 4.4 per cent in Madugula mandal and 21.1 per cent in Paderu mandal. Regarding availability of Playground, (7.8 per cent) respond in Chintapalli mandal and 3.3 per cent in Madugula mandal. The obtained chi-square value is 20.95 which is significant at 0.01 level because it is more than the Table value (13.3).

How distant is the school in your village

S. No.		*Srikakulam*		
		Palakonda	*Polaki*	*Seethampeta*
1	1-2 Km	77 (85.6)	4 (4.4)	64 (71.1)
2	2-3 Km	13 (14.4)	86 (95.6)	26 (28.9)
3	3 Km			
4	Above 3 Km			
	Chi-square value		**135.53****	

S. No.		*Vizianagaram*		
		GLP	*Kurupam*	*Pachipenta*
1	1-2 Km	37 (41.1)	16 (57.1)	7 (7.8)
2	2-3 Km	50 (55.6)	2 (7.1)	82 (91.1)
3	3 Km	3 (3.3)	10 (35.7)	1 (1.1)
4	Above 3 Km			
	Chi-square value		**92.34****	

		Visakhapatnam		
S. No.		*Chintapalli*	*Madugula*	*Paderu*
1	1-2 Km	53 (58.9)	75 (83.3)	25 (27.8)
2	2-3 Km	36 (40.0)	15 (16.7)	65 (72.2)
3	3 Km	1 (1.1)		
4	Above 3 Km			
	Chi-square value	**59.22****		

How distant is the school in your village?

Srikakulam

The Table infers the response of the sample respondents of Srikakulam district regarding the distance of the school in village for their children's education. As about distance of 1-2 km, 85.6 per cent are in Palakonda mandal, with 4.4 per cent in Polaki mandal and 71.1 per cent in Seethampeta mandal. As regards the distance of 2-3 km, 14.4 per cent in Palakonda mandal, 95.6 per cent in Polaki mandal and 28.9 per cent in Seethampeta mandal. The obtained chi-square value is 135.53 which is significant at 0.01 level because it is more than the Table value (6.63).

Vizianagaram

The Table analyses the response of the sample respondents of Vizianagaram district regarding the distance of the school in the village for their children's education. As regards the distance of 1-2 km, 41.1 per cent are in GLP mandal, with 57.1 per cent in Kurupam mandal and 7.8 per cent in Pachipenta mandal. Regarding the distance of 2-3 km, 55.6 per cent are in GLP mandal, with 7.1 per cent in Kurupam mandal and 91.1 per cent in Pachipenta mandal. Regarding the distance of 3 km, 3.3 per cent are in GLP mandal, with 35.7 per cent in Kurupam mandal and 1.1 per cent in Pachipenta mandal. The obtained chi-square value 92.34 is significant at 0.01 level as it is more than the Table value (13.3).

Visakhapatnam

The Table explains the response of the sample respondents of Visakhapatnam district regarding the distance of the school in village for their children's education. As about distance of 1-2 km, 58.9 per cent are in Chintapalli mandal, with 83.3 per cent in Madugula mandal and 27.8 per cent in Paderu mandal. As regards distance of 2-3 km, 40.0 per cent are in Chintapalli mandal, with 16.7 per cent in Madugula mandal and 72.2 per cent in Paderu mandal. In case of 3 km distance

1.1 per cent are in Chintapalli mandal. The obtained chi-square value is 59.22 which is significant at 0.01 level as it is more than the Table value (13.3).

Sl. No.	*Item*	*Srikakulam*											
		Palakonda				*Polaki*				*Seethampeta*			
		Yes	*%*	*No*	*%*	*Yes*	*%*	*No*	*%*	*Yes*	*%*	*No*	*%*
19	Are your children regularly attending the school daily?	83	92.2	7	7.8	88	97.8	2	2.2	68	75.6	22	24.4
21	In case of your children not present in the school, are the teachers bringing that to parents notice?	68	75.6	22	24.4	81	90.0	9	10.0	61	67.8	29	32.2

Sl. No.	*Item*	*Vizianagaram*											
		GLP				*Kurupam*				*Pachipenta*			
		Yes	*%*	*No*	*%*	*Yes*	*%*	*No*	*%*	*Yes*	*%*	*No*	*%*
19	Are your children regularly attending the school daily?	84	93.3	6	6.7	13	46.4	15	53.6	77	85.6	13	14.4
21	In case your children are not present in the school, are the teachers bringing that to parents notice?	74	82.2	16	17.8	12	42.9	16	57.1	57	63.3	33	36.7

Sl. No.	Item	Visakhapatnam											
		Chintapalli				Madugula				Paderu			
		Yes	%	No	%	Yes	%	No	%	Yes	%	No	%
19	Are your children regularly attending the school daily?	83	92.2	7	7.8	81	90.0	9	10.0	52	57.8	38	42.2
21	In case your children not present in the school, are the teachers bringing that to parents notice?	61	67.8	29	32.2	52	57.8	38	42.2	46	51.1	44	48.9

Are your children regularly attending the school daily? In case your children not present in the school, are the teachers bringing that to parents notice?

Srikakulam

The Table analyses the responses of the sample respondents of Palakonda mandal of Srikakulam district on children regularly attending the school daily. Out of the total sample majority group (92.2 per cent) responded that their children are regularly attending the school daily and, while the remaining few (7.8 per cent) were not attending the school. From the total sample of Polaki mandal, majority group (97.8 per cent) responded that their children are regular in school attendance and the remaining few (2.2 per cent) were not attending school. Of the total sample from Seethampeta mandal, a significant group (75.6 per cent) responded that their children are regular in school and the remaining (24.4 per cent) not attending school.

Regarding responses of the sample respondents of Palakonda mandal of Srikakulam district, in case children not present in the school, whether the teachers are bringing that to parents' notice, majority group (75.6 per cent) of Palakonda mandal responded that their children are regularly attending the school and the remaining few (24.4 per cent) were not. From the total sample of Polaki mandal, majority group (90.0 per cent) responded that in case of children not present in the school, the teachers are bringing that to parents notice and the remaining few (10.0 per cent) were not. And from the total sample from Seethampeta mandal, a significant group (67.8 per cent) responded that in case of their children not present in the school the teachers are bringing to parents' notice and the remaining few (32.2 per cent) did not respond.

Vizianagaram

The Table explains about the responses of the sample respondents of GLP mandal of Vizianagaram district whether their children are regularly attending the school daily. Out of the total sample, majority group (93.3 per cent) responded that children are regularly attending the school daily and the remaining few respondents hold they (6.7 per cent) were not. In the total sample of Kurupam mandal, majority group (53.6 per cent) responded that children are regularly attending the school daily and the remaining few (46.4 per cent) responded negatively. And from the total sample from Pachipenta mandal, a significant group (85.6 per cent) responded that their children are regularly attending the school daily and the remaining few (14.4 per cent) did not respond.

Regarding the responses of the sample respondents of GLP mandal of Vizianagaram district that in case, of their children not present in the school, the teachers are bringing to their notice. Out of the total sample, majority group (82.2 per cent) hold in case their children are not present in the school, the teachers are bringing that to their notice and the remaining ones (17.8 per cent) were not. From the total sample of Kurupam mandal, majority group (57.1 per cent) responded negatively in case, children are not present in the school, the teachers are bringing that to their notice and the remaining (42.9 per cent) responded positively. And from the total sample from Pachipenta mandal, significant group (63.3 per cent) responded that in case, children were not present in the school, the teachers were bringing that to their notice with the remaining few (36.7 per cent) responded negatively.

Visakhapatnam

The Table analyses the responses of the sample respondents of Chintapalli mandal of Visakhapatnam district on their children regularly attending the school daily. Out of the total sample of Chintapalli majority group (92.2 per cent) responded that their children are regularly attending the school daily and, while the remaining few (7.8 per cent) were not attending the school. From the total sample of Madugula mandal, majority group (90.0 per cent) responded that their children are regularly attending the school daily and the remaining few (10.0 per cent) were not attending the school. And from the total sample from Paderu mandal, a significant group (57.8 per cent) responded that their children are regularly attending the school daily and the remaining (42.2 per cent) did not respond.

From the responses of the sample respondents of Chintapalli mandal of Visakhapatnam district that in case when children are not present in the school, whether teachers are bringing that to parents notice about their children's education, majority group (67.8 per cent) responded that in case their children are not present in the school, teachers are bringing that to their notice and the remaining (32.2 per cent) were not bringing to parents notice. From the total sample of Madugula mandal, majority group (57.8 per cent) responded that In case their children are not present in the school, teachers were bringing that to their notice, while the remaining respondents (42.2 per cent) were not. And in the total sample of Paderu mandal, a significant group (51.1 per cent) responded that in case, their children were not present in the school, the teachers were bringing that to their notice about their children's education and the remaining respondents (48.9 per cent) had not responded.

In case children are not going to school, what are the reasons?

Sl. No.		*Srikakulam*		
		Palakonda	*Polaki*	*Seethampeta*
1	Agriculture work	79 (87.8)	27 (30.0)	78 (86.7)
2	Domestic work	4 (4.4)	31 (34.4)	8 (8.9)
3	Looking after infants	5 (5.6)	26 (28.9)	4 (4.4)
4	Illness	2 (2.2)	6 (6.7)	
5	Disability to understand the class lesson			
	Chi-square value		**91.92****	

S. No.		*Vizianagaram*		
		GLP	*Kurupam*	*Pachipenta*
1	Agriculture work	41 (45.6)	18 (64.3)	66 (73.3)
2	Domestic work	5 (5.6)	7 (25.0)	5 (5.6)
3	Looking after infants	38 (4.2)	3 (10.7)	18 (20.0)
4	Illness	6 (6.7)		1 (1.1)
5	Disability to underst and the class lesson			
	Chi-square value		**33.68****	

S. No.		*Visakhapatnam*		
		Chintapalli	*Madugula*	*Paderu*
1	Agriculture work	22 (24.4)	50 (55.6)	31 (34.4)
2	Domestic work	8 (8.9)	6 (6.7)	38 (42.2)
3	Looking after infants	58 (64.4)	24 (26.7)	21 (23.3)
4	Illness	2 (2.2)	10 (11.1)	
5	Disability to understand the class lesson			
	Chi-square value		87.58**	

In case children are not going to school, what are the reasons?

Srikakulam

The Table explains the responses of the sample respondents of Srikakulam district, regarding the reasons for their children not going to school. Going for the sake of Agriculture work, 87.8 per cent children are from Palakonda mandal, with 30.0 per cent from Polaki mandal and 86.7 per cent from Seethampeta mandal. For going to Domestic work, 4.4 per cent children from Palakonda mandal, with 34.4 per cent from Polaki mandal and 8.9 per cent from Seethampeta mandal. Regarding looking after infants, 5.6 per cent children are from Palakonda mandal, with 28.9 per cent from Polaki mandal and 4.4 per cent from Seethampeta mandal. Owing to illness 2.2 per cent children are from Palakonda mandal with 6.7 per cent from Polaki mandal. The obtained chi-square value 91.92 is significant at 0.01 level as it is more than the Table value (16.8).

Vizianagaram

The Table analyses the responses of the sample respondents of Vizianagaram district, regarding reasons for their children not going to school. Because of the Agriculture work, 45.6 per cent children are from GLP mandal, with 64.3 per cent from Kurupam mandal and 73.3 per cent from Pachipenta mandal. For domestic work, 5.6 per cent children are from GLP mandal, with 25.0 per cent from Kurupam mandal and 5.6 per cent from Pachipenta mandal. For looking after infants, 4.2 per cent children are from GLP mandal, with 10.7 per cent from Kurupam mandal and 20.0 per cent from Pachipenta mandal. Owing to illness, 6.7 per cent children are from GLP mandal, with 1.1 per cent from Pachipenta mandal. The obtained chi-square value 33.68 is significant at 0.01 level as it is more than the Table value (16.8).

Visakhapatnam

The Table explains the responses of the sample respondents of Visakhapatnam district, regarding the reasons for their children not going to school. On Agriculture work, (24.4 per cent) are from Chintapalli mandal, wioth 55.6 per cent from Madugula mandal and 34.4 per cent from Paderu mandal. For domestic work, 8.9 per cent children are from Chintapalli mandal, with 6.7 per cent from Madugula mandal and 42.2 per cent from Paderu mandal. On looking after infants, 64.4 per cent children are from Chintapalli mandal, with 26.7 per cent from Madugula mandal and 23.3 per cent from Paderu mandal. Owing to illness, 2.2 per cent children are from Chintapalli mandal, with 11.1 per cent from Madugula mandal. The obtained chi-square value 87.58 is significant at 0.01 level as it is more than the Table value (16.8).

Sl.	*Item*	*Srikakulam*											
No.		*Palakonda*				*Polaki*				*Seethampeta*			
		Yes	*%*	*No*	*%*	*Yes*	*%*	*No*	*%*	*Yes*	*%*	*No*	*%*
22	Are you satisfied about your children's competence in getting the level of their learning	70	77.8	20	22.2	6	6.7	84	93.3	48	53.3	42	46.7

Sl.	*Item*	*Vizianagaram*											
No.		*GLP*				*Kurupam*				*Pachipenta*			
		Yes	*%*	*No*	*%*	*Yes*	*%*	*No*	*%*	*Yes*	*%*	*No*	*%*
22	Are you satisfied about your children's competence in getting the level of their learning	81	90.0	9	10.0	13	46.4	15	53.6	60	66.7	30	33.3

Sl. No.	*Item*	*Visakhapatnam*											
		Chintapalli				*Madugula*				*Paderu*			
		Yes	*%*	*No*	*%*	*Yes*	*%*	*No*	*%*	*Yes*	*%*	*No*	*%*
22	Are you satisfied about your children's competence in getting the level of their learning	87	96.7	3	3.3	25	27.8	65	72.2	50	55.6	40	44.4

Are you satisfied about your children's competence in getting the level of their learning?

Srikakulam

The Table analyses the responses of the sample respondents of Palakonda mandal of Srikakulam district on the satisfaction about children's competence in getting the level of their learning. Out of the total sample, majority group of 77.8 per cent responded that they are satisfied about children's competence in getting the level of their learning and the remaining few 22.2 per cent are not satisfied. From the total sample of Polaki mandal, 93.3 per cent did not respond positively that they are satisfied about their children's competence in getting the level of their learning, with the remaining 6.7 per cent did not respond. And from the total sample from Seethampeta mandal, a significant group of 53.3 per cent have responded that they are satisfied about their children's competence in getting the level of their learning and the remaining 46.7 per cent are not satisfied.

Vizianagaram

The Table analyses the responses of the sample respondents of GLP mandal of Vizianagaram district, about children's competence in getting the level of their learning. Out of the total sample, majority group of 90.0 per cent responded that they are satisfied about children's competence in getting the level of their learning and the remaining few

(10.0 per cent) were not satisfied. From the total sample, majority group (53.6 per cent) did not respond that they are satisfied about their children's competence in getting the level of their learning, while the remaining (46.4 per cent) responded positively. And in the total sample from Paderu mandal, a significant group of 66.7 per cent responded that they are satisfied about their children's competence in their learning, with the remaining (33.3 per cent) remaining not satisfied.

Visakhapatnam

The Table explains the responses of the sample respondents of Chintapalli mandal of Visakhapatnam district about their children's competence in getting the level of their learning. Out of the total sample, majority group of 96.7 per cent responded that they are satisfied about their children's competence in getting the level of their learning and the remaining 3.3 per cent are not satisfied. From the total sample, 72.2 per cent have not responded that they are satisfied about their children's competence in getting the level of their learning and the remaining (27.8 per cent) have not responded. And from the total sample of Paderu mandal, a significant group of 55.6 per cent responded that they are satisfied about their children's competence in getting the level of their learning and the remaining (44.4 per cent) are not satisfied.

In case, it is not so, what are the reasons?

Sl. No.		*Srikakulam*		
		Palakonda	*Polaki*	*Seethampeta*
1	Children's illness	31 (35.2)	83 (93.3)	60 (62.5)
2	Lack of teachers' interest	15 (17.0)	5 (5.6)	12 (12.5)
3	Impact of other students	8 (9.1)	1 (1.1)	20 (20.8)

4	Deficiency of Home Environment	34 (38.6)		4 (4.2)
5	Disability to understand class lessons			
	Chi-square value		**103.17****	

Sl. No.		*Vizianagaram*		
		GLP	*Kurupam*	*Pachipenta*
1	Children's illness	50 (55.6)	8 (28.6)	77 (85.6)
2	Lack of teachers' interest	21 (23.3)	12 (42.9)	8 (8.9)
3	Impact of other students	1 (1.1)	5 (17.9)	5 (5.6)
4	Deficiency of Home Environment	18 (20.0)	3 (10.7)	
5	Disability to understand class lessons			
	Chi-square value		**55.56****	

Sl. No.		*Visakhapatnam*		
		Chintapalli	*Madugula*	*Paderu*
1	Children's illness	84 (93.3)	84 (93.3)	46 (51.1)
2	Lack of teachers' interest	5 (5.6)	5 (5.6)	29 (32.2)
3	Impact of other students		1 (1.1)	6 (6.7)
4	Deficiency of Home Environment	1 (1.1)		9 (10.0)
5	Disability to understand class lessons			
	Chi-square value		**66.48****	

In case, it is not so, what are the reasons

Srikakulam

The Table explains the responses of the sample respondents of Srikakulam district, regarding causes of dissatisfaction. As regards the Children's illness, 35.2 per cent are from Palakonda mandal, with 93.3 per cent from Polaki mandal and 62.5 per cent from Seethampeta mandal. Regarding the Lack of teachers' interest, 17.0 per cent is from Palakonda mandal, with 5.6 per cent from Polaki mandal and 12.5 per cent Seethampeta mandal. Regarding impact of other students, 9.1 per cent are from Palakonda mandal, with 1.1 per cent from Polaki mandal and 20.8 per cent from Seethampeta mandal. As regards deficiency of home environment, 38.6 per cent are from Palakonda mandal and 4.2 per cent from Seethampeta mandal. The obtained chi-square value 103.17 is significant at 0.01 level, as it is more than the Table value (16.8).

Vizianagaram

The Table Infers the responses of the sample respondents of Vizianagaram district regarding causes of dissatisfaction about their children's education. Regarding Children's illness, 55.6 per cent are from GLP mandal, with 28.6 per cent from Kurupam mandal and 85.6 per cent from Pachipenta mandal. As regards lack of teachers' interest, 23.3 per cent are from GLP mandal, with 42.9 per cent from Kurupam mandal and 8.9 per cent from Pachipenta mandal. Regarding impact of other students, 1.1 per cent are from GLP mandal, 17.9 per cent from Kurupam mandal and 5.6 per cent from Pachipenta mandal. Regarding deficiency of home environment, 20.0 per cent are from GLP mandal, with 10.7 per cent from Kurupam mandal. The obtained chi-square value 55.56 is significant at 0.01 level, as it is more than the Table value (16.8).

Visakhapatnam

The Table analyses the responses of the sample respondents of Visakhapatnam district, regarding causes of dissatisfaction. Regarding Children's illness, 93.3 per cent are from Chintapalli mandal, with 93.3 per cent from Madugula mandal and 51.1 per cent from Paderu mandal. As regards lack of teachers; interest, 5.6 per cent is from Chintapalli mandal, with 5.6 per cent from Madugula mandal and 32.2 per cent from Paderu mandal. Regarding impact of other students, 1.1 per cent are from Chintapalli mandal, with 6.7 per cent from Paderu mandal. Regarding deficiency of home environment, 1.1 per cent are from Chintapalli mandal and 10.0 per cent from Paderu mandal. The obtained chi-square value 66.48 is significant at 0.01 level, as it is more than the Table value (16.8).

Sl. No.	*Item*	*Srikakulam*											
		Palakonda				*Polaki*				*Seethampeta*			
		Yes	*%*	*No*	*%*	*Yes*	*%*	*No*	*%*	*Yes*	*%*	*No*	*%*
24	Do you agree that children's education is spoiled / lagged and indiscipline taking place by the appointment of contract teachers, as they are untrained and belong to a strong political and social group in the village?	81	90.0	9	10.0	89	98.9	1	1.1	70	77.8	20	22.2

Sl. No.	*Item*	*Vizianagaram*											
		GLP				*Kurupam*				*Pachipenta*			
		Yes	*%*	*No*	*%*	*Yes*	*%*	*No*	*%*	*Yes*	*%*	*No*	*%*
	1	*2*	*3*	*4*	*5*	*6*	*7*	*8*	*9*	*10*	*11*	*12*	*13*
24	Do you agree that children's	77	85.6	13	14.4	26	92.9	2	7.1	86	95.6	4	4.4

Contd...

1	*2*	*3*	*4*	*5*	*6*	*7*	*8*	*9*	*10*	*11*	*12*	*13*
education is spoiled/ lagged and indiscipline taking place by the appointment of contract teachers as they are untrained and belong to a strong political and social group in the village?												

Sl. No.	*Item*	*Visakhapatnam*											
		Chintapalli				*Madugula*				*Paderu*			
		Yes	*%*	*No*	*%*	*Yes*	*%*	*No*	*%*	*Yes*	*%*	*No*	*%*
24	Do you agree that children's education is spoiled/ lagged with indiscipline taking place by the appointment of contract teachers as they are untrained and belong to a strong political and social group in the village?	44	48.9	46	51.1	88	97.8	2	2.2	79	87.8	11	12.2

Do you agree that children's education is spoiled / lagged and indiscipline taking place by the appointment of contract teachers, as they are untrained and belong to a strong political and social group in the village?

Srikakulam

The Table infers the responses of the sample respondents of Palakonda mandal of Srikakulam district, on the view that children's education is spoiled / lagged and indiscipline taking place by the appointment of contract teachers, as they are untrained and belong to a strong political and social group in the village. Out of the total sample, majority group of 90.0 per cent responded favourably and the remaining (10.0 per cent) were not favourable. In the total sample of Polaki mandal, majority group of 98.9 per cent responded that they agree that children's education is spoiled / lagged and indiscipline taking place by the appointment of contract teachers as they are untrained and belong to a strong political and social group in the village and the remaining few (1.1 per cent) did not respond favourably. And from the total sample from Seethampeta mandal, a significant group of 77.8 per cent responded that they agree as to the children's education is spoiled / lagged and indiscipline taking place by the appointment of contract teachers as they are untrained and belong to a strong political and social group in the village, while the remaining few (22.2 per cent) did not agree.

Vizianagaram

The Table analyses the responses of the sample respondents of GLP mandal of Vizianagaram district, on the view that children's education is spoiled / lagged and indiscipline taking place by the appointment of contract teachers as they are untrained and belong to a strong political and social group in the village. Out of the total sample, majority group of 85.6 per cent responded favourably, with the remaining (14.4 per cent) not responding favourably. From the total sample of Kurupam mandal, majority group of 92.9 per cent responded that they agree that the children's education is spoiled / lagged and indiscipline taking place by the appointment of contract teachers as they are untrained and belong to a strong political and social group in the village, with the remaining few (7.1 per cent) not responding favourably. And from the total sample from Paderu mandal, a significant group of 95.6 per cent responded that they agree that children's education is spoiled / lagged and indiscipline taking place by the appointment of contract teachers, as they are untrained and belong to a strong political and social group in the village and the remaining (4.4 per cent) did not respond favourably.

Visakhapatnam

The Table analyses the responses of the sample respondents of Chintapalli mandal of Visakhapatnam district, on the view that children's education is spoiled / lagged and indiscipline taking place by the appointment of contract teachers, as they are untrained and belong to a strong political and social group. Out of the total sample at Chintapalli mandal majority group of 51.1 per cent did not respond favourably and the remaining (48.9 per cent) responded favourably. From the total sample of Madugula mandal, majority group of 97.8 per cent responded that they agree that children's education is spoiled / lagged and indiscipline taking place by the appointment of contract teachers as they are untrained and belong to a strong political and social group in the village and the remaining (2.2 per cent) did not respond. And from the total sample from Paderu mandal, a significant group of 87.8 per cent responded that they agree as to children's education is spoiled / lagged and indiscipline taking place by the appointment of contract teachers, as they are untrained and belong to a strong political and social group in the village and the remaining (12.2 per cent) did not respond favourably.

Sl. No.	Item	Srikakulam											
		Palakonda				Polaki				Seethampeta			
		Yes	%	No	%	Yes	%	No	%	Yes	%	No	%
25	Are the teachers residing in the same village	20	22.2	70	77.8	1	1.1	89	98.9	14	15.6	76	84.4
26	Are the teachers coming regularly to the school	80	88.9	10	11.1	88	97.8	2	2.2	79	87.8	11	12.2
27	Are the teachers observing regular school times	82	91.1	8	8.9	3	3.3	87	96.7	72	80.0	18	20.0

Sl. No.	Item	Vizianagaram											
		GLP				Kurupam				Pachipenta			
		Yes	%	No	%	Yes	%	No	%	Yes	%	No	%
25	Are the teachers residing in the same village	36	40.0	54	60.0	3	10.7	25	89.3	3	3.3	87	96.7
26	Are the teachers coming regularly to school	82	91.1	8	8.9	10	35.7	18	64.3	59	65.6	31	34.4
27	Are the teachers observing regular school times	83	92.2	7	7.8	7	25.0	21	75.0	42	46.7	48	53.3

Sl. No.	*Item*	*Visakhapatnam*											
		Chintapalli				*Madugula*				*Paderu*			
		Yes	*%*	*No*	*%*	*Yes*	*%*	*No*	*%*	*Yes*	*%*	*No*	*%*
25	Are the teachers residing in the same village	5	5.6	85	94.4	4	4.4	86	95.6	5	5.6	85	94.4
26	Are the teachers coming regularly to school	86	95.6	4	4.4	74	82.2	16	17.8	49	54.4	41	45.6
27	Are the teachers observing regular school times	86	95.6	4	4.4	85	94.4	5	5.6	50	55.6	40	44.4

Srikakulam

The Table analyses the responses of the sample respondents of Palakonda mandal of Srikakulam district on the view whether teachers reside in the same village. Out of the total sample majority group of 77.8 per cent did not respond favourably that the teachers are residing in the same village, with the remaining few (22.2 per cent) favourably responding. From the total sample of Polaki mandal, majority group of 98.9 per cent did not respond favourably that the teachers are residing in the same village, with the remaining few (1.1 per cent) favourably responding. And from the total sample from Seethampeta mandal, a significant group of (84.4 per cent) did not respond that the teachers are residing in the same village, with the remaining few 15.6 per cent having responded favourably.

From the responses of the sample respondents of Palakonda mandal of Srikakulam district, on teachers coming regularly to school, majority group of 88.9 per cent responded that teachers are coming regularly to school and the remaining 11.1 per cent did not responded favourably. From the total sample of Polaki mandal, majority group, 97.8 per cent responded that teachers are observing regular school times and the remaining 2.2 per cent did not responded favourably. And from the total sample from Seethampeta mandal, a significant group of 87.8 per cent responded that teachers are coming regularly to school and the remaining 12.2 per cent did not respond favourably.

Regarding the sample respondents of Palakonda mandal of Srikakulam district, teachers are observing regular school times. In the total sample, majority group 91.1 per cent responded that teachers are observing regular school times and the remaining 8.9 per cent did not respond favourably. From the total sample of Polaki mandal, majority group 96.7 per cent did not respond as to the teachers observing regular school times, while the remaining 3.3 per cent responded favourably. And from the total sample from Seethampeta mandal, a significant group 80.0 per cent responded that teachers are observing regular school times, while the remaining few (20.0 per cent) did not respond favourably.

Vizianagaram

The Table explains the responses of the sample respondents of GLP mandal of Vizianagaram district, on teachers residing in the same village. Out of the total sample majority group, 60.0 per cent did not respond as to teachers residing in the same village, while the remaining 40.0 per cent did not respond favourably. From the total sample of Kurupam mandal, majority group 89.3 per cent did not respond favourably that teachers residing in the same village, with the remaining 10.7 per cent responding favourably. And from the total sample from Pachipenta mandal, a significant group of 96.7 per cent did not respond that teachers are residing in the same village, with the remaining few (3.3 per cent) responding favourably.

From the responses of the sample respondents of GLP mandal of Vizianagaram district, whether the teachers are coming regularly to school, majority group, 91.1 per cent responded that teachers are coming regularly to school, with the remaining (8.9 per cent) not responding favourably. From the total sample of Kurupam mandal, majority group, 64.3 per cent did not respond favourably that teachers are observing regular school times and the remaining few (35.7 per cent) responding favourably. And from the total sample from Pachipenta mandal, a significant group 65.6 per cent have responded that teachers are coming regularly to school, with the remaining few (34.4 per cent) are not favourable.

Regarding responses of the GLP mandal of Vizianagaram district, on the teachers observing regular school times, majority group, 92.2 per cent responded that the teachers are observing regular school times, with the remaining few (7.8 per cent) not responding favourably. From the total sample of Kurupam mandal, majority group, 75.0 per cent did not respond favourably as to the teachers observing regular school times, with the remaining few (25.0 per cent) responding favourably. And the total sample from Pachipenta mandal, a significant group, 53.3 per cent did not respond favourably that teachers are observing regular school times, with the remaining (46.7 per cent) responding favourably.

Visakhapatnam

The Table analyses about the responses of the sample respondents of Chintapalli mandal of Visakhapatnam district on the item whether teachers reside in the same village. Out of the total sample majority group of 94.4 per cent did not respond that teachers are residing in the same village, while the remaining few 5.6 per cent responded favourably. From the total sample of Madugula mandal, majority group of 95.6 per cent did not respond favourably as to teachers residing in the same village, with the remaining 4.4 per cent responding favourably. And from the total sample from Paderu mandal, a significant group of 94.4 per cent did not respond favourably that teachers are residing in the same village, with the remaining 5.6 per cent responding favourably.

From the response of the sample respondents of Chintapalli mandal of Visakhapatnam district, on teachers coming regularly to the school, out of the total sample, majority group, 95.6 per cent responded that the teachers are coming regularly to school, while the remaining 4.4 per cent did not responded favourably. From the total sample of Madugula mandal, majority group, 82.2 per cent responded that teachers are observing regular school times and the remaining few (17.8 per cent) did not respond favourably. And from the total sample from Paderu mandal, a significant group 54.4 per cent responded that teachers are coming regularly to school and the remaining (45.6 per cent) did not respond favourably.

Regarding responses of the Chintapalli mandal of Visakhapatnam district, the teachers are observing regular school times. Out of the total sample, majority group 95.6 per cent, responded that teachers are observing regular school times, with the remaining few (4.4 per cent) did not respond favourably. From the total sample of Madugula mandal, majority group 94.4 per cent responded that teachers are observing regular school times, while the remaining few (5.6 per cent) did not respond favourably. And from the total sample of Paderu mandal, a significant group, 55.6 per cent responded that teachers are observing regular school times, with the remaining few (44.4 per cent) not responding favourably.

Sl. No.	*Item*	*Srikakulam*											
		Palakonda				*Polaki*				*Seethampeta*			
		Yes	*%*	*No*	*%*	*Yes*	*%*	*No*	*%*	*Yes*	*%*	*No*	*%*
28	Are you thinking that the teachers are having proper competency and efficiency in teaching your children?	86	95.6	4	4.4	88	97.8	2	2.2	85	94.4	5	5.6
29	Are you thinking teachers are observing responsibilities in teaching?	63	70.0	27	30.0	89	98.9	1	1.1	74	82.2	16	17.8
30	Are you supporting those teachers who are not taking proper responsibility in teaching?	28	31.1	62	68.9	89	98.9	1	1.1	72	80.0	18	20.0
31	Have you complained against any teacher for his irresponsibility?	23	25.6	67	74.4	11	12.2	79	87.8	49	54.4	41	45.6

Sl. No	*Item*	*Vizianagaram*											
		GLP				*Kurupam*				*Pachipenta*			
		Yes	*%*	*No*	*%*	*Yes*	*%*	*No*	*%*	*Yes*	*%*	*No*	*%*
28	Are you thinking that the teachers are having proper competency and efficiency in teaching your children?	83	92.2	7	7.8	19	67.9	9	32.1	78	86.7	12	13.3

29	Are you thinking that the teachers are observing responsibilities in teaching?	85	94.4	5	5.6	24	85.7	4	14.3	47	52.2	43	47.8
30	Are you supporting those teachers who are not taking proper responsibility in teaching?	79	87.8	11	12.2	18	64.3	10	35.7	69	76.7	21	23.3
31	Have you complained against any teacher for his irresponsibility?	58	64.4	32	35.6	11	39.3	17	60.7	37	41.1	53	58.9

Sl. No.	*Item*	*Visakhapatnam*											
		Chintapalli				*Madugula*				*Paderu*			
		Yes	*%*	*No*	*%*	*Yes*	*%*	*No*	*%*	*Yes*	*%*	*No*	*%*
28	Are you thinking that teachers are having proper competency and efficiency in teaching your children?	85	94.4	5	5.6	89	98.9	1	1.1	56	62.2	34	37.8
29	Are you thinking that teachers are observing responsibilities in teaching?	84	93.3	6	6.7	81	90.0	9	10.0	72	80.0	18	20.0
30	Are you supporting those teachers who are not taking proper responsibility in teaching?	57	63.3	33	36.7	57	63.3	33	36.7	50	55.6	40	44.4
31	Have you complained against any teacher for his irresponsibility?	8	8.9	91.1	90	28	31.1	62	68.9	14	15.6	76	84.4

Srikakulam

The Table analyses the responses of the sample respondents of Palakonda mandal of Srikakulam district, whether teachers are having proper competency and efficiency in teaching their children. Out of the total sample, majority group, 95.6 per cent, responded that teachers are having proper competency and efficiency in teaching their children and the remaining few (4.4 per cent) did not respond favourably. From the total sample of Polaki mandal, majority group 97.8 per cent, responded that teachers are having proper competency and efficiency in teaching their children and the remaining few (2.2 per cent) did respond favourably. Out of the total sample from Seethampeta mandal, a significant group 94.4 per cent, responded that teachers are having proper competency and efficiency in teaching their children and the remaining (5.6 per cent) did not respond favourably.

Regarding the responses of the sample respondents of Palakonda mandal of Srikakulam district, whether the teachers are observing responsibilities in teaching their children, out of the total sample, majority group, 70.0 per cent responded that the teachers are observing responsibilities in teaching their children and the remaining (30.0 per cent) have not responded favourably. From the total sample of Polaki mandal, majority group 98.9 per cent have responded that teachers are observing responsibilities in teaching their children and the remaining (1.1 per cent) have not responded favourably. And from the total sample from Seethampeta mandal, a significant group, 82.2 per cent have responded that teachers are observing responsibilities in teaching their children and the remaining (17.8 per cent) said 'no'.

This indicates the responses of Palakonda mandal of Srikakulam district, on the support to those teachers who are not taking proper responsibility in teaching their children, that out of the total sample majority group, 68.9 per cent have not responded supporting those teachers who are not taking proper responsibility in teaching their children and the remaining (31.1 per cent) have responded favourably. From the total sample of Polaki mandal, majority group, 98.9 per cent, have responded supporting those teachers who are not taking proper responsibility in teaching their children and the remaining (1.1 per cent) have not responded favourably. And from the total sample from Seethampeta mandal, a significant group, 80.0 per cent, responded that they support those teachers who are not taking proper responsibility in teaching in their children and the remaining (20.0 per cent) said 'no'.

Regarding the responses of Palakonda mandal of Srikakulam district, whether they lodged complaint against any teacher for irresponsibility towards their children, out of the total sample majority group, 74.4 per cent have not responded that they complained against any teacher for his irresponsibility in teaching their children and the remaining 25.6 per cent, have responded favourably. From the total sample of Polaki mandal, majority group, 87.8 per cent have responded that they complained against a teacher for his irresponsibility in teaching their children and the remaining (12.2 per cent) have not responded favourably. And from the total sample from Seethampeta mandal, a significant group of 54.4 per cent have not responded that they complained against any teacher for his irresponsibility in teaching their children and the remaining (45.6 per cent) said 'no'.

Vizianagaram

The Table analyses the responses of the sample respondents of GLP Mandal of Vizianagaram district, whether teachers are having proper competency and efficiency in teaching children, out of the total sample, majority group,

92.2 per cent have responded favourably and remaining (5.6 per cent) have not responded favourably. From the total sample of Kurupam mandal, majority group of more than sixty per cent (67.9 per cent) responded that teachers are having proper competency and efficiency in teaching their children and the remaining (32.1 per cent) have not responded favourably. And from the total sample from Pachipenta mandal, a significant group of 86.7 per cent have responded that teachers are having proper competency and efficiency in teaching their children and the remaining (13.3 per cent) said 'no'.

Regarding responses of the sample respondents of GLP mandal of Vizianagaram district whether teachers are observing responsibilities in teaching their children, out of the total sample, majority group of more than ninety per cent (94.4 per cent) responded that the teachers are observing responsibilities in teaching their children and the remaining (5.6 per cent) have not responded favourably. From the total sample of Kurupam mandal, majority group of 85.7 per cent responded that the teachers are observing responsibilities in teaching their children and the remaining (14.3 per cent have responded favourably. And from the total sample from Pachipenta mandal, a significant group, 52.2 per cent, have responded that teachers are observing responsibilities in teaching their children and the remaining 47.8 per cent said 'no'.

From the responses of the sample respondents of GLP mandal of Vizianagaram district, whether they support those teachers who do not take proper responsibility in teaching their children, out of the total sample, majority group of 87.8 per cent responded favourably and supported those teachers who are not taking proper responsibility in teaching their children and the remaining few (12.2 per cent) have not responded favourably. From the total sample of Kurupam mandal, more than sixty per cent (64.3 per cent) have responded supporting those teachers who are not taking proper responsibility in teaching their children and the remaining 35.7 per cent have not responded favourably. And from the total sample from Pachipenta mandal, a significant group of 76.7 per cent responded that they support those teachers who are not taking proper responsibility in teaching their children, while the remaining 23.3 per cent said 'no'.

Visakhapatnam

The Table analyses the responses of the sample respondents of Chintapalli mandal of Visakhapatnam district, whether teachers are having proper competency and efficiency in teaching their children, out of the total sample, majority group, 94.4 per cent, said that the teachers are having proper competency and efficiency in teaching their children and the remaining (5.6 per cent) have not responded favourably. From the total sample of Madugula mandal, majority group of more than ninety per cent (98.9 per cent) responded that teachers are having proper competency and efficiency in teaching their children and the remaining (1.1 per cent) have not responded favourably. And from the total sample from Paderu mandal, a significant group, 62.2 per cent have responded that teachers are having proper competency and efficiency in teaching their children and the remaining (37.8 per cent) said 'no'.

From the responses of the sample respondents of Chintapalli mandal of Visakhapatnam district, whether the teachers are observing responsibilities in teaching their children, out of the total sample, majority group, of more than ninety per cent (93.3 per cent) have responded that teachers are observing responsibilities in teaching their children and the remaining (6.7 per cent) have not responded favourably. From the total sample of Madugula mandal, majority group of 90.0 per cent, have responded that teachers are observing responsibilities in teaching their children and the remaining (10.0 per cent) have not responded favourably. And from the total sample from Paderu mandal, a significant group, (80.0 per cent), responded that teachers are observing responsibilities in teaching their children and the remaining 20.0 per cent said 'no'.

Responses of the sample respondents of Chintapalli mandal of Visakhapatnam district, show that teachers who are not taking proper responsibility in teaching towards their children. Out of the total sample, majority group, 63.3 per cent, responded, that they support those teachers who are not taking proper responsibility in teaching their children and the remaining few (36.7 per cent) have not responded. From the total sample of Madugula mandal, more than sixty per cent (63.3 per cent) responded in supporting those teachers who are not taking proper responsibility in teaching their children and the remaining (36.7 per cent) have not responded favourably. And from the total sample from Paderu mandal, a significant group, 55.6 per cent, responded that they support those teachers who do not take proper responsibility in teaching their children and the remaining few (44.4 per cent) said 'no'.

Regarding responses of the sample respondents of Chintapalli mandal of Visakhapatnam district, whether they complained against any teacher for his irresponsibility towards their children, out of the total sample majority group, 91.1 per cent have not complained against any teacher for their irresponsibility in teaching their children and the remaining few (8.9 per cent) have responded favourably. From the total sample of Madugula mandal, more than sixty per cent (68.9 per cent) have not complained against any teacher for irresponsibility in teaching their children and the remaining (31.1 per cent) responded favourably. And from the total sample from Paderu mandal, a significant group of

84.4 per cent have not complained against any teacher for irresponsibility in teaching their children and the remaining (15.6 per cent) responded 'yes'.

Sl. No.	*Item*	*Srikakulam*											
		Palakonda				*Polaki*				*Seethampeta*			
		Yes	*%*	*No*	*%*	*Yes*	*%*	*No*	*%*	*Yes*	*%*	*No*	*%*
32	Were you present in some of the parents meetings in the school?	41	45.6	49	54.4	82	91.1	8	8.9	50	55.6	40	44.4
33	Were you discussing in parental meetings about your children's education in the school?	53	58.9	37	41.1	89	98.9	1	1.1	55	61.1	35	38.9

Sl. No.	*Item*	*Vizianagaram*											
		GLP				*Kurupam*				*Pachipenta*			
		Yes	*%*	*No*	*%*	*Yes*	*%*	*No*	*%*	*Yes*	*%*	*No*	*%*
32	Were you present in some of the parents meetings in the school?	78	86.7	12	13.3	4	14.3	24	85.7	48	53.3	42	46.7
33	Were you discussing in parental meetings about your children's education in the school?	76	84.4	14	15.6	15	53.6	13	46.4	52	57.8	38	42.2

Sl. No.	Item	Visakhapatnam											
		Chintapalli				Madugula				Paderu			
		Yes	%	No	%	Yes	%	No	%	Yes	%	No	%
32	Were you present in some of the parents meetings in the school?	27	30.0	63	70.0	20	22.2	70	77.8	39	43.3	51	56.7
33	Were you discussing in parental meetings about your children's education in the school?	40	44.4	50	55.6	34	37.8	56	62.2	41	45.6	49	54.4

Srikakulam

The Table indicates the responses of the sample respondents of Palakonda mandal of Srikakulam district, on their presence in some of the parents' meetings in school. Out of the total sample, majority group, 54.4 per cent have not responded that they were present in some of the parents' meetings in the school and the remaining 45.6 per cent have not responded favourably. From the total sample of Polaki mandal, majority group, 91.1 per cent have responded that they were present in some of the parents' meetings and the remaining 8.9 per cent said 'no'. And from the total sample from Seethampeta mandal, a significant group of 55.6 per cent have responded that they were present in some of the parents' meetings in the school and the remaining 44.4 per cent said 'no'.

From the responses of the sample respondents of Palakonda mandal of Srikakulam district whether they were present in parental meetings about children's education in the school. Out of the total sample, majority group, 58.9 per cent responded that they were present in parental meetings, about children's education in the school and the remaining 41.1 per cent have not responded favourably. From the total sample of Polaki mandal, majority group of 98.9 per cent responded they were present in parental meetings about children's education in the school and the remaining 1.1 per cent have not responded favourably. And from the total sample from Seethampeta mandal, a significant group of 61.1 per cent responded that they were present in parental meetings to know about their children's education in the school and the remaining 38.9 per cent said 'no'.

Vizianagaram

The Table analyses the responses of the sample respondents of GLP mandal of Vizianagaram district, on their presence in some of the parents' meetings in school. Out of the total sample, majority group of more than eighty per cent (86.7 per cent) responded that they were present in some of the parents meetings in the school and the remaining (13.3 per cent) have not responded favourably. From the total sample of Kurupam mandal, majority group of 85.7 per cent have not responded to have been present in some of the parents' meetings to know about their children education and the remaining (14.3 per cent) have responded favourably. And from the total sample from Pachipenta mandal, a significant group of 53.3 per cent have responded that they were present in some of the parents' meetings in the school and the remaining 46.7 per cent said 'no'.

From the response of the sample respondents of GLP mandal of Vizianagaram district about discussing in parental meetings on their children's education in school, out of the total sample majority group of 84.4 per cent responded favourably discussing in parental meetings about their children's education in the school and the remaining 15.6 per cent have not responded favourably. From the total sample of Kurupam mandal, majority group of more than fifty per cent (53.6 per cent) have responded favourably about discussing in parental meetings on their children's education in the school and the remaining 46.4 per cent have not responded favourably. And from the total sample from Pachipenta mandal, a significant group of 57.8 per cent have responded favourably about discussing in parental meetings on their children's education in the school and the remaining 42.2 per cent have not responded favourably.

Visakhapatnam

The Table analyses the responses of the sample respondents of Chintapalli mandal of Visakhapatnam district, on presence in some of the parents' meetings in school. Out of the total sample, majority group of more than seventy per cent (70.0 per cent) responded that they were present in some of the parents' meetings in the school and the remaining 30.0 per cent have not responded favourably. From the total sample of Madugula mandal, majority group of 77.8 per cent responded that they were present in some of the parents' meetings and the remaining 22.2 per cent said 'no'. And from the total sample from Paderu mandal, a significant group, 56.7 per cent have not responded as to their presence in some of the parents' meetings in school and the remaining (43.3 per cent) have not responded.

From the responses of the sample respondents of Chintapalli mandal of Visakhapatnam district, whether they were present in discussing in parental meetings about children's education in the school. Out of the total sample majority group, 55.6 per cent have not responded favourably about discussing in parental meetings on children's education in the school and the remaining 44.4 per cent have responded favourably. From the total sample of Madugula mandal, majority group of more than sixty per cent (62.2 per cent) have not responded as to discussing in parental meetings about their children's education in the school and the remaining 37.8 per cent have responded favourably. And from the total sample from Paderu mandal, a significant group of 54.4 per cent have not responded on discussing in parental meetings about their children's education in the school and the remaining of 45.6 per cent said 'yes'.

Sl. No.	*Item*	*Srikakulam*											
		Palakonda				*Polaki*				*Seethampeta*			
		Yes	*%*	*No*	*%*	*Yes*	*%*	*No*	*%*	*Yes*	*%*	*No*	*%*
34	Were you aware of your children properly learning in the school regularly?	57	63.3	33	36.7	86	95.6	4	4.4	64	71.1	26	28.9
35	Are the school management committees overseeing the school discipline?	28	31.1	62	68.9	16	17.8	74	82.2	63	70.0	27	30.0

Sl. No.	*Item*	*Vizianagaram*											
		GLP				*Kurupam*				*Pachipenta*			
		Yes	*%*	*No*	*%*	*Yes*	*%*	*No*	*%*	*Yes*	*%*	*No*	*%*
34	Were you aware that your children are properly learning in the school regularly?	81	90.0	9	10.0	18	64.3	10	35.7	58	64.4	32	35.6
35	Are the school management committees overseeing the school discipline?	76	84.4	14	15.6	16	57.1	12	42.9	63	70.0	27	30.0

Sl.	*Item*	*Visakhapatnam*											
No.		*Chintapalli*				*Madugula*				*Paderu*			
		Yes	*%*	*No*	*%*	*Yes*	*%*	*No*	*%*	*Yes*	*%*	*No*	*%*
34	Were you aware of your children properly learning in the school regularly?	80	88.9	10	11.1	43	47.8	47	52.2	49	54.4	41	45.6
35	Are the school management committees overseeing the school discipline?	52	57.8	38	42.2	24	26.7	66	73.3	9	10.0	81	90.0

Srikakulam

The Table analyses the responses of the sample respondents of Palakonda mandal of Srikakulam district, on their awareness of children properly learning in their school regularly, out of the total sample, majority group of 63.3 per cent have responded favourably that they were aware of their children properly learning in the school and the remaining 36.7 per cent have not responded favourably. From the total sample of Polaki mandal, majority group of 95.6 per cent have favourably responded that they were aware of their children's education and the remaining 4.4 per cent have not responded favourably. And from the total sample from Seethampeta mandal, a significant group of 71.1 per cent have favourably responded that they were aware of their children properly learning in the school regularly and the remaining 28.9 per cent said 'no'.

From the responses of the sample respondents of Palakonda mandal of Srikakulam district, on the school management committees overseeing the school discipline of their children, out of the total sample, majority group of 68.9

per cent have not responded favourably about the school management committees overseeing the school discipline of their children and the remaining 31.1 per cent have not responded favourably. From the total sample of Polaki mandal, majority group of 82.2 per cent have not responded favourably as to school management committees overseeing the school discipline regarding their children and the remaining 17.8 per cent responded favourably. And from the total sample from Seethampeta mandal, a significant group of 70.0 per cent responded favourably that they were in the school management committees overseeing the school discipline regarding their children's education and the remaining 30.0 per cent said 'no'.

Vizianagaram

The Table analyses the responses of the sample respondents of GLP mandal of Vizianagaram district, on their awareness of children properly learning in the school regularly, out of the total sample, majority group of 90.0 per cent responded that they are aware that their children are properly learning in the school regularly and the remaining 10.0 per cent have not responded favourably. On the total sample of Kurupam mandal, majority group of 64.3 per cent have responded favourably and aware of their children are properly learning in the school regularly and the remaining 35.7 per cent have not responded favourably. And from the total sample from Pachipenta mandal, a significant group of 64.4 per cent favourably responded and that they are aware of children properly learning in the school regularly and the remaining 35.6 per cent said 'no'.

Regarding responses of the sample respondents of GLP mandal of Vizianagaram district, on the school management committees overseeing the school discipline of their children, out of the total sample, majority group of 84.4 per cent have responded favourably as to the school management committees overseeing the school discipline, while the remaining 15.6 per cent not have responded favourably. About the total sample of Kurupam mandal, majority group of more than fifty per cent (57.1 per cent) responded that the school management committees are overseeing the school discipline and the remaining 42.9 per cent have not responded favourably. And from the total sample from Pachipenta mandal, a significant group of 70.0 per cent have responded favourably that the school management committees are overseeing the school discipline and the remaining 30.0 per cent said 'no'.

Visakhapatnam

The Table analyses the responses of the sample respondents of Chintapalli mandal of Visakhapatnam district, on their awareness of children properly learning in the school regularly. Out of the total sample, majority group of more than eighty per cent (88.9 per cent) responded favourably that they are aware of their children properly learning in the school and the remaining 11.1 per cent have not responded favourably. From the total sample of Madugula mandal, majority group of 52.2 per cent were not aware of their children properly learning in the school regularly and the remaining 47.8 per cent responded favourably. And from the total sample from Paderu mandal, a significant group of 54.4 per cent have responded favourably that they were aware of children properly learning in the school regularly and the remaining 45.6 per cent said 'no'.

As regards the responses of the sample respondents of Chintapalli mandal of Visakhapatnam district, on the school management committees overseeing the school discipline of their children, out of the total sample, majority group of 57.8 per cent responded that the school management committees oversee the school discipline regarding their children's education, while the remaining 42.2 per cent have not responded favourably. From the total sample of Madugula mandal, majority group of more than seventy per cent (73.3

per cent) have not responded favourably on school management committees overseeing the school discipline regarding their children's education, while the remaining 26.7 per cent responded favourably. And from the total sample from Paderu mandal, a significant group of 90.0 per cent have not responded favourably as to the school management committees overseeing the school discipline regarding their children's education, while the remaining (10.0 per cent) have responded favourably.

Sl. No.	*Item*	*Srikakulam*											
		Palakonda				*Polaki*				*Seethampeta*			
		Yes	*%*	*No*	*%*	*Yes*	*%*	*No*	*%*	*Yes*	*%*	*No*	*%*
36	By sending to school are you thinking that your children are neither studying in the school, nor useful for domestic work?	40	44.4	50	55.6	79	87.8	11	12.2	64	71.1	26	28.9

Sl. No.	*Item*	*Vizianagaram*											
		GLP				*Kurupam*				*Pachipenta*			
		Yes	*%*	*No*	*%*	*Yes*	*%*	*No*	*%*	*Yes*	*%*	*No*	*%*
36	By sending to school are you thinking that your children are neither studying in the school, nor useful for domestic work?	46	51.1	44	48.9	17	60.7	11	39.3	47	52.2	43	47.8

Sl. No.	Item	Visakhapatnam											
		Chintapalli				Madugula				Paderu			
		Yes	%	No	%	Yes	%	No	%	Yes	%	No	%
36	By sending to school are you thinking that your children are neither studying in the school, nor useful for domestic work?	9	10.0	81	90.0	44	48.9	46	51.1	15	16.7	75	83.3

By sending to school are you thinking that your children are neither studying in the school, nor useful for domestic work?

Srikakulam

The Table analyses the responses of the sample respondents of Palakonda mandal of Srikakulam district, on the view that by sending to school, their children are neither studying in the school nor useful for domestic work. Out of the total sample, majority group, 55.6 per cent have not responded favourably and the remaining 44.4 per cent responded favourably. From the total sample of Polaki mandal, majority group, 87.8 per cent, responded that by sending to school they think that children are neither studying in the school, nor useful for domestic work, while the remaining 12.2 per cent said ‘no’. And from the total sample from Seethampeta mandal, a significant group of 71.1 per cent, have responded that by sending to school they think that children are neither studying in the school, nor useful for domestic work, while the remaining 28.9 per cent, said ‘no’.

Vizianagaram

The Table analyses the responses of the sample respondents of GLP mandal of Vizianagaram district, on the view that by sending to school their children are neither studying in the school, nor useful for domestic work, out of the total sample majority group of 51.1 per cent have not responded favourably and the remaining 48.9 per cent have responded favourably. From the total sample of Kurupam mandal, majority group of 60.7 per cent have responded that by sending to school they think that children are neither studying in the school, nor useful for domestic work, while the remaining 39.3 per cent have not responded favourably. And from the total sample from Pachipenta mandal, a significant group of 52.2 per cent have responded that by sending to school they think that children are neither studying in the school, nor useful for domestic work and the remaining 47.8 per cent said 'no'.

Visakhapatnam

The Table analyses the responses of the sample respondents of Chintapalli mandal of Visakhapatnam district, on the view that by sending to school, their children are neither studying in the school, nor useful for domestic work out of the total sample, majority group of 90.0 per cent have not responded favourably and the remaining 10.0 per cent have responded favourably. From the total sample of Madugula mandal, majority group of 51.1 per cent have not responded favourably that by sending to school their children are neither studying in the school, nor useful for domestic work, while the remaining 48.9 per cent have responded favourably. And from the total sample from Paderu mandal, a significant group of 83.3 per cent have not responded favourably that by sending to school they think that their children are neither studying in the school, nor useful for domestic work, while the remaining 16.7 per cent have responded favourably.

Sl. No.	Item	Srikakulam											
		Palakonda				Polaki				Seethampeta			
		Yes	%	No	%	Yes	%	No	%	Yes	%	No	%
37	Even though the Government is providing incentives like waiver of school fees, giving free books and also providing mid-day meals, why do you opt for domestic work for your children?	68	75.6	22	24.4	86	95.6	4	4.4	74	82.2	16	17.8

Sl. No.	Item	Vizianagaram											
		GLP				Kurupam				Pachipenta			
		Yes	%	No	%	Yes	%	No	%	Yes	%	No	%
37	Even though the Government is providing incentives like waiver of school fees, giving free books and also providing mid-day meals, why do you opt for domestic work for your children?	49	54.4	41	45.6	24	85.7	4	14.3	85	94.4	5	5.6

Sl. No.	Item	Visakhapatnam											
		Chintapalli				Madugula				Paderu			
		Yes	%	No	%	Yes	%	No	%	Yes	%	No	%
37	Even though the Government is providing incentives like waiver of school fees, giving free books and also providing mid-day meals, why do you opt for domestic work for your children?	78	86.7	12	13.3	86	95.6	4	4.4	70	77.8	20	22.2

Even though the Government is providing incentives like waiver of school fees, giving free books and also providing mid-day meals, why do you opt for domestic work for your children?

Srikakulam

The Table analyses the responses of the sample respondents of Palakonda mandal of Srikakulam district, on Government incentives like waiver of school fees, giving free books and also providing mid-day meals, why do parents opt for domestic work for their children, out of the total sample, majority group of 75.6 per cent have responded that even though Government is providing incentives like waiver of school fees, giving free books and giving free books and also providing mid-day meals, option for their children is domestic work, while the remaining 24.4 per cent have not responded favourably. From the total sample of Polaki mandal, majority group of 95.6 per cent responded that even though Government is providing incentives like mid-day meals, they opt for domestic work to their children and the remaining 4.4 per cent said 'no'. And from the total sample from Seethampeta mandal, a significant group of 74.0 per cent have responded favourably for domestic work for their children while the remaining 17.8 per cent said 'no'.

Vizianagaram

The Table analyses the responses of the sample respondents of GLP mandal of Vizianagaram district, even though Government is providing incentives like waiver of school fees, free books and also providing mid-day meals, they opt for domestic work for their children, out of the total sample, majority group of 54.4 per cent have responded that even though Government is providing incentives like providing mid-day meals, their option is for domestic work for their children and the remaining 45.6 per cent have not responded favourably. From the total sample of Kurupam mandal, majority group of 85.7 per cent responded that even though Government is providing incentives like providing mid-day meals, they opt for domestic work for their children while the remaining 14.3 per cent did not respond favourably. And from the total sample from Pachipenta mandal, a significant group, 94.4 per cent have responded that they opt for domestic work for their children while the remaining 5.6 per cent did not respond favourably.

Visakhapatnam

The Table analyses the responses of the sample respondents of Chintapalli mandal of Visakhapatnam district, on Government incentives like waiver of school fees, giving free books and also providing mid-day meals they opt for domestic work for their children, out of the total sample majority group of 86.7 per cent have responded that even though Government is providing incentives like providing mid-day meals, their option for their children is domestic work and the remaining 13.3 per cent have not responded favourably. From the total sample of Madugula mandal, majority group of 95.6 per cent responded that even though Government is providing incentives like providing mid-day meals but parents opt for domestic work for their children, while remaining 4.4 per cent did not respond favourably.

And from the total sample from Paderu mandal, a significant group of 77.8 per cent responded favourably for domestic work for their children and the remaining 22.2 per cent did not respond favourably.

Sl.	*Item*	*Srikakulam*											
No.		*Palakonda*				*Polaki*				*Seethampeta*			
		Yes	*%*	*No*	*%*	*Yes*	*%*	*No*	*%*	*Yes*	*%*	*No*	*%*
38	Are you thinking that your children are afraid of the teachers are giving physical punishment in the school?	47	52.2	43	47.8	13	14.4	77	85.6	43	47.8	47	52.2

Sl.	*Item*	*Vizianagaram*											
No.		*GLP*				*Kurupam*				*Pachipenta*			
		Yes	*%*	*No*	*%*	*Yes*	*%*	*No*	*%*	*Yes*	*%*	*No*	*%*
38	Are you thinking that your children are afraid of the teachers are giving physical punishment in the school?	65	72.2	25	27.8	11	39.3	17	60.7	16	17.8	74	82.2

Sl.	*Item*	*Visakhapatnam*											
No.		*Chintapalli*				*Madugula*				*Paderu*			
		Yes	*%*	*No*	*%*	*Yes*	*%*	*No*	*%*	*Yes*	*%*	*No*	*%*
38	Are you thinking that your children are afraid of the teachers are giving physical punishment in the school?	28	31.1	62	68.9	66	73.3	24	26.7	36	40.0	54	60.0

Are you thinking that your children are afraid of the teachers are giving physical punishment in the school?

Srikakulam

The Table analyses the responses of the sample respondents of Palakonda mandal of Srikakulam district, on their view that their children are afraid that teachers are giving physical punishment in the school, out of the total sample, majority group of 52.2 per cent responded favourably while 47.8 per cent have not responded favourably. From the total sample of Polaki mandal, majority group of 85.6 per cent have not responded favourably that children are afraid that the teachers are giving physical punishment in the school, while the remaining 14.4 per cent have responded favourably. And from the total sample from Seethampeta mandal, a significant group of 52.2 per cent have not responded favourably that their children are afraid that the teachers are giving physical punishment in the school for their children and the remaining 47.8 per cent have responded favourably.

Vizianagaram

The Table analyses the responses of the sample respondents of GLP mandal of Vizianagaram district, on the view that children are afraid that the teachers are giving physical punishment in the school, out of the total sample, majority group of 72.2 per cent have responded favourably but 27.8 per cent have not responded favourably. From the total sample of Kurupam mandal, majority group of 60.7 per cent have not responded favourably that the children are afraid that the teachers are giving physical punishment in the school, while the remaining 39.3 per cent have responded favourably. And from the total sample from Pachipenta mandal, a significant group, 82.2 per cent have not responded favourably for physical punishment is given in the school, while the remaining 17.8 per cent responded favourably.

Visakhapatnam

The Table analyses the responses of the sample

respondents of Chintapalli mandal of Visakhapatnam district, on the view that children are afraid that the teachers are giving physical punishment in the school, out of the total sample majority group of 68.9 per cent have not responded favourably but 31.1 per cent responded favourably. From the total sample of Madugula mandal, majority group of 73.3 per cent responded that children are afraid that the teachers are giving physical punishment in the school while the remaining 26.7 per cent have responded favourably. And from the total sample from Paderu mandal, a significant group of 60.0 per cent hve not responded favourably and the remaining 40.0 per cent responded favourably.

Sl. No.	*Item*	*Srikakulam*											
		Palakonda				*Polaki*				*Seethampeta*			
		Yes	*%*	*No*	*%*	*Yes*	*%*	*No*	*%*	*Yes*	*%*	*No*	*%*
39	In case your children are not properly progressing in the school are you going to question the teachers?	52	57.8	38	42.2	77	85.6	13	14.4	55	61.1	35	38.9

Sl. No.	*Item*	*Vizianagaram*											
		GLP				*Kurupam*				*Pachipenta*			
		Yes	*%*	*No*	*%*	*Yes*	*%*	*No*	*%*	*Yes*	*%*	*No*	*%*
39	In case your children are not properly progressing in the school are you going to question the teachers?	63	70.0	27	30.0	7	25.0	21	75.0	60	66.7	30	33.3

Sl. No.	*Item*	*Visakhapatnam*											
		Chintapalli				*Madugula*				*Paderu*			
		Yes	*%*	*No*	*%*	*Yes*	*%*	*No*	*%*	*Yes*	*%*	*No*	*%*
39	In case your children are not properly progressing in the school are you going to question the teachers?	45	50.0	45	50.0	53	58.9	37	41.1	33	36.7	57	63.3

In case your children are not properly progressing in the school are you going to question the teachers?

Srikakulam

The Table analyses the responses of the sample respondents of Palakonda mandal of Srikakulam district, on children not properly progressing in the school are you going to question the teachers, out of the total sample, majority group of 57.8 per cent, responded favourably while 42.2 per cent have not responded favourably. From the total sample of Polaki mandal, majority group of more than eighty per cent (85.6 per cent) have responded that their children are not properly progressing in the school and that they are going to question the teachers, while the remaining 14.4 per cent responded favourably. And from the total sample from Seethampeta mandal, a significant group of 61.1 per cent responded favourably and the remaining 38.9 per cent have not responded favourably.

Vizianagaram

The Table analyses the responses of the sample respondents of GLP mandal of Vizianagaram District on children not properly progressing in the school whether they are going to question the teachers. Out of the total sample, majority group of 70.0 per cent have not responded with 30.0 per cent of them not responding. From the total sample of Kurupam mandal, majority group of more than seventy five (75.0 per cent) have not responded with the remaining 25.0 per cent responding. And from the total sample from Pachipenta mandal, a significant group of 66.7 per cent have responded and the remaining 33.3 per cent have not responded.

Visakhapatnam

The Table analyses the responses of the sample respondents of Chintapalli mandal of Visakhapatnam district, on children not properly progressing in the school they are going to question the teachers that out of the total sample, majority group of 50.0 per cent have not responded favourably, while are 50.0 per cent responded favourably. From the total sample of Madugula mandal, majority group of more than fifty per cent (58.9 per cent) responded that their children are not properly progressing in the school and as such they are going to question the teachers, while the remaining 41.1 per cent have not responded favourably. And from the total sample from Paderu mandal, a significant group of 63.3 per cent have not responded favourably and the remaining 36.7 per cent have responded favourably.

Sl. No.	*Item*	*Srikakulam*											
		Palakonda				*Polaki*				*Seethampeta*			
		Yes	*%*	*No*	*%*	*Yes*	*%*	*No*	*%*	*Yes*	*%*	*No*	*%*
40	The reasons for your children taking back seat because of teachers telling so to you. Are you convinced about it?	64	71.1	26	28.9	17	18.9	73	81.1	65	72.2	25	27.8

Sl. No.	Item	Vizianagaram											
		GLP				Kurupam				Pachipenta			
		Yes	%	No	%	Yes	%	No	%	Yes	%	No	%
40	The reasons for your children taking back seat because of teachers telling so to you. Are you convinced about it?	68	75.6	22	24.4	18	64.3	10	35.7	32	35.6	58	64.4

Sl. No.	Item	Visakhapatnam											
		Chintapalli				Madugula				Paderu			
		Yes	%	No	%	Yes	%	No	%	Yes	%	No	%
40	The reasons for your children taking back seat because of teachers telling so to you. Are you convinced about it?	61	67.8	29	32.2	42	46.7	48	53.3	38	42.2	52	57.8

The reasons for your children taking back seat because of teachers telling so to you. Are you convinced about it?

Srikakulam

The Table analyses the responses of the sample respondents of Palakonda mandal of Srikakulam District on children taking back-seat because of teachers telling so to them. Out of the total sample majority group of 71.1 per cent have responded and 28.9 per cent have not responded. From the total sample of Polaki mandal, majority group of more than eighty per cent (81.1 per cent) have not responded that their children take back-seat because of teachers telling so to them and the remaining 18.9 per cent have responded. And from the total sample from Seethampeta mandal, the reasons for their children taking back-seat because of teachers telling so to them. A significant group of 72.2 per cent have responded and the remaining 27.8 per cent were have not responded.

Vizianagaram

The Table analyses the responses of the sample respondents of GLP mandal of Vizianagaram District on children taking back-seat because of teachers telling so to them. Out of the total sample, majority group of 75.6 per cent have responded and 24.4 per cent have not responded. From the total sample of Kurupam mandal, majority group of more than sixty per cent (64.3 per cent) have responded for children taking back-seat because of teachers telling so to them and the remaining 35.7 per cent have not responded. And from the total sample from Pachipenta mandal, the reasons for children taking back-seat because of teachers telling so to them. A significant group of 64.4 per cent have not responded and the remaining 35.6 per cent have responded.

Visakhapatnam

The Table analyses the responses of the sample respondents of Chintapalli mandal of Visakhapatnam District on children taking back-seat because of teachers telling so to them. Out of the total sample, majority group of 67.8 per cent have responded and 32.2 per cent were have responded. From the total sample of Madugula mandal, majority group of more than fifty per cent (53.3 per cent) have not responded about the reasons for children taking back seat because of teachers telling so to them and the remaining 46.7 per cent have responded. And from the total sample from Paderu mandal, the reasons for their children taking back-seat because of the teachers telling so to them, a significant group of 57.8 per cent have not responded and the remaining 42.2 per cent have responded.

Sl.	*Item*	*Srikakulam*											
No.		*Palakonda*				*Polaki*				*Seethampeta*			
		Yes	*%*	*No*	*%*	*Yes*	*%*	*No*	*%*	*Yes*	*%*	*No*	*%*
41	Recently private schools are prospering more than the Government schools. The private schools in 1993-94 were 12.5 lakh and they went up to 48 lakhs in the year 2007-08. And parents are attracted to the private schools and ultimately losing economically. Are you feeling unhappy about it?	77	85.6	13	14.4	83	92.2	7	7.8	83	92.2	7	7.8

Sl.	*Item*	*Vizianagaram*											
No.		*GLP*				*Kurupam*				*Pachipenta*			
		Yes	*%*	*No*	*%*	*Yes*	*%*	*No*	*%*	*Yes*	*%*	*No*	*%*
41	Recently private schools are prospering more than the Government schools. The private schools in 1993-94 were 12.5 lakh and	69	76.7	21	23.3	27	96.4	1	3.6	88	97.8	2	2.2

Contd...

they went up to 48 lakh in the year 2007-08. And the parents are attracted to the private schools and ultimately losing economically. Are you feeling unhappy about it?

Sl. No.	*Item*	*Visakhapatnam*											
		Chintapalli				*Madugula*				*Paderu*			
		Yes	*%*	*No*	*%*	*Yes*	*%*	*No*	*%*	*Yes*	*%*	*No*	*%*
41	Recently private schools are prospering more than the Government schools. The private schools in 1993-94 were 12.5 lakh and they went up to 48 lakh in the year 2007-08. And the parents are attracted to the private schools and ultimately losing economically. Are you feeling unhappy about it?	80	88.0	10	11.1	85	94.4	5	5.6	58	64.4	32	35.6

Recently private schools are prospering more than the Government schools. The private schools in 1993-94 were 12.5 lakh and they went up to 48 lakh in the year 2007-08. And the parents are attracted to the private schools and ultimately losing economically. Are you feeling unhappy about it?

Srikakulam

The Table analyses the responses of the sample respondents of Palakonda mandal of Srikakulam district on private schools prospering more than the Government schools. The private schools in 1993- 94 are 12.5 lakh and they went up to 48 lakhs in the year 2007-08. And the parents are attracted to the private schools and ultimately losing economically. Out of the total sample, majority group (85.6 per cent) have responded and the remaining (14.4 per cent) have not responded. From the total sample of Polaki mandal, majority group (92.2 per cent) have responded that private schools are prospering more than the Government schools and the remaining 7.8 per cent have not responded. And from the total sample from Polaki as well as Seethampeta mandals, a significant group of 92.2 per cent have responded and the remaining 7.8 per cent have not responded.

Vizianagaram

The above Table analyses about the responses of the sample respondents of GLP mandal of Vizianagaram district with private schools are prospering more than the Government schools. The private schools in 1993-94 while 12.5 lakh and went up to 48 lakh in the year 2007-08. And the parents are attracted by the private schools and ultimately losing economically. Out of the total sample, a majority group of 76.7 per cent has responded and the remaining (23.3 per cent) has not responded. From the total sample of Kurupam mandal, a majority group of 96.4 per cent responded that private schools are prospering more than the Government schools, while the remaining (3.6 per cent) has not responded. And from the total sample from Pachipenta mandal, a significant group of 97.8 per cent has responded and the remaining (2.2 per cent) has not responded.

Visakhapatnam

The Table explains about the responses of the sample respondents of Chintapalli mandal of Visakhapatnam district on recently private schools prospering more than the

Government schools. The private schools in 1993- 94 were 12.5 lakh and went up to 48 lakh in the year 2007-08. And the parents are attracted by private schools and ultimately losing economically. Out of the total sample, a majority group of 88.0 per cent has responded and the remaining (11.1 per cent) had not responded. From the total sample of Madugula mandal, majority group of 94.4 per cent had responded as to private schools prospering more than the Government schools and the remaining (5.6 per cent) has not responded. And from the total sample from Paderu mandal, a significant group of 64.4 per cent has responded while the remaining 35.6 per cent have not responded.

What are the main reasons for your children joining private schools instead of Government schools?

Sl. No.		*Srikakulam*		
		Palakonda	*Polaki*	*Seethampeta*
1	Teaching is not up to the mark	72 (80.0)	83 (92.2)	63 (70.0)
2	Facilities not available	17 (18.9)	6 (6.7)	21 (23.3)
3	Prosperity of children's parents	1 (1.1)		5 (5.6)
4	Teachers' lack of moral commitment		1 (1.1)	1 (1.1)
	Chi-square value		**18.98****	

Sl. No.		*Vizianagaram*		
		GLP	*Kurupam*	*Pachipenta*
1	Teaching is not up to the mark	46 (51.1)	21 (75.0)	82 (91.1)
2	Facilities not available	14 (15.6)	4 (14.3)	3 (3.3)
3	Prosperity of children's parents	22 (24.4)	2 (7.1)	4 (4.4)
4	Teachers' lack moral commitment	8 (8.9)	1 (3.6)	1 (1.1)
	Chi-square value		**37.42****	

S. No.		Visakhapatnam		
		Chintapalli	*Madugula*	*Paderu*
1	Teaching is not up to the mark	81 (90.0)	88 (97.8)	72 (80.0)
2	Facilities not available	8 (8.9)	2 (2.2)	17 (18.9)
3	Prosperity of children's parents	1 (1.1)		1 (1.1)
4	Teachers' lack moral commitment			
	Chi-square value		15.27**	

What are the main reasons for your children joining private schools instead of Government schools?

Srikakulam

The Table explains the responses of the sample respondents of Srikakulam district regarding the main reason for their children joining private schools, instead of Government schools. In Government schools, teaching is not up to the mark according to a total (80.0 per cent) from Palakonda mandal, alogn with 92.2 per cent from Polaki mandal and 70.0 per cent from Seethampeta mandals. As about the facilities not available, (18.9 per cent) from Palakonda mandal, 6.7 per cent from Polaki mandal and 23.3 per cent from Seethampeta mandal has responded. Regarding prosperity of children's parents, only 1.1 per cent from Palakonda mandal and 5.6 per cent from Seethampeta mandal, have responded as to teachers' lack of moral commitment, only 1.1 per cent from Polaki mandal have responded. The obtained chi-square value is 18.98 which is significant at 0.01 level more than the Table value (16.8).

Vizianagaram

The above Table analyses responses of the sample respondents of Vizianagaram district regarding the main reason for their children joining in private schools, instead of Government schools. Out of them as to teaching is not up to the mark, for a total of 51.1 per cent from GLP mandal, 75.0 per cent from Kurupam mandal and 91.1 per cent from Pachipenta mandal. For the facilities not available, 15.6 per cent of GLP mandal, 14.3 per cent of Kurupam mandal and 3.3 per cent in Pachipenta mandal, think so. Regarding Prosperity of children's parents, 24.4 per cent is from GLP mandal, 7.1 per cent from Kurupam mandal and 4.4 per cent from Pachipenta mandal. Towards Teachers' lack of moral commitment, 8.9 per cent from GLP mandal, 3.6 per cent from Kurupam mandal and 1.1 per cent from Pachipenta mandal opine so. The obtained chi-square value is 37.42 which is significant at 0.01 level is more than the Table value (16.8).

Visakhapatnam

The Table analyses the responses of the sample respondents of Visakhapatnam district on the main reasons for their children joining in private schools instead of Government schools. Out of them, the main reason is that teaching is not up to the mark, while a total (90.0 per cent from Chintapalli mandal, 97.8 per cent from Madugula mandal and 80.0 per cent from Paderu mandal think so. For the facilities not available, 8.9 per cent from Chintapalli mandal, 2.2 per cent from Madugula mandal and 18.9 per cent from Paderu mandal think so. Regarding prosperity of children's parents, only 1.1 per cent from Chintapalli mandal and 1.1 per cent Paderu mandal, think so. The obtained chi-square value is 15.27, which is significant at 0.01 level more than the Table value (13.3).

Sl. No.	*Item*	*Srikakulam*											
		Palakonda				*Polaki*				*Seethampeta*			
		Yes	*%*	*No*	*%*	*Yes*	*%*	*No*	*%*	*Yes*	*%*	*No*	*%*
43	In future, Government school will be for very poor people. As per this are you feeling that the Government schools are becoming nominal tokens of educating children?	87	96.7	3	3.3	88	97.8	2	2.2	82	91.1	8	8.9

Sl. No.	*Item*	*Vizianagaram*											
		GLP				*Kurupam*				*Pachipenta*			
		Yes	*%*	*No*	*%*	*Yes*	*%*	*No*	*%*	*Yes*	*%*	*No*	*%*
43	In future, Government school will be for very poor people. As per this are you feeling that the Government schools are becoming nominal tokens of educating children?	74	82.2	16	17.8	27	96.4	1	3.6	88	97.8	2	2.2

Sl. No.	Item	Visakhapatnam											
		Chintapalli				Madugula				Paderu			
		Yes	%	No	%	Yes	%	No	%	Yes	%	No	%
43	In future, Government school will be for very poor people. As per this are you feeling that the Government schools are becoming nominal tokens of educating children?	86	95.6	4	4.4	90	100.0			74	82.2	16	17.8

In future, Government school will be for very poor people. As per this are you feeling that the Government schools are becoming nominal tokens of educating children?

Srikakulam

The Table explains about the responses of the sample respondents of Palakonda mandal of Srikakulam district, as to future Government schools will be for very poor people and are becoming nominal tokens of educating their children. Out of the total sample, majority group of 96.7 per cent from Palakonda have responded and remaining few (3.3 per cent) have not responded. From the total sample of Polaki mandal, a majority group of 97.8 per cent has responded that Government schools will be for very poor people and are becoming nominal tokens of educating children and the remaining 2.2 per cent have not responded. And from the total sample from Seethampeta mandal, a significant group of 91.1 per cent has responded that In future, Government schools will be for very poor people, and are becoming nominal tokens of educating children and the remaining 8.9 per cent has responded so.

Vizianagaram

The Table explains the responses of the sample respondents of GLP mandal of Vizianagaram district, that, in future Government schools will be for very poor people, and are becoming nominal tokens of educating children. Out of the total sample, majority group of 82.2 per cent has responded, while the remaining few (17.8 per cent) have not responded so. From the total sample of Kurupam mandal, majority group of 96.4 per cent has responded that in future, Government schools will be for very poor people and as such, are becoming nominal tokens of educating children, while the remaining 3.6 per cent have not responded in that way. And from the total sample from Pachipenta mandal, a significant number (97.8 per cent) has responded that, in future, Government schools will be for very poor people, and as such, becoming are nominal tokens of educating children, while the remaining 2.2 per cent have not responded in that manner.

Visakhapatnam

The Table explains the responses of the sample respondents of Chintapalli mandal of Visakhapatnam district that, in future, Government schools will be for very poor people, and are becoming nominal tokens of educating children. Out of the total sample, majority group of 95.6 per cent has responded so and the remaining few (4.4 per cent) have not responded. From the total sample of Madugula mandal, cent per cent responded that, in future, Government schools will be for very poor people and are becoming nominal tokens of educating children. And from the total sample from Paderu mandal, a significant group of 82.2 per cent has responded that, in future, Government schools will be for very poor people and are becoming nominal tokens of educating children and the remaining 17.8 per cent has not responded in that manner.

Sl. No.	*Item*	*Srikakulam*											
		Palakonda				*Polaki*				*Seethampeta*			
		Yes	*%*	*No*	*%*	*Yes*	*%*	*No*	*%*	*Yes*	*%*	*No*	*%*
44	With the recent D.S.C 52 thousand teachers are to be recruited and the school assistants, becoming head masters from S.G.T to school assistants. Are you thinking that the Government schools will be providing better quality of education in the future?	81	90.0	8	8.9	12	13.3	78	86.7	71	78.9	19	21.1

Sl. No.	*Item*	*Vizianagaram*											
		GLP				*Kurupam*				*Pachipenta*			
		Yes	*%*	*No*	*%*	*Yes*	*%*	*No*	*%*	*Yes*	*%*	*No*	*%*
44	With the recent D.S.C 52 thousand teachers are to be recruited and the school assistants, becoming head masters from S.G.T to school assistants. Are you thinking that the Government schools will be providing better quality of education in the future?	85	94.4	5	5.6	90	100.0			86	95.6	4	4.4

Sl. No.	Item	Visakhapatnam											
		Chintapalli				Madugula				Paderu			
		Yes	%	No	%	Yes	%	No	%	Yes	%	No	%
44	With the recent D.S.C 52 thousand teachers are to be recruited and the school assistants, becoming head masters from S.G.T to school assistants. Are you thinking that the Government schools will be providing better quality of education in the future?	86	95.6	4	4.4	83	92.2	7	7.8	81	90.0	9	10.0

With the recent D.S.C 52 thousand teachers are going recruited and the school assistants, becoming head masters from S.G.T to school assistants. Are you thinking that the Government schools will be providing better quality of education in the future?

Srikakulam

The Table explains the responses of the sample respondents of Palakonda mandal of Srikakulam district on the recent D.S.C 52 that thousand teachers are getting to be recruited and the school assistants become head masters from S.G.T to school assistants. Do you think that the Government schools will be providing better quality of education in the future towards children's education. Out of the total sample, majority group of 90.0 per cent has responded and remaining few (8.9 per cent) have not responded. From the total sample of Polaki mandal, majority group of 86.7 per cent has not responded that with the recent D.S.C 52 thousand teachers are getting to be recruited and the school assistants become head-masters from S.G.T to school assistants and that the Government schools will be providing better quality of education in future while the remaining (13.3 per cent) have responded. And from the total sample from Seethampeta mandal, a significant group (78.9 per cent) responded that with the recent D.S.C 52 thousand teachers are going to be recruited and the school assistants become head-masters from S.G.T become school-assistants, which make Government schools providing better quality of education in future while the remaining (21.1 per cent) have not responded.

Vizianagaram

The Table explains the responses of the sample respondents of GLP mandal of Vizianagaram district with the recent D.S.C, 52 thousand teachers are getting recruited and the school-assistants become head-masters from S.G.T to school assistants and the Government schools will be providing better quality of education in future. Out of the total sample, majority group of 94.4 per cent have responded with the remaining few (5.6 per cent) not responding. From the total sample of Kurupam mandal, cent per cent said 'yes', that with the recent D.S.C, 52 thousand teachers are getting to be recruited and the school-assistants become head-masters from S.G.T to school assistants and the Government schools will be providing better quality of education in the future. And from the total sample from Pachipenta mandal, a significant group of 95.6 per cent responded that with the recent D.S.C, 52 thousand teachers are getting to be recruited and the school-assistants as head-masters from S.G.T to school assistants and that the Government schools will be providing better quality of education in the future with the remaining 4.4 per cent has not responded.

Visakhapatnam

The Table explains the responses of the sample respondents of Chintapalli mandal of Visakhapatnam district on the recent D.S.C, 52 thousand teachers are getting recruited and the school-assistants, become head-masters from S.G.T to school assistants and the Government schools will be providing better quality of children's education in future. Out of the total sample, majority group of 95.6 per cent has responded and the remaining few (4.4 per cent) have not responded. From the total sample of Madugula mandal, majority group of (92.2 per cent) has responded that with the recent D.S.C, 52 thousand teachers are getting recruited and the school-assistants become head-masters from S.G.T to school assistants and the Government schools will be providing better quality of education in future, while the remaining (7.8 per cent) have not responded. And from the total sample from Paderu mandal, a significant group of 90.0 per cent has responded that with the recent D.S.C 52 thousand teachers are getting recruited and the school-assistants become head-masters from S.G.T to school assistants and the Government schools will be providing better quality of education in future and the remaining (10.0 per cent) have said 'no'.

Sl. No.	*Item*	*Srikakulam*											
		Palakonda				*Polaki*				*Seethampeta*			
		Yes	*%*	*No*	*%*	*Yes*	*%*	*No*	*%*	*Yes*	*%*	*No*	*%*
45	What do you think that in case the primary schools will appoint women teachers completely?	13	14.4	76	84.4	4	4.4	86	95.6	46	51.1	44	48.9

Sl. No.	*Item*	*Vizianagaram*											
		GLP				*Kurupam*				*Pachipenta*			
		Yes	*%*	*No*	*%*	*Yes*	*%*	*No*	*%*	*Yes*	*%*	*No*	*%*
45	What do you think that in case the primary schools will appoint women teachers completely?	50	55.6	40	44.4	27	96.4	1	3.6	15	16.7	75	83.3

Sl. No.	*Item*	*Visakhapatnam*											
		Chintapalli				*Madugula*				*Paderu*			
		Yes	*%*	*No*	*%*	*Yes*	*%*	*No*	*%*	*Yes*	*%*	*No*	*%*
45	What do you think that in case the primary schools will appoint women teachers completely?	15	16.7	75	83.3	21	23.3	69	76.7	18	20.0	72	80.0

What do you think that in case the primary schools will appoint women teachers completely?

Srikakulam

The Table explains the responses of the sample respondents of Palakonda mandal of Srikakulam district whether the primary schools will appoint women teachers completely to children's education. Out of the total sample, majority group of 84.4 per cent have not responded and remaining few (14.4 per cent) only responded. From the total sample of Polaki mandal, majority group of 95.6 per cent have not responded favourably that in case the primary schools will appoint women teachers completing their children's education with the remaining (4.4 per cent) responding favourably. And from the total sample from Seethampeta mandal, a significant group (51.1 per cent) has responded favourably that in case the primary schools will appoint women teachers completely for their children's education with the remaining (48.9 per cent) said 'no'.

Vizianagaram

The Table analyses the responses of the sample respondents of GLP mandal of Vizianagaram District, to know about as to the primary schools appoint only women teachers completely as regards their children's education. Out of the total sample, majority group of 55.6 per cent responded favourably and remaining (44.4 per cent) have not responded favourably. From the total sample of Kurupam mandal, majority group of 96.4 per cent responded that primary schools run by woman teachers completely held their children's education, with the remaining (3.6 per cent) has not responded favourably. And from the total sample from Pachipenta mandal, a significant group of 83.3 per cent has not favourably responded that they think it as good. In case the primary schools will appoint only woman teachers in their children's education with and the remaining (16.7 per cent) favourably responded.

Visakhapatnam

The Table explains the responses of the sample respondents of Chintapalli mandal of Visakhapatnam district, that in case the primary schools will appoint women teachers completely what happens to their children's education. Out of the total sample majority group of 83.3 per cent did not respond favourably, with the remaining few (16.7 per cent) did not respond favourably. From the total sample of Madugula mandal, majority group (76.7 per cent) has not responded favourably that in case the primary schools will appoint women teachers completely, with the remaining (23.3 per cent) responding favourably. And from the total sample from Paderu mandal, a significant group of 80.0 per cent has not responded favourably that in case the primary schools will appoint women teachers completely in change of the children's education, with the remaining (20.0 per cent) responding with 'yes'.

Sl. No.	Item	Srikakulam											
		Palakonda				Polaki				Seethampeta			
		Yes	%	No	%	Yes	%	No	%	Yes	%	No	%
	1	2	3	4	5	6	7	8	9	10	11	12	13
46	Are you supporting that the school children can be promoted on the basis of their age?	10	11.1	80	88.9	1	1.1	89	98.9	74	82.2	16	17.8
47	Are you supporting abolishing public examination in 7th standard exams and giving them the natural promotion?	37	41.1	53	58.9	3	3.3	87	96.7	72	80.0	18	20.0
48	Is the success school getting access to be approved by Government.	18	20.0	72	80	1	1.1	89	98.9	49	54.4	41	45.6
49	Are you thinking that English medium schools are more useful to your children in future?	48	53.3	42	46.7	17	18.9	73	81.1	82	91.1	8	8.9

Contd...

	1	*2*	*3*	*4*	*5*	*6*	*7*	*8*	*9*	*10*	*11*	*12*	*13*
50	Are you thinking that success schools are going to reflect future progress of English medium schools?	46	51.1	44	48.9	84	93.3	6	6.7	79	87.8	11	12.2

Sl. No.	*Item*	*Vizianagaram*											
		GLP				*Kurupam*				*Pachipenta*			
		Yes	*%*	*No*	*%*	*Yes*	*%*	*No*	*%*	*Yes*	*%*	*No*	*%*
46	Are you supporting the view the school children can be promoted on the basis of their age?	76	84.4	14	15.6	1	3.6	27	96.4	37	41.1	53	58.9
47	Are you supporting abolishing of public examination in 7th standard exams and giving natural promotion?	75	83.3	15	16.7	5	17.9	23	82.1	4	4.4	86	95.6
48	Is the success school getting access with approval by Government.	43	47.8	47	52.2	7	25.0	21	75.0	4	4.4	86	95.6
49	Are you thinking that English medium schools are more useful to your children in future?	51	56.7	39	43.3	18	64.3	10	35.7	65	72.2	25	27.8

Contd...

1		*2*	*3*	*4*	*5*	*6*	*7*	*8*	*9*	*10*	*11*	*12*	*13*
50	Are you thinking that success schools are going to reflect the future progress of English medium schools?	78	86.7	12	13.3	28	100.0			71	78.9	19	21.1

Sl. No.	*Item*	*Visakhapatnam*											
		Chintapalli				*Madugula*				*Paderu*			
		Yes	*%*	*No*	*%*	*Yes*	*%*	*No*	*%*	*Yes*	*%*	*No*	*%*
46	Are you supporting that school children can be promoted on the basis of their age?	78	86.7	12	13.3	7	7.8	83	92.2	43	47.8	47	52.2
47	Are you supporting abolishing of public examination in 7th standard and giving them natural promotion?	78	86.7	12	13.3	10	11.1	80	88.9	43	47.8	47	52.2
48	Is the success school to be getting access be approved by Government.	7	7.8	83	92.2	13	14.4	77	85.6	9	10.0	80	88.9
49	Are you thinking that English medium schools are more useful to children future?	85	94.4	5	5.6	87	96.7	3	3.3	24	26.7	66	73.3

Contd...

1		2	3	4	5	6	7	8	9	10	11	12	13
50	Are you thinking that success schools are going to reflect future progress of English medium schools?	87	96.7	3	3.3	88	97.8	2	2.2	77	85.6	13	14.4

Srikakulam

The Table analyses the responses of the sample respondents of Palakonda mandal of Srikakulam district on supporting that school children getting promoted on the basis of their age. Out of the total sample majority group of 88.9 per cent has not responded favourably with the remaining (11.1 per cent) responding favourably. From the total sample of Polaki mandal, majority group of (98.9 per cent) has not responded supporting the school children to promoted on the basis of their age and the remaining (1.1 per cent) said 'no'. And from the total sample from Seethampeta mandal, a significant group (82.2 per cent) has responded that they are supporting the school children being promoted on the basis of their age, with the remaining (17.8 per cent) saying 'no'.

From the responses of the sample respondents of Palakonda mandal of Srikakulam district on supporting the abolishing of public examination in 7th standard exams and giving natural promoting process in their children's education. Out of the total sample, majority group of 58.9 per cent have not responded favourably, with their remaining (41.1 per cent) responding favourably. From the total sample of Polaki mandal, majority of (96.7 per cent) have not responded supporting of the abolishing of public examination in 7th standard exams and giving the natural process of promoting their children's education, with the remaining (1.1 per cent) not responding favourably. And from the total sample from Seethampeta mandal, a significant group of 80.0 per cent has responded that they are supporting abolishing of public examination in 7th standard exams and giving natural promotion in their children's education, with the remaining (20.0 per cent) not responding favourably.

Regarding responses of the sample respondents of Palakonda mandal of Srikakulam district on the success school in getting access should be approved by Government in their children's education. Out of the total sample majority group of 80.0 per cent have not responded favourably and remaining (20.0 per cent) responding favourably. From the total sample of Polaki mandal, majority group of 98.9 per cent has not responded on the success school getting access should be approved by Government in their children's education, with the remaining (1.1 per cent) has not responded favourably. And from the total sample from Seethampeta mandal, a significant group of 54.4 per cent has responded on the success school getting access to them should be approved by Government in their children's education and the remaining (45.6 per cent) said 'no'.

From the responses of the sample respondents of Palakonda mandal of Srikakulam district on English medium schools being more useful to their children in future. Out of the total sample majority group of 53.3 per cent has responded favourably, with remaining (46.7 per cent) not responding favourably. From the total sample of Polaki mandal, majority group of 81.1 per cent has not responded favourably that English medium schools are more useful to their children in their children's education, with the remaining (18.9 per cent) having responded favourably. And from the total sample from Seethampeta mandal, a significant group of 91.1 per cent has responded that English medium schools are more useful to their children in future, with remaining (8.9 per cent) were not responding favourably.

From the responses of the sample respondents of Palakonda mandal of Srikakulam district on success schools to reflect the future progress of English medium schools in their children's education, majority group of 51.1 per cent has responded favourably, with the remaining (48.9 per cent) not responding favourably. From the total sample of Polaki mandal, majority group of 93.3 per cent has responded as to success schools going to reflect future progress of English medium schools in their children's education, with the remaining (6.7 per cent) not responding favourably. And from the total sample from Seethampeta mandal, a significant group of 87.8 per cent has responded that success schools are going to reflect the future progress of English medium schools, with the remaining (12.2 per cent) were not responding favourably.

Vizianagaram

The Table analyses the responses of the sample respondents of GLP mandal of Vizianagaram district, in supporting the view that school children can be promoted on the basis of their age. Out of the total sample, majority group of 84.4 per cent has responded, with the remaining 15.6 per cent not responding favourably. From the total sample of Kurupam mandal majority group of 96.4 per cent has not responded in supporting the view that school children can be promoted on the basis of their age, with the remaining (3.6 per cent) responding favourably. And from the total sample from Pachipenta mandal, a significant group (58.9 per cent) has not responded as to supporting the view that the school children can be promoted on the basis of their age, with the remaining (41.1 per cent) responding favourably.

From the responses of the sample respondents of GLP mandal of Vizianagaram district in supporting the view point in abolishing public examination in 7th standard and giving them natural promotion, out of the total sample, majority group of 83.3 per cent has responded favourably, with the remaining (16.7 per cent) not responding favourably. From the total sample of Kurupam mandal, a majority group of more than eighty per cent (82.1 per cent) have not responded in supporting abolishing public examination in 7th standard and giving natural promotion to their children, with the remaining (17.9 per cent) responding favourably. And from the total sample from Pachipenta mandal, a significant group of 95.6 per cent has not responded that they are supporting abolishing of public examination in 7th standard and in giving natural promotion to their children, with the remaining (4.4 per cent) has responded favourably.

Regarding the response of the sample respondents of GLP mandal of Vizianagaram district, on the success schools is getting access as approved by Government in their children's education. Out of the total sample, majority group of 52.2 per cent have not responded favourably and remaining (47.8 per cent) responding favourably. From the total sample of Kurupam mandal, majority group of more than seventy per cent (75.0 per cent) have not responded to the success school getting access as approved by Government in children's education and the remaining (25.0 per cent) have responded favourably. And from the total sample from Pachipenta mandal, a significant group of 95.6 per cent has not responded to the success school is getting access as approved by Government in their children's education and the remaining (4.4 per cent) has responded favourably.

As per the responses of the sample respondents of GLP mandal of Vizianagaram district, on English medium schools being more useful to their children in future, a majority group of 56.7 per cent has responded favourably and the remaining of 43.3 per cent not responding favourably. From the total sample of Kurupam mandal, a majority group of more than sixty per cent (64.3 per cent) has responded as to English medium schools being more useful to their children in future and the remaining (35.7 per cent) has not responded favourably. And from the total sample from Pachipenta mandal, a significant group (72.2 per cent) responded in thinking that English medium schools are more useful to their children in future and the remaining (27.8 per cent) said 'no'.

From the responses of the sample respondents of GLP mandal of Vizianagaram district, it is seen that success schools are going to reflect future progress of English medium schools in their children's education, a majority group of 86.7 per cent has responded favourably and the remaining (13.3 per cent) have not responded favourably. From the total sample of Kurupam mandal, (100.0 per cent) have responded in thinking that success schools are going to reflect future progress of English medium schools in their children's education. And from the total sample from Pachipenta mandal, it is seen that a significant group (78.9 per cent) have responded in thinking that success schools are going to reflect future progress of English medium schools in their children's education, with the remaining (21.1 per cent) not responding favourably.

Visakhapatnam

The Table analyses the responses of the sample respondents of Chintapalli mandal of Visakhapatnam district on supporting the school children being promoted on the basis of their age. Out of the total sample, majority group of 86.7 per cent has responded favourably and remaining (13.3 per cent) did not respond favourably. From the total sample of Madugula mandal, majority group of 92.2 per cent have not responded in supporting the promotion on the basis of their age and the remaining (7.8 per cent) have responded with 'no'. And from the total sample from Paderu mandal, a significant group of 52.2 per cent has not responded in supporting school children promoting on the basis of their age, with the remaining (47.8 per cent) did not respond.

From the responses of the sample respondents of Chintapalli mandal of Visakhapatnam district, it can be seen that supporting abolishing of public examination in 7th standard exams giving natural promotion. Out of the total sample, majority group of 86.7 per cent has responded favourably, with the remaining (13.3 per cent) not responding favourably. From the total sample of Madugula mandal, majority group (88.9 per cent) has not responded favourably in supporting abolishing of Public Examination of 7th standard while giving natural promotion to their children, with the remaining (11.1 per cent) responding favourably. And from the total sample from Paderu mandal, a significant group (52.2 per cent) have not responded in supporting of abolishing Public Examination in 7th standard, giving natural promotion to their children with remaining (47.8 per cent) responding favourably.

Regarding responses of the sample respondents of Chintapalli mandal of Visakhapatnam district, on the success school getting access as approved by Government for their children's education. Out of the total sample majority group (92.2 per cent) have not responded favourably, with the remaining (7.8 per cent) responding favourably. From the total sample of Madugula mandal, majority of more than fifty per cent (85.6 per cent) have not responded favourably to the success school getting access to them as approved by Government and the remaining (14.4 per cent) responding positively. And from the total sample from Paderu mandal, a significant group of 88.9 per cent have not responded to the success school in getting access to them as approved by

Government, with the remaining (10.0 per cent) responding favourably.

This indicates the responses of the sample respondents of Chintapalli mandal of Visakhapatnam district on the English medium schools being more useful to their children. Out of the total sample, majority group of 94.4 per cent have not responded favourably and to remaining 5.6 per cent responded favourably. From the total sample of Madugula mandal, majority group of 96.7 per cent has responded by thinking that English medium schools are more useful in their children's education with and the remaining (3.3 per cent) not responding favourably. And the total sample from Paderu mandal, a significant group of 73.3 per cent have not responded to think that English medium schools are more useful to their children's future education and the remaining (26.7 per cent) have responded favourably.

Regarding the responses of the sample respondents of Chintapalli mandal of Visakhapatnam district on success schools going to reflect future progress of English medium schools for their children's education, majority group of 96.7 per cent responded favourably, with the remaining (3.3 per cent) not responding favourably. From the total sample of Madugula mandal, a majority group of 97.8 per cent responded by thinking that success schools are going to reflect future progress of English medium schools in their children's education, with the remaining (2.2 per cent) not responding favourably. And from the total sample from Paderu mandal, a significant group (85.6 per cent) responded by thinking that success schools are going to reflect the future progress of English medium schools in their children's education, with the remaining (14.4 per cent) not responding favourably.

Sl. No.	*Item*	*Srikakulam*											
		Palakonda				*Polaki*				*Seethampeta*			
		Yes	*%*	*No*	*%*	*Yes*	*%*	*No*	*%*	*Yes*	*%*	*No*	*%*
51	Are Anganwadi/ Balwadi Centres/ and Pre play schools available in your village?	40	44.4	50	55.5	86	95.6	3	3.3	78	86.7	12	13.3
52	Are the Anganwadi Centers and pre-play schools available in different places of your village?	80	88.9	10	11.1	88	97.8	2	2.2	63	70.0	27	30.0

Sl. No.	*Item*	*Vizianagaram*											
		GLP				*Kurupam*				*Pachipenta*			
		Yes	*%*	*No*	*%*	*Yes*	*%*	*No*	*%*	*Yes*	*%*	*No*	*%*
51	Are Anganwadis/ Balwadi Centers/ and Pre play schools available in your village?	76	84.4	14	15.6	26	92.9	2	7.1	68	75.6	22	24.4
52	Are Anganwadi Centers and Pre-play schools available in different places of your village?	77	85.6	13	14.4	26	92.9	2	7.1	68	75.6	22	24.4

Sl. No.	Item	Visakhapatnam											
		Chintapalli				Madugula				Paderu			
		Yes	%	No	%	Yes	%	No	%	Yes	%	No	%
51	Are Anganwadi/ Balwadi Centers/ and Pre play schools available in your village?	80	88.9	10	11.1	83	92.2	7	7.8	77	86.5	12	13.5
52	Are Anganwadi Centers and pre-play schools available in different places in your village?	26	28.9	64	71.1	77	85.6	13	14.4	70	78.7	19	21.3

Srikakulam

The Table explains the responses of the sample respondents of Palakonda mandal of Srikakulam district, whether Anganwadis / Balwadi Centers / and Pre play schools are available in their village for their children's education, with the total sample majority group of 55.5 per cent not responding favourably and the remaining (44.4 per cent) responding favourably. From the total sample of Polaki mandal, majority group of 95.6 per cent has responded that Anganwadis / Balwadi Centers / and Pre play schools are available in their village for their children's education and the remaining (3.3 per cent) have not responded about their existence. And from the total sample from Seethampeta mandal, a significant group of 86.7 per cent has responded that Anganwadis / Balwadi Centers and Pre play schools available in their village for their children's education and the remaining (13.3 per cent) has not responded favourably.

From the responses of the sample respondents of Palakonda mandal of Srikakulam district, on the availability of Anganwadi Centers and pre-play school in different places in their village, 88.9 per cent had responded favourably and the remaining 11.1 per cent have not responded favourably. From the total sample of Polaki mandal, majority group of 97.8 per cent has responded that Anganwadi Centers and pre-play schools are available in different places in their village for their children's education and the remaining 2.2 per cent have not responded favourably. And from the total sample of Seethampeta mandal, a significant group of 70.0 per cent have responded that Anganwadi Centers and pre-play schools are available in different places of their village for their children's education and the remaining (30.0 per cent) said 'no'.

Vizianagaram

The Table explains the responses of the sample respondents of GLP mandal of Vizianagaram district, on the availability of Anganwadis / Balwadi Centers / and Pre-play schools in their village, a majority group of 84.4 per cent has responded favourably and the remaining (15.6 per cent) not responding favourably. From the total sample of Kurupam mandal, majority group of 92.9 per cent has responded that Anganwadis / Balwadi Centers / and Pre-play schools are available in their village for their children's education and the remaining (7.1 per cent) has not responded favourably. And from the total sample from Pachipenta mandal, a significant group of 75.6 per cent has responded that Anganwadis / Balwadi Centers and Pre-play schools are available in their village for their children's education and the remaining (24.4 per cent) have not responded favourably.

From the responses of the sample respondents of GLP mandal of Vizianagaram district, on the availability of Anganwadi Centers and Pre-play schools in different places of their village for children's education, a majority group of 85.6 per cent has responded and the remaining (14.4 per cent) not responding favourably. From the total sample of

Kurupam mandal, majority group of 92.9 per cent have responded that Anganwadi Centers and Pre-play schools are available in different places of their village and the remaining (7.1 per cent) have not responded favourably. And from the total sample from Pachipenta mandal, a significant group of 75.6 per cent have responded that Anganwadi Centers and Pre-play schools are available in different places of their village for their children's education and the remaining (24.4 per cent) said 'no'.

Visakhapatnam

The Table explains the responses of the sample respondents of Chintapalli mandal of Visakhapatnam district, whether Anganwadis / Balwadi Centers / and Pre-play schools are available in their village for their children education, majority group of 88.9 per cent have responded favourably and remaining 11.1 per cent have not responded favourably. From the total sample of Madugula mandal, a majority group of 92.2 per cent have responded that Anganwadis / Balwadi Centers / and Pre-play schools are available in their village for their children's education, with the remaining (7.8 per cent) not responding favourably. And from the total sample from Paderu mandal, a significant group (86.5 per cent) have responded that Anganwadis / Balwadi Centers and Pre play schools are available in their village for their children's education and the remaining (13.5 per cent) have not responded favourably.

From the response of the sample respondents of Chintapalli mandal of Visakhapatnam district, on the availability of Anganwadi Centers and pre-play schools in different places of their village for their children's education, a majority group of 71.1 per cent have not responded favourably and remaining 28.9 per cent have responded favourably. From the total sample of Madugula mandal, a majority group (85.6 per cent) have responded that Anganwadi Centers and Pre-play schools are available in different places of their village and the remaining (14.4 per cent) have not responded favourably. And from the total sample from Paderu mandal, a significant group of 78.7 per cent have responded that Anganwadi Centers and Pre-play schools are available in different places of their village for their children's education and the remaining (21.3 per cent) said 'no'.

Sl. No.	*Item*	*Srikakulam*											
		Palakonda				*Polaki*				*Seethampeta*			
		Yes	*%*	*No*	*%*	*Yes*	*%*	*No*	*%*	*Yes*	*%*	*No*	*%*
	1	*2*	*3*	*4*	*5*	*6*	*7*	*8*	*9*	*10*	*11*	*12*	*13*
53	Are you thinking that mid - day meals for your children in the schools will be more useful for your children?	76	84.4	14	15.5	70	77.8	20	22.2	80	88.9	10	11.1
54	Are you children satisfied over the provision of mid – day meals in the school?	73	81.1	17	18.9	28	31.1	62	68.9	77	85.6	13	14.4

Sl. No.	*Item*	*Vizianagaram*											
		GLP				*Kurupam*				*Pachipenta*			
		Yes	*%*	*No*	*%*	*Yes*	*%*	*No*	*%*	*Yes*	*%*	*No*	*%*
53	Are you thinking that mid-day meals for your children in the school will be more useful for children?	77	85.6	13	14.4	27	96.4	1	3.6	85	94.4	5	5.6

Contd...

1		2	3	4	5	6	7	8	9	10	11	12	13
54	Are your children satisfied for the provision of mid-day meals in the school?	55	61.1	35	38.9	27	96.4	1	3.6	57	63.3	33	36.7

Sl. No.	*Item*	*Visakhapatnam*											
		Chintapalli				*Madugula*				*Paderu*			
		Yes	*%*	*No*	*%*	*Yes*	*%*	*No*	*%*	*Yes*	*%*	*No*	*%*
53	Are you thinking that mid – day meals for your children in the schools will be more useful for children?	82	91.1	8	8.9	79	87.8	11	12.2	67	75.3	22	24.7
54	Are your children satisfied with the provision of mid-day meals in the school?	68	75.6	22	22.4	37	41.1	52	57.8	59	66.3	30	33.7

Srikakulam

The Table explains the responses of the sample respondents of Palakonda mandal of Srikakulam district on the availability of mid-day meals for their children in the schools as it will be more useful for their children's education, a majority group of 84.4 per cent have responded favourably and the remaining (15.5 per cent) have not responded favourably. From the total sample of Polaki mandal, a majority group of more than seventy per cent (77.8 per cent) has responded favourably that mid-day meals for their children in the schools will be more useful for children's education and the remaining (22.2 per cent) have not responded favourably. And from the total sample from Seethampeta mandal, a significant group of 88.9 per cent have responded that mid-day meals for their children in the schools will be more useful in their children's education and the remaining (11.1 per cent) have not responded favourably.

Regarding responses of the sample respondents of Palakonda mandal of Srikakulam district, whether children were satisfied for the provision of mid- day meals in the school, a majority group of 81.1 per cent have responded favourably and the remaining (18.9 per cent) have not responded favourably. From the total sample of Polaki mandal, majority group of more than sixty per cent (68.9 per cent) have not responded that their children were satisfied on the provision of mid-day meals in the school, with the remaining (31.1 per cent) responding favourably. And from the total sample from Seethampeta mandal, a significant group of 85.6 per cent have responded that their children were satisfied on the provision of mid-day meals in the school and the remaining (14.4 per cent) said 'no'.

Vizianagaram

The Table explains the responses of the sample respondents of GLP mandal of Vizianagaram district, whether mid-day meals for their children in the schools will be more useful. Majority group of 85.6 per cent have responded favourably and remaining (14.4 per cent) has not responded favourably. From the total sample of Kurupam mandal, majority group of 96.4 per cent have responded that mid-day meals for their children in the schools will be more useful for children's education and the remaining (3.6 per cent) have not responded favourably. And as per total sample from

Pachipenta mandal, a significant group of 94.4 per cent responded that they think of mid-day meals for their children in the schools will be more useful for their education and the remaining (5.6 per cent) have not responded favourably.

From the responses of the sample respondents of GLP mandal of Vizianagaram district, it is seen that children are satisfied for the provision of mid- day meals in the school, with majority group of 61.1 per cent responding favourably remaining (38.9 per cent) have not responded favourably. From the total sample of Kurupam mandal, majority group of 96.4 per cent have responded that the children were satisfied for the provision of mid-day meals in the school for their children and the remaining (3.6 per cent) responding favourably. And from the total sample from Pachipenta mandal, a significant group of 63.3 per cent have responded that children were satisfied for the provision of mid-day meals in the school and the remaining (36.7 per cent) said 'no'.

Visakhapatnam

The Table explains the responses of the sample respondents of Chintapalli mandal of Visakhapatnam district whether they think that mid-day meals for their children in the schools will be more useful for their children's education, majority group of 91.1 per cent has responded and the remaining 8.9 per cent has not responded favourably. From the total sample of Madugula mandal, majority group of more than eighty per cent (87.8 per cent) have responded that mid-day meals for their children in the school will be more useful for their children's education and the remaining (12.2 per cent) have not responded favourably. And from the total sample from Paderu mandal, a significant group of 75.3 per cent have responded that they think about mid-day meals for their children in the schools will be more useful in children's education and the remaining (24.7 per cent) have not responded favourably.

From the responses of the sample respondents of Chintapalli mandal of Visakhapatnam district on children getting satisfied for the provision of mid- day meals in the school, majority group of 75.6 per cent have responded favourably and the remaining (22.4 per cent) not responding favourably. From the total sample of Madugula mandal, majority group of more than fifty per cent (57.8 per cent) have not responded that the children were satisfied for the provision of mid-day meals in the school and the remaining (41.1 per cent) have responded favourably. And from the total sample from Paderu mandal, a significant group of 66.3 per cent have responded that their children were satisfied for the provision of mid-day meals in the school for their children's education and the remaining (33.7 per cent) said 'no'.

In case you are not happy what are the reason?

Sl. No.		*Srikakulam*		
		Palakonda	*Polaki*	*Seethampeta*
1	Prevalence of corruption	80 (89.9)	76 (84.4)	60 (66.7)
2	Government providing money is not sufficient.	9 (10.1)	10 (11.1)	24 (26.7)
3	Teachers are not showing proper interest		3 (3.3)	2 (2.2)
4	Mahila group members are not cooking properly		1 (1.1)	2 (2.2)
5	Lack of supervision			2 (2.2)
	Chi-square value		**21.69****	

S. No.		*Vizianagaram*		
		GLP	*Kurupam*	*Pachipenta*
1	As they are corrupt	33 (36.7)	17 (60.7)	75 (83.3)
2	Government is providing money is not sufficient.	17 (18.9)	6 (21.4)	2 (2.2)
3	Teachers are not showing proper interest	16 (17.8)	5 (17.9)	2 (2.2)
4	Mahila group members not cooking food properly	19 (21.1)		9 (10.0)
5	Lack of supervision	5 (5.6)		2 (2.2)
	Chi-square value		**51.35****	

Sl. No.		*Visakhapatnam*		
		Chintapalli	*Madugula*	*Paderu*
1	As they are corrupt	50 (55.6)	64 (71.1)	49 (55.1)
2	Government is providing money is not sufficient.	16 (17.8)	12 (13.3)	27 (30.3)
3	Teachers not showing proper interest	2 (2.2)	9 (10.0)	3 (3.4)
4	Mahila group members not cooking food properly	6 (6.7)		2 (2.2)
5	Lack of supervision	16 (17.8)	5 (5.6)	8 (9.0)
	Chi-square value		**28.95****	

In case you are not happy what are the reason?

Srikakulam

The Table explains the responses of the sample respondents of Srikakulam district, as to their not being happy about their children's education. Out of the reasons, prevalence of corruption is 89.9 per cent in Palakonda mandal with 84.4 per cent in Polaki mandal and 66.7 per cent in Seethampeta mandal. As about Government's providing money being not sufficient, 10.1 per cent are from Palakonda mandal, 11.1 per cent are from Polaki mandal and 26.7 per cent are from Seethampeta mandal. Regarding teachers not showing proper interest, 3.3 per cent are from Polaki mandal and 2.2 per cent are from Seethampeta mandal. Regarding mahila group members, not cooking properly, 1.1 per cent are from Polaki mandal and 2.2 per cent are from Seethampeta mandal. Regarding opinions of lack of supervision, 2.2 per cent are from Seethampeta mandal. The obtained chi-square value of 21.69 is significant at 0.01 level more than the Table value (20.1).

Vizianagaram

The Table explains the responses of the sample respondents of Vizianagaram District, regarding why they are not happy in their children's education. Out of the reasons, due to corruption, 36.7 per cent are from GLP mandal, 60.7 per cent from Kurupam mandal and 83.3 per cent from Pachipenta mandal. On the Government's providing money being not sufficient, 18.9 per cent are from GLP mandal, 21.4 per cent from Kurupam mandal and 2.2 per cent from Pachipenta mandal. Regarding teachers not showing proper interest, 17.8 per cent) are from GLP mandal, 17.9 per cent from Kurupam mandal and 2.2 per cent from Pachipenta mandal. Towards Mahila group members not cooking food properly, 21.1 per cent are from GLP mandal and 10.0 per cent are from Pachipenta mandal. As regards lack of supervision, 5.6 per cent are from GLP mandal and 2.2 per cent from Pachipenta mandal. The obtained chi-square value of 51.35 is significant at 0.01 level more than the Table value (20.1).

Visakhapatnam

The Table analyses the responses of sample respondents of Visakhapatnam District, regarding why they are not happy about their children's education. They opine it is due to corruption, with 55.6 per cent being from Chintapalli mandal, 71.1 per cent from Madugula mandal and 55.1 per cent from Paderu mandal. On the Government providing money is not being sufficient, 17.8 per cent opine from Chintapalli mandal, 13.3 per cent from Madugula mandal and 30.0 per cent from Paderu mandal. Regarding teachers not showing proper interest, 2.2 per cent from Chintapalli mandal, 10.0 per cent from Madugula mandal and 3.4 per cent from Paderu mandal. Regarding Mahila group members not cooking food properly, 6.7 per cent are from Chintapalli mandal and 2.2 per cent are from Paderu mandal. As regards lack of supervision, 17.8 per cent are from Chintapalli mandal, 5.6 per cent are from Madugula mandal and 9.0 per cent from Paderu mandal. The obtained chi-square value of 28.95 is significant at 0.01 level more than the Table value (20.1).

Sl. No.	*Item*	*Srikakulam*											
		Palakonda				*Polaki*				*Seethampeta*			
		Yes	*%*	*No*	*%*	*Yes*	*%*	*No*	*%*	*Yes*	*%*	*No*	*%*
56	Do you feel that the evil of corruption is very much prevalent in the department of education?	72	80.0	18	20.0	89	98.9	1	1.1	79	87.8	11	12.2

Sl. No.	Item	Vizianagaram											
		GLP				Kurupam				Pachipenta			
		Yes	%	No	%	Yes	%	No	%	Yes	%	No	%
56	Do you feel that the evil of corruption is very much prevalent in the department of education?	85	94.4	5	5.6	21	75.0	7	25.0	65	72.2	25	27.8

Sl. No.	Item	Visakhapatnam											
		Chintapalli				Madugula				Paderu			
		Yes	%	No	%	Yes	%	No	%	Yes	%	No	%
56	Do you feel that the evil of corruption is very much prevalent in the department of education?	44	48.9	46	51.1	84	93.3	6	6.7	47	52.8	42	47.2

Do you feel that the evil of corruption is very much prevalent in the department of education?

Srikakulam

The Table analyses the responses of the sample respondents of Palakonda mandal of Srikakulam district on the evil of corruption being very much prevalent in the Department of Education. Out of the total sample, majority of 80.0 per cent have responded that they feel that the evil of corruption is very much there in the Department of Education and the remaining (20.0 per cent) do not feel so. From the total sample of Polaki mandal, majority group of 98.9 per cent responded that they feel that the evil of corruption is very much prevalent in the Department of Education and the remaining (1.1 per cent) do not feel so. And from the total sample from Seethampeta mandal, a significant group of 87.8 per cent responded that they feel about the evil of corruption is very much prevalent in the Department of Education in respect of their children's education, with the remaining (12.2 per cent) not feeling so.

Vizianagaram

The Table explains the responses of the sample respondents of GLP mandal of Vizianagaram district on the evil of corruption being very much prevalent in the Department of Education. Out of the total sample majority group (94.4 per cent) have responded that they feel that the evil of corruption is very prevalent in the Department of Education and the remaining (5.6 per cent) do not feel so. From the total sample of Kurupam mandal, majority group of more than seventy per cent (75.0 per cent) have responded that they feel that the evil of corruption is very much prevalent in the Department of Education and the remaining (25.0 per cent) do not feel so. And from the total sample from Pachipenta mandal, a significant group of 72.2 per cent have responded that they feel that the evil of corruption is very much prevalent in the Department of Education and the remaining (27.8 per cent) do not feel so.

Visakhapatnam

The Table explains the responses of the sample respondents of Chintapalli mandal of Visakhapatnam district on the evil of corruption being very much prevalent in the Department of Education as regards their children's education. Out of the total sample majority group of 51.1 per cent has not responded that they feel that the evil of corruption is very much prevalent in the Department of Education and the remaining (48.9 per cent) do not feel so. From the total sample of Madugula mandal, majority (93.3 per cent) have responded that they feel that the evil of corruption is very much prevalent in the Department of Education and the remaining (6.7 per cent) do not so. From the total sample from Paderu mandal, a significant group (52.8 per cent) have responded that they, feel that the evil of corruption is very much prevalent in the Department of Education and the remaining (47.2 per cent) do not feel so. were not.

Sl. No.	*Item*	*Srikakulam*											
		Palakonda				*Polaki*				*Seethampeta*			
		Yes	*%*	*No*	*%*	*Yes*	*%*	*No*	*%*	*Yes*	*%*	*No*	*%*
57	Do you suggest that salaries and promotions be given on the basis of talent, punctuality, sincerity of the teacher as well as the results of the school?	74	82.2	16	17.8	89	98.9	1	1.1	81	90.0	9	10.0

Sl. No.	*Item*	*Vizianagaram*											
		GLP				*Kurupam*				*Pachipenta*			
		Yes	*%*	*No*	*%*	*Yes*	*%*	*No*	*%*	*Yes*	*%*	*No*	*%*
57	Do you suggest that salaries and promotions be given on the basis of talent, punctuality, sincerity of the teacher as well as the results of the school?	86	95.6	4	4.4	22	78.6	6	21.4	87	96.7	3	3.3

Sl. No.	*Item*	*Visakhapatnam*											
		Chintapalli				*Madugula*				*Paderu*			
		Yes	*%*	*No*	*%*	*Yes*	*%*	*No*	*%*	*Yes*	*%*	*No*	*%*
57	Do you suggest that salaries and promotions be given on the basis of talent, punctuality, sincerity of the teacher as well as the results of the school?	71	78.9	19	21.1	89	98.9	1	1.1	83	93.3	6	6.7

Do you suggest that salaries and promotions be given on the basis of talent, punctuality, sincerity of the teacher as well as the results of the school?

Srikakulam

The Table analyses the responses of the sample respondents of Palakonda mandal of Srikakulam district on the suggestion that salaries and promotions be given on the basis of talent, punctuality, sincerity of teacher as well as results of the school. Out of the total sample, majority group of 82.2 per cent have responded positively and the remaining (17.8 per cent) do not feel so. From the total sample of Polaki mandal, majority group (98.9 per cent) have responded that they suggest that salaries and promotions be given on the basis of talent, punctuality and sincerity of teacher as well as the results of the school and the remaining (1.1 per cent) do not feel so. And from the total sample from Seethampeta mandal, a significant group of 90.0 per cent have responded that they suggest salaries be given on the basis of talent, punctuality, sincerity of teacher as well as the results of the school and the remaining (10.0 per cent) do not feel so.

Vizianagaram

The Table analyses about the responses of the sample respondents of GLP mandal of Vizianagaram district that salaries and promotions be given on the basis of talent, punctuality, sincerity of the teacher as well as result of the school. Out of the total sample, majority group of 95.6 per cent has responded favourably and the remaining (4.4 per cent) has not responded favourably. From the total sample of Kurupam mandal, majority group of 78.6 per cent has responded that they suggest that salaries and promotions be given on the basis of talent, punctuality, sincerity of the teacher as well as results of the school and the remaining (21.4 per cent) has not responded favorably. And from the total sample from Pachipenta mandal, a significant group (96.7 per cent) has responded that salaries be given on the basis of talent, punctuality and sincerity of the teacher as well as results of the school and the remaining (3.3 per cent) has not responded favourably.

Visakhapatnam

The Table analyses the responses of the sample respondents of Chintapalli mandal of Visakhapatnam district, that salaries and promotions be given on the basis of talent, punctuality and sincerity of the teacher as well as the results of the school. Out of the total sample, majority group (78.9 per cent) has responded favourably and the remaining (21.1 per cent) have not responded favourably. From the total sample of Madugula mandal, majority group of 98.9 per cent has responded that salaries and promotions be given on the basis of talent, punctuality and sincerity of the teacher as well as results of the school and the remaining (1.1 per cent) has not responded favourably. And from the total sample from Paderu mandal, a significant group of 93.3 per cent has responded that salaries and promotion be given on the basis of talent, punctuality, sincerity of the teacher as well as the results of the school and the remaining (6.7 per cent) has not responded favourably.

Major Findings of the Study

The researcher made an attempt to know whether children are regular to the school, take education seriously. Are the teachers make a note of their absence to school to contact and alert parents. The children of all the tree districts and nine mandals are regular to school and as and when they are absent the teachers are bringing it to the notice of parents. It is a welcome trend towards right to education act and universalization of primary education.

It was learnt that those who do not send their children to school is either to engage their children in agricultural work or sibling care in the absence of their parents. The chi square test is significant at 0.01 level indicating the relation between independent and dependent variable.

Attempt was made to learn the parental perceptions on their child's academic performance, satisfied the reasons for deficiencies. Respondents from six out of nine mandals expressed happiness over their child's performance. The unhappy parents were from Polaki, Madugula, Kurupam mandals of Srikakulam, Visakhapatnam and Vijayanagaram districts respectively.

The chi square test of association is significant at 0.01 level indicating the association between dependent and independent variables i.e. inability to learn as dependent variable and ill health as independent variable. It was observed that health of children in these villages is found be the major hurdle for their learning. It is necessary that along with education health of these children is also to be taken into consideration. Another most significant factor for dearth in child's education is apathy of teachers.

Respondents' opinion on their children's failure to learn was attributed to lack of training, insufficient pay scales and indiscipline among teachers.

It was evident from the study that the teachers were regular and punctual to school except in one mandal i.e. Polaki of Srikakulam district.

When enquired about the competency and responsiveness of teachers majority opined that the teachers are competent and responsive.

It was learnt that the respondents of Srikakulam and Vizianagaram districts have little interest in attending the parent-teacher meetings where as Visakhapatnam respondents were not at all keen. But all of them said they discuss their children's academic issues as and when they attend the meetings.

It was evident from the study that the respondents/ parents were not very enthusiastic to send their children to school they feel their children are neither helpful in domestic works nor are they learning anything by going to school.

It heartening to know that in spite of governmental sops like mid-day meal, fee waiver and free books they opt work for school for their children due to poverty. It is the vicious circle of poverty which has to be broken to make education program successful.

Majority respondents would go and talk to the teachers whenever their wards failed to achieve academic targets and one set of respondents said they are not convinced with the teacher's explanation on their wards failures.

The respondents strongly feel that the private schools are gaining prominence to government schools. The reasons they expressed for opting private schools are lack of infrastructural facilities and apathy of teachers in

Government schools. The chi square test is significant at 0.01 level indicates the hypotheses that the private schools are gaining prominence to Government schools.

The respondents feel that with the DSC appointments and promotion of SGTs to school assistant the government schools would gain prominence.

It was learnt from the respondents that the success schools started by government were not accessible to them. They would certainly help their children and they be started from primary level onwards for better results.

All the respondents strongly feel that the midday meal scheme would enhance the school attendance and majority of them also said they are content with the food given.

The response pattern on failure of mid-day meal suggests it is corruption which is responsible for the failure of the scheme and chi square test which is significant at 0.0 level also supports the hypotheses.

6

Observations and Suggestions

The researcher would like to make an effort to spell out some of the aspects identified during the study.

Observations made by the Researcher

It is learnt that those who do not send their children to school is either to engage their children in agricultural work or sibiling care in the absence of their parents.

Attempt was made to learn the parental perceptions on their children's educational performance. Respondents from six out of nine mandals expressed satisfaction over their children's performance. The unhappy parents were from Polaki, Madugula, Kurupam mandals of Srikakulam, Visakhapatnam and Vijayanagaram districts respectively.

It was observed that health of children in these villages are found to be the major hurdle for their learning. It is necessary that along with education, health of these children is also to be taken into consideration. Another most significant factor for dearth in child's education is apathy of teachers.

Respondents' opinion on their children's failure to learn was attributed to lack of training, insufficient pay scales and indiscipline and absenteeism among teachers.

It was learnt that the respondents of Srikakulam and Vizianagaram districts have little interest in attending the parent teacher meetings whereas Visakhapatnam (except towns) respondents were not at all keen. But most of them said they will not discuss their children's academic issues with teachers. Further, parents do not know about teacher and parent meetings.

It was evident from the study that the respondents/ parents were not very enthusiastic to send their children to school as they feel their children are neither helpful in domestic works nor learning anything by going to school.

In spite of governmental sops like mid-day meal, fee waiver and free books, stationary and dress, parents are opting to send their children for work. This parental option can be attributed to poverty. So, it is the vicious circle of poverty which has to be broken to make the education programme successful.

Majority respondents would go and talk to the teachers whenever their wards failed to achieve academic targets and one set of respondents said they are not convinced with the teacher's explanation on their wards failures.

The respondents strongly feel that the private schools are gaining prominence to government schools. The reasons they expressed for opting private schools instead of Govenemnt schools which are having lack of infrastructural facilities and apathy of teachers in Government schools. The chi square test is significant at 0.01 level supports the hypotheses that the private schools are gaining prominence to Government schools.

The respondents feel that with the DSC (District Selection Committee) appointments and promotion of SGTs to school assistants, the government schools would gain prominence.

It was learnt from the respondents that the success schools started by government are not accessible to them. They would certainly help their children and they be started from primary level onwards for better results.

All the respondents strongly feel that the mid-day meal scheme would enhance the school attendance and majority of them also said *they are contented with the food given.*

The response pattern on failure of mid-day meal suggests, it is corruption which is responsible for the failure of the scheme and chi square test which is significant at 0.01 level also supports the hypothesis.

It is observed a school in tribal area of Visakhapatnam, has a pucca building with spacious play ground and infrastructure facilities, teaching aids including equipment and also it is located side of the block top road. But neither pupils nor teachers are available during the school hours. Further it is noticed, another school which has also pucca building with well structured doors which were not locked and barely opened. It indicates no individual in the village including vidya committee member(s) or village panchayat do not care or look after whether the school is running regularly or not. During the interview, conducted with villagers regarding the school, the villagers expressed that the concerned teacher(s)/vidya volunteer(s) do not come regularly. Therefore some children dropped out from the school and the other children are admitted into neibouring private school.

In Paderu Mandalam Vonthadavalasa village, Visakhapatnam district the school is locked though it is located in a road side during the school hours. Regarding this the respondents expressed with anguish mood that no one could take care of running of the school.

In Paderu Mandalam it is observed a single lady teacher appeared in school with 9-10 children in a dilapidated school building which is built with wooden poles. The structure of the building may collapse at any moment. In Chintapalli Mandalam one of the schools was permanently occupied by the local sadhus and it is used as residence.

It is over all observation of the researcher of these three districts, instead of the permanent school teachers Vidya Volunteers are appeared in schools who are appointed by the village committee in more cases whereas in other cases the teachers are also appointed as substitutes in their absence. Due to the absence of the qualified permanent teachers, abysmal quality of education is prevailing in such schools.

Further it is observed in almost all the schools of the three districts, teacher's absenteeism is significantly high for various reasons. And most of the schools have poor infrastructure, including no separate toilets for girls, no playground, no compound wall, no supply of safety drinking water, poor maintenance of records.

When interview was held with slum people of Visakhapatnam, all of whom belong to fishermen community and deprived sections of the society expressed their anguish over state and condition of the their school as well as performance of the teachers and quality of teaching. Further they commented upon teachers that due to their poverty the teachers are neglecting their children education with an apathetic attitude, negligency and strong feeling of job security. Further, teachers came to know that we are not in a position to proceed either to court of law we lodge a complaint to the authorities but no concern officers take any action over irregular teachers or question them directly for, our children education due to our poverty as we are on searching for our daily bread.

Most of the housewives are literally worried for imposing ban on alcohol as their spouses are not at all showing any kind of interest towards their children education. Sometimes they ransacked their home and terrorise the entire family members including children; even they never spare old people for demanding money. Therefore there is no room for congenial atmosphere for study of their children.

In Jalaripeta a housewife Mrs. Ramanamma in Visakhapatnam city responded with pathetic voice that recently 3 children between the age group of 12-14 died before Pongal with aids and venereal diseases since they followed elders as role model and they are gradually habituated for consumption of alcohol of which condition tends to lead promiscuous. Further she expressed that instead of staying in school presently they are at arrack shops or searching for girls.

There was an eye witness of another fisherman who said that teachers were sitting together and started gossip on their interested topic during the school hours but they do not take care of children education whether they are studying or not and even they do not observe whether they quarrel or fight among themselves. That is the state of school condition and apathetic attitude of the teachers due to job security.

During the interview a parent who confessed himself his weakness of addiction of alcohol but he has pinned all his hopes on their children education by government schools but he is in desperate mood due to abysmal quality of education. (poor performance of their children education)

Another housewife said that the standard and quality of education of the school that "my child was to be 7th std as per his age but he is in 2nd std who does not even know or identify alphabets (Telugu)" in our own language.

While visiting during the working hours of schools, there has been a large scale absenteeism of teachers, (absenteeism more than 50% in remote rural and tribal areas, it may not appear in urban areas).

It is thoroughly observed that a teacher who belongs to dominant caste in a particular village shows some kind of apathetic attitude and negligency towards his duty, and whereas some of the teachers have affinity with some political party or politicians may also have the same attitude.

While conducting the interviews, some of the teachers expressed that they are deviated and diverted due to the assignment of election duty and census work, (which is only 7% of the total working days in a year). Minimum days of school functioning in a year (200 and 250 for primary and upper primary respectively).

There is a lack of sincerity and commitment that appears in the attitude of teachers, since they used to come to school and leaving the school without timings.

Some of the teachers do not come down to the level of the students.

A majority of teachers stay long in the same school without transfer after three years or they are transferred to neighbouring village. They will actively participate in local politics/caste politics, which is one of the main reasons for not concentration on duty.

Some of the local teachers instead of duty they will concentrate on farming the land and other agricultural activities existing locally.

During the learning hours in school some of the teachers actively participated in local politics and caste politics and other activities; when a teachers would starts a discussion, (otherwise it is called gossip): Therefore the other teachers are also influenced by him and they may also join with him for gossip. It leads to great indiscipline among the children.

During the field work the researcher identifies the appearance of a dim view of schooling system, which will not attract the child at all. This is one of the main reasons of child absenteeism. Due to the apathetic attitude of the teacher the school appears as dim and dull.

While teaching, some of the teachers do not make use of various techniques of methods in teaching or teaching aids like maps, globe, pictures etc for attracting or drawing children attention towards education.

Due to frequent absence of teacher to the class. Pupil may not turn to school and they will be going outside for playing or will wander with the peer group it also leads to indiscipline among children.

When teacher teaches regularly, as per the curriculum/ syllabus, there is no scope for students' absenteeism. In a normal practice, when a child is not regularly coming to the school, concerned teacher(s) must identify the particular child and go to his home and bring back the child to the school by his way of convincing.

Corporal punishment tends to further increase children absenteeism, students fail to give proper answer to the question of the teachers. The researcher observes, due to the frequency of teacher absenteeism the students do not follow or understand or due to the discontinuity of particular topic or lesson the student naturally may not answer the question. In this scenario, a teacher who himself identifies his mistake of his absenteeism and it is suggested they never show any kind of corporal punishment as which is the one of the main reason of the absenteeism.

In some schools, the children are being given severe corporal punishments, physical punishment by teacher(s) by three reasons- a) though a teacher who teaches well but child is not properly answering when teacher ask him question. b) In other cases though the teaching is not good such a teacher blames the child and punishing him without reasoning as he does not realize himself that his quality of teaching is not up to the level of child. C) Whereas in some schools, though the teacher is attending school, but he will be available outside the classroom. In a situation the tender children quarrel with each other and exchange of filthy and abusive language among them ultimately that lead to the deficiencies of the school system.

Despite schemes like Mid Day Meal, free education, free uniform etc the government schools are looked down upon by parents. The enrollment of govt schools has come down from higher to lower. Therefore, although declining birth rate could be an important reason, there is no denying the fact that the general community trust on the quality of education and child care provided at government schools are also a significant reason for declining enrolment rate at the government schools. However, wide spread awareness is very much required on the importance of education.

Primary education in Andhra Pradesh stands 31st rank in India. The education mill is on the grind always. Although one can not claim all school-going age children or in school, one can say the trend is comfortable except for the hazard of child labour in some pockets of Andhra Pradesh. The number of out of school children in the state is reported to be high. Due to various reasons some of the children did not pursue school education, despite the existence of anti child labour legislations, and SSA effort of 100% enrolment running of mid day meal programme, child labour/out of school children or non-enrolled children are present significantly.

Perhaps, migration of parents in search of employment uninterested children of unaware parents, disability of children could be taken as reasons for non enrolment as well as child labour.

Observations about Teachers

On different aspects, some of the teachers are responsible for the following:

Morale and commitment: The procedural selection of teachers of primary level is really appreciable to the Govt. like Andhra Pradesh as any person wants to become a school

Teacher either primary or secondary, who should be qualified at the three levels – the first one is acquiring the minimum bachelor degree in Education (B.Ed) or Diploma in Education (DIET), secondly she/he will have to qualify Teacher Eligibility Test (TET) examination and thirdly he/she will have to qualify District Selection Committee Test (DSC). One must qualify these three tests to get teacher post.

According to the system of selection no one can doubt about the standard and quality of the teacher(s) and the way of teacher's selection. But here low morale and commitment of the same individual(s) leads to abysmal quality of education which leads to dim view of school system, which creates detraction and aversion to the parents not to either enroll their children or continue or shift another private school. In the result presently more than 26 per cent children are admitted in private schools. If the same situation continues in the government schools system ultimately the small cannot develop (economically weaker sections and socially disadvantaged children).

It is well known fact as far as concerned to Japan and China where morale and commitment are very high, when compared to the other countries like India. Therefore there is high quality and quantity of production is yielded in all respects.

1) Teacher absenteeism, apathetic attitude, lack of commitment and accountability are main cause of non-implementation of RTE ACT.

2) Participation in local politics and caste domination: working in the same place for more than three years or transferred to neighboring village leads to unwanted social network established which tends to deviate their original duty of work.

3) Some teachers who belong to dominant caste may neglect his duty, (exploiting dominant casteeism) so the

rest of the people in the village never question him due to his dominant caste, as they belong to weaker community rather than teacher's community. Mandal Education Officer (MEO) will also be managed by some teachers because of active participation in local politics.

4) Out of 220 working days in the year–as per the official statistics only 7% the working days teachers are engaged for election duty and census duty including any other official work so that such assignment is not over burden to teachers to complete the syllabus. It is an open fact such duty is the obligation of every employee.

5) Some of the teachers have lack of values, morale, self introspection and accountability especially in the field of education further decline the progress and development of the nation as the teachers and teaching community played a crucial role to promote principles of democracy and transforming the society in the way of right direction.

6) It is the obligation of the teachers to bring back the children to the school who are frequently absentees when parents are illiterates.

7) When researcher interacted with the parents and general community clearly put across that where the school head master/teacher(s) have been active the schools have good image among the general community. Wherever teachers come to school on time, the image has been good. Wherever the teachers share the performance of children with the parents the school image has also been good.

8) Wherever the school children go to private school though the government (paid teachers') schools are accessible the image has been poor.

9) Where the teacher is a moneylender or active and in the local politics or pursuing his own agriculture or owner of a grocery or any kind of business, he is viewed secondarily a teacher.

Types of Absenteeism of Teachers

- Unofficial substitute teacher who teaches instead of regular teacher in his absence is paid some money by understanding (as a substitute) for his work.
- It is further observed regarding teachers absenteeism that there has been mutual understanding among teachers eg. Out of four teachers only one or two teachers would attend on the day and the rest of the two may attend next day or the other day. It indicates 50% of the regular teacher stands absent which is a general practice in tribal and remote rural villages.
- A teacher whenever he comes to school takes classes otherwise not as per his convenience.
- Schools run by single teacher-there is no accountability to anyone as there is no strict vigilance, therefore such schools are working so-so.
- Long Medical leaves.
- Frequent absenteeism without intimation.
- Go on deputation other than the teaching profession.

Suggestions for Teachers

1) Teachers shall have these qualities for promoting the society especially in Regularity, Sincerity, Integrity and self-introspection.
2) Tame the child and mould the child not to be absent to the school.
3) Commitment towards institution, towards the children education and welfare of the state.

4) Teacher will have to establish rapport with the parents of the child.

5) Teachers are suggested to impart social values and value based education to the children for healthy society.

6) Teachers should not participate in the local caste/politics.

7) Teacher shall follow prescribed teaching methodology while teaching.

Suggestion for Teachers Union

Teachers union play a very significant role in creating congenial atmosphere and environment.

Absenteeism of comparatively well-paid teachers, particularly where bulk of the students come from scheduled castes and tribes, poses a major problem. Students are circumstantially forced to go in for private tuitions.

The teachers' unions, which have a very positive role to play in protecting the interests of teachers and have played that part well in the past, are often turning into an influence that reinforces the neglect of the interests of children from desperately underpriviledged families. There is evidence of hardening of class barriers that separate the newly affluent teachers from the impoverished rural poor. (The *Argumentative Indian*, Amartya Sen)

- It is important to recognize the role that the teacher unions can play in the enhancement of culture of learning and teaching as well as in the professionalism and motivation of teachers.

- The role of a teachers union in the improvement teacher motivation and professionalism as prerequisite the enhancement of the culture of learning and teaching is important in education. The enhancement of the culture of learning and teaching is important in education. To achieve this aim, teachers play an important role because they are responsible for the one crucial part namely teaching. The teachers' motivation to perform well and their professionalism in the delivery of a high level performance is important in this aspect. The professional attitude of teacher and the perspective of teaching as a profession can also play an important role in the enhancement of learning and teaching.

- It is also advised the union though they have some demands but have strong commitment and obligation to take it as the primary duty to endeavor to promote education for the public good.
- Teachers federation/union should create a public opinion which should serve as adequate sanction against such unsocial acts.
- In this connection the researcher advise either to pass some strictures themselves with their open heart or a ban on unions or postpone their demands for at least ten years (in a positive way) for attainment of 100% literacy.

Suggestion to the Parents

1) Nodoubt there is a consistency between parent's aspiration and constitutional goal of 8 years education, but the first generation of going school children are unable to achieve certain level of targeted education. However, the rural and tribal parents and other deprived sections of the society are all most all illiterates as they are unable to recognize the fruits of education, even after attainment of 65 years of Independence therefore they motivate themselves by observing educated persons who got benefited.

2) Illiteracy is the root cause of all the socio-economic, cultural problems so that rural and tribal parents shall

have to concentrate their children's education by getting awareness (socialization) through watching electronic media (T.V.) and radio programmes.

3) Further it is suggested that regularly they have to send their child to the school as it is duty of the parents under (Article 15K).

4) Parents will have to interact with school management and visit concerned teacher, periodically.

5) It is the duty of parents to send a child to the school on the regular basis otherwise the growing children will loose the fruits of globalization, liberalisation, natural resources etc. on par with main stream of the society.

6) It is advised to follow the suggestion of the Former Chief Justice of India Balakrishnan gave a judgment that their parents shall be punished if they fail to send their children to school and further he expressed that their services do not make use other than education upto 18 years.

7) While child is pursuing education, it is the duty of the parents to encourage; proper guidance and encouragement are necessary for every child.

8) It is advised to utilize all the schemes and benefits like mid-day meal, supply of free books, zero fee and other benefits like scholarships etc. for pursing higher education and employment.

Suggestions for Government Schools vs. Private Schools

Privately-managed and government-aided schools have also joined the government primary schools providing universal education for all. However, the strength in Primary Schools in rural areas is losing ground very fast. In fact, some of the schools have shuttered down for want of children, some of schools closed down but on records are shown especially in remote rural and tribal. The privately managed schools are thriving and making headway increasing the number of enrolment each year. At the same time the community in general has become sceptical about the quality of education and the childcare provided by the government-run primary schools. However, poor it might be in terms of infrastructure, private schools tend to thrive. It is a blind of myth-and-reality that all the private schools offer quality education. But they have gained the parent's validation and support, notwithstanding high tution fees, and other paraphernalia.

Despite schemes like mid day meal, free education, free uniforms, free transportation facilities etc. the Primary School is looked down upon by parents. The enrolment in government schools has come down year after year. Therefore, although declining birth rate could be an important reason, there is no denying the fact that the general community trust on the quality of education and childcare provided at Primary Schools is also a significant reason for declining enrolment rate at the government schools in the State. However, there is widespread awareness on the importance of education even amongst the poorest of families.

Involvement of Public & NGOs

Public inaction is one of the important reasons for dull Primary schools in the State. The public are fast washing their hands off Primary School, mainly because they have an easy alternative available (privately run schools with van facilities for picking up and dropping back children) that suit different types of income categories. The rest of the states take Kerala as the role model as at the beginning of Independence the people of kerala started social movements for development of education management. Kerala has the highest literacy rate among the state of India. Kerala undertook a "campaign for total literacy" in Ernakulam district in the late 1980s, with a "fusion between the district administration headed by its Collector on one side and, on the other side, voluntary groups, social activists and others". On February 4, 1990, The Government of Kerala then replicated the initiative on a statewide level, launching the Kerala State Literacy Campaign. First, households were surveyed with door-to-door, multistage survey visits to form an accurate picture of the literacy landscape and areas that needed special focus. Then, Kala Jathan (cultural troupes) and Saksharata Pada Yatras (Literacy Foot Marches) were organized to generate awareness of the campaign and create a receptive social atmosphere for the program. An integrated management system was created involving state officials, prominent social figures, local officials and senior voluntary workers to oversee the execution of the campaign.

Role of Panchayats and School Management Committee (SMC)

The role of Panchayats as well as village level educational committee as a way of decentralization in ensuring transparency, accountability and good governance at the local level. They are very important to make all children are educated but the panchayats play very little role in managing or setting right the problems of enrolment, retention or in improving the school infrastructure, or quality of education. The administrative structure of Primary Schools and place of local Panchayats is such that the Panchayat functionaries feel that they have no role to play in matters relating to basic education.

Panchayats as well as school management committee shall keep their eye on functioning of the school relating to pupils attendance, retention, enroll the non-enrollment, and drop out and also pay particular attention on teachers absenteeism and quality of education.

Comments

1. Right to Education Act is a significant piece of legislation passed by the UPA government. Millions of children,

regardless of caste, colour or creed will now have access to, and more importantly the right to be in school. Raising literacy levels among the young is essential for our overall socioeconomic development. The right will serve as the springboard for the success of deprived children.

2. It needs to be translated into action at the ground level by the collective efforts of all concerned-parents, teachers, students and the government, especially local governments. However, the major handicap of the act as rightly opined in the article "India's children have a precarious right," is that the beneficiary cannot demand it nor fight a legal battle when the right is denied or violated.

3. In the village where it has a school, there are no proper classrooms. If there is a classroom, there is no blackboard. And if there is a blackboard, there is no teacher. We need to provide the necessary infrastructure in schools to make education meaningful.

4. Ministry of Human Resource Development has not made any effort to back it up with legislation. Instead the draft bill has been sent to the States. The Centre continues to fail in its duty to provide education for all, as even after lapse of more than Two years the RTE Act does implementation some states.

5. In India, policies are formulated with the best possible intentions but the flaw lies at the implementation level.

6. The magnitude and implications of the right are far-reaching. Even today not many are aware of the enormous task involved in putting every child in school.

7. There was a time when getting admission in government schools was considered a matter of pride. But today, even the poor want to educate their children

in private schools. Can this situation be reversed by the new law?

8. The prime stakeholder in the group is the parent. If the parent is poor, as it is true in many cases, he may opt for income rather than education. Let us hence look at it as a wider societal issue which cannot be addressed only through the RTE Act.

9. No method is prescribed for selecting the 25 per cent poor students for admission into unaided private schools. Selection by lottery would be ridiculous. In the absence of a viable provision, the private unaided (de facto commercial) schools can choose the 25 per cent poor children in a way that the choice would benefit the school. So far no corporate school has not implemented 25 per cent reservation for the deprived sections or stake holders. At the same time the stake holders do not come forward for seeking admission perhaps due to their poverty and backwardness.

10. There is nothing in the Act or its rules and regulations that will prevent unaided private schools from charging students for activities that are not mentioned in the Act or its Rules & Regulations. Examples would be laboratory fee, computer fee, building fee, sports fee, fee for stationery, fee for school uniform, fee for extra-curricular activities such as music, painting, pottery, and so on.

11. Sec 2n. IV article 19.1g: (All the citizens shall have the right to practice any profession or to carry out any occupation, trade or business). RTE Act does not rule out educational institutions to set up for profit. Whether primary institutions or Higher Educational institutions is not made clear. Therefore it is necessary to read with Article 19.6 of the Indian constitution that no one in the country can set up Nuclear Power Plants or narcotic plants etc.

12. Education has no profit motive since it is not a trade business. But education has been taken over by education mafia'. There are long queues outside private schools to secure admission forms, followed by interviews' for parents and children, which include questions on parent's salaries, occupation, family background, etc.

13. Sec. 11. 1b. if education to be run for profit it would not get recognition of the government. But RTE Act is State Act. Therefore the Centre should make it a part of the Act. Therefore we have to distinguish before education for a citizen to know the rights and responsibilities and professional courses like Medicine and Engineering.

Suggestions

Basing on the major findings of the study the following suggestions are made to both the central and state Governments, parents, government school teachers and concerned government officials, NGOs and social activists to run the schools successfully to eradicate illiteracy apart from a documentary film is made for 45 miniutes for illiterate people in Vernacular language to motivate them and also made the film in English medium for official purpose.

1. It must not remain a mere right to school enrolment. There should be a corresponding obligation on the part of teachers, students and parents to ensure that children have a minimum attendance of 75 per cent, and minimum standards of academic attainment (quality). Otherwise, vast resources will be squandered away without any tangible benefits.

2. Health care would go long way to make the education programme successful. The major reason that the respondents said for missing school is due to ill health; hence, attention to be paid to provide proper health care in these areas.

3. Poverty is another major hurdle coming in the way of education and poverty eradication programmes are also to be given importance in these villages.

4. Failure of Government schools is attributed to lack of infrastructure facilities, apathy and lack of commitment of teachers to their duties.

5. The respondents opine and suggest that success of schools be made accessible to all and they be introduced from primary level onwards to make it more effective.

6. The school committee should be responsible and see the proper functioning of the school in all aspects.

7. Steps to be taken to eradicate corruption in education department.

8. It is good to link up promotions to talent, punctuality, sincerity of the teacher and of the result of the students in the school. This approach can improve the teacher's performance.

9. The successful Kerala methodology and action plans are to be emulated by rest of the country for successful implementation of any educational programme intended for eradication of illiteracy.

10. Motivating teachers is utmost important step in taking the literacy programme ahead. Motivation of teachers in the sense of regular and punctual attendence to school to inculcate morale and commitment to teach the students with interest of progress of pupil as well as national interest at large.

11. It is an important question that needs to be addressed is that quality and responsiability for which local authorities, school principals, teachers should ensure that children attend school regularly.

12. It is suggested to both the Central government and the State government to release the budgetary funds

atleast in the first quarter of the financial year (budget). Instead of vote on account funds.

13. To maintain quality education not only at the elementary level but also the level of private teaching institutes, Secondary Grade Teachers (SGT) and Bachelor of Education (B.Ed) as most of the teaching training institutes do not follow the rules and regulations of NCTE. Though there is conducting Teacher Eligibility Test (TET) and District Selection Committee (DSC), the teacher institutes shall be sanctioned in a strict manner.

14. The salaries of the teachers will be paid basing on the results/imparting of quality education (performance based salary).

15. It is suggested that until reaching 100% literacy, the Government of India as well as the concerned State governments provide further rural employment programmes like (MGNREGA) and financial support by which parents will have a breath to send their children to schools.

16. As every body knows that the Act does not send the children to school; the government shall take stringent action against concerned persons until to attain national goal.

17. Teachers are no doubt the foundation stone to mould children in a right path. A teacher, who does not use third degree force (beating, using abusive language, shouting and punishment) on the pupil.

18. The scope of the Act should be extended to college degree-level or at (+) Plus Two Level to secure education meaningfully and to make the downtrodden enlightened and competent to face global competition.

19. The government should not treat this as an amendment to the Constitution. There is need to work further at the grass-root level to reduce dropouts and enhance enrolment. The responsibility of motivating parents, proper publicity by showing documentary films, film strips, advertisement in T.Vs and also better to socialize through news reel in movies to admit their children into schools.

20. The provision for reservation of 25 per cent seats in private institutions would be resisted, out of fear that it may affect their "quality". The best way to effect the fruits of the Act reach the targeted beneficiaries would be to nationalize education, employing, of course, strict conditions of accountability on the teachers. This will also arrest the tendency of vested interests to find ways of commercializing education. The government should be strict in according recognition.

21. Mere enactment of laws will not do the miracle. It may be worth giving cash incentives to families engaged in labour and encouraging them to send their children to school.

22. It is advised that in tribal areas a local teacher shall be appointed, with knowledge of tribal vernacular language, as most of the tribals do not know other than their own vernacular language.

23. Women teachers are to be given more preference at least at the primary level, till attainment of 100% literacy.

24. As a reformative method certain backward areas like tribal and remote rural areas people should be socialized and mobilized and lead a social movement regarding eradication of illiteracy. In this regard NGOs as well as the Government officials either individually or

collectively as groups take initiative for social movements to create awareness among deprived sections with the support of the local people, for example, due to the social movements the state of Kerala achieved highest percentage of literacy attained in the state though it is poor when compared with other Indian States.

25. As most of the studies spelt out there has been high percentage of teachers absenteeism in tribal and remote rural areas so that the high illiteracy is very much prevalent. If the same trend continues we cannot achieve literacy goal in a stipulated period or time bound. Therefore it is advised to take help of nuns or NGOs if available who dedicate their lives to the God and the society welfare that "they believe work is worship".

26. It is also recommended that State Government to allocate atleast 30% of the State budget like Kerala for Elementary Education in the State.

27. The researcher has further emphasized that education is essential for adult illiterates which is very important for farmers to know the skills and knowledge and techniques in the field of agriculture for making use of inputs such as fertilizers, Pesticides and the quality of seeds so that the minimum education is a pre-requisite to such people for improvement optimum production.

28. The adult education resource persons and local petty agricultural officers join together and impart knowledge, techniques and skills relating to agriculture for good farming and high yielding of production.

29. Due to the laxity of values and morale there is a lack of accountability in some teachers who do not feel responsibility or obligation therefore strict vigilance is very essential to correct them.

30. Due to lack of vigilance by the concerned Government officials some of the schools have shown fictitious enrolment in their school records.

31. Even today, an illiterate parent does not recognise the importance of education and unwilling to send their children to the school. Therefore concerned officials, social workers NGOs, electronic and print media shall take iniative and create awareness among parents to send their children to the school.

32. Poverty is one of the main reasons which discourage parents to send their children as they are always searching for their daily bread. They cannot wait for long goal of education. Therefore under Mahatma Gandhi National Rural Employment guarantee programme MGNREGP: it is suggested to increase employability from 100 to 150 or 200 days for those who come under BPL, which indirectly supports enrolment of the children, to decrease drop outs, and to insure continuity of education.

33. Right to have equality and social justice of every citizen in the country the people for the it is the primary duty of the nation to provide primary health, and education to the people for the development and prosperity of the nation.

34. There are two myths regarding parent's opinion over the children's education. A number of recent studies helped to dispel two myths that have tended to cloud official thinking and public debate on the subject. The first myth is that Indian parents have little interest in education as per the official circles rational to avoid of the failure in order to achieve universal elementary education. For example, according to probe survey in India's most educational backward states, parents expressed that their children to be educated as high as 98% for boys, 89% for girls only 3% parents opposed.

35. *Kerala Model:* It is encouraging to note that the success story of DPEP in the state of Kerala which is intended to improve female literacy, control dropout rate and increase the enrollment rate of socially disadvantaged groups, along with motivating parents, children and teachers through various activities. In the light of the above findings and observations Kerala state programs are emulated. It is not difficult to reach the success in education programme in our state too if we adopt the efficacious methods.

36. It is suggested that, where children are unable to reach, school where schools are run by single teacher where the children enrolment is very low. Where there is no pucca building without infrastructure facilities, these are to be centrally located apart from providing transport facility for both to the children and to the teachers who are residing in remote tribal and rural areas to attend the schools with in 1-3 Kms of distance. Since most of the single teacher schools are not run due to high absenteeism of teachers. Who fails to attend the school that will lead to children absenteeism.

37. The Government should make it mandatory for parents to submit their children's proof of attendance in school to get family ration cards or for getting any welfare facilities and banking loans and public facilites etc.

38. It is suggested that states should not shift its responsibility to private schools. It is the states duty to provide free, quality education to ever child.

39. Parents engage their children in work for daily wages. The government should establish more schools with boarding facilities and improve the infrastructure in existing schools.

40. People should save the money which they spend on IPL cricket, for the crackers on Diwali and shopping

malls in order to invest it in government schemes to promote noble causes.

41. In a country with 42 per cent of children malnourished and the largest number of street children, the foremost step is to ensure the complete participation of children by providing the basic necessities. Let the government do first by further extended welfare schemes without corruption.

42. Corporate giants should earmark some of their profits for promoting elementary education, especially in rural areas like Premji School Education Foundation.

43. Salaries and promotions shall be linked up with quality of teaching, accountability and integrity and sincerity of the teacher.

44. Rewards will be given to encourage sincere teachers; as they will become role model to other teachers.

45. Dropout-prevention shall be their primary objective. The intervening review provides a mix of services, such as counsling, monitoring school restructuring, curriculum redesign, financial incentives and community services to mitigate factors impeding academic success.

46. *Importance of pre-primary education:* Pre-primary lays the foundations of a child's knowledge, skills and rules of behaviour and conduct that create prerequisites for successful progress in daily life and in school. Further pre-primary education lays the foundation for the development of reading, writing and number work. It is a programme which encourages interaction with environment, active participation in group activities and enhances creativity and problem solving in children. It stresses on providing first hand experience. Pre-primary education indirectly promotes self-control and thereby

inner discipline in children. It provides plenty of opportunity for socialization.

47. It is now virtually universally recognised that 12 years of school education beginning at the age of six, preceded by appropriate pre-school education, is a minimum requirement for further progress. Therefore, in all developed countries, a vast majority of children including those of the rich and powerful go to government schools for 12 years of totally free education. The RTE Act is unconcerned about the four most important years of school education – that is, from Class IX to Class XII.

48. The 25 per cent reservation is really laudable. But the painful fact is: the remaining 75 per cent of underprivileged children will have to attend the same government schools. It seems the state wants to shift its "responsibility" to private schools. It is the state's duty to provide free, quality education to every child. Therefore the government take steps to improve its own school infrastructure. It recruit good teachers. The mere sharing of school fees will not automatically make the poor children comfortable among their elite classmates in private schools. There are other expenses. The private schools we are talking about are located in urban pockets. But the vast majority of children live in villages and tribal areas who are unable to compete with urban elite.

49. Even after lapse of over 2 years some state governments failed to take serious steps whereas some state governments even if they are taking initiation at which stage the funds for (mid-day meal, infrastructure facilities) are being misused at various levels by the bureaucrat and local petty leaders. Without doing or using funds falsely they have shown on papers and

further withdrawing from the banks. There are some cases of deliberate mischief. to be corrected.

50. The RTE Act gives enough powers to the village education committee/school management committee, which includes parents as members. But many parents are unaware of it. It will be very useful if such information appears in the media.

51. Either the teacher or an employee of the government schools have no self confidence of their children's improved education in their schools and as such they are also sending their children to corporate schools. Therefore they have to buildup confidence themselves first and create confidence in public by way of improving quality of education.

52. Quality of Education: Unless teachers are trained properly, one could not expect them to deliver quality education to the children. "From various independent surveys have come to show that despite increase in enrollment there has been notable deterioration in learning skills of the students all over the country.

There are many dimensions of quality which includes the spirtual development of a child's physical mental and emotional faculties. Even we excludes these 'higher' levels of aspirations and examine the basics of development of basic skills the situation is alarming. Reforms in education initiated in India, aims at rapidly expanding the education, achieving the equity in the provision of education, and significantly improving the quality of education. Talking in practical terms, all these if implemented sincerely should be able to produce far-reaching results. Besides this, two other things required are: (i) liberal social sector budget provisions to make it operational; and (ii) a determination on the part of the teachers in government schools to change their outlook and enhance their commitment levels.

53. Some of the state governments like Andhra Pradesh which has recently imposed a strict rule that 10 years of schooling in government schools shall be eligible for scholarship which is really good to enhance the image of government schools and attract the children towards the government schools provided there is knowledgeable standards maintained by the school and the teachers working therein with commitment. Otherwise children's career will be spoiled.

54. In view of the demands of rapidly changing technology and the growth of knowledge in economy, a mere eight years of elementary education would be grossly inadequate for our young children to acquire necessary skills to compete in the job market. Therefore a mission for higher secondary education is essential to consolidate the gains of SSA and to move forward in establishing a knowledgeable society.

Summary and Conclusion

The appropriate government introduced various committees, educational programmes and schemes as well as different models of schools as desired by the contemporary Indian society to face global challenges to improve quality of life of deprived and weaker sections of the society by enjoying socioeconomic development and natural resources on par with privileged sections of the society. In this backdrop the Union Government enacted law as "Right to Education" and free and compulsory education to the children between 6 to 14 years as part of national endeavour of development so that it is the duty of every right thinking citizen especially it is on the shoulders of the teaching community to mobilize those who are not eager to get their children educated.

Availability of teachers in schools during working hours is an important variable for quality of education. It is well-known fact that a teacher is the rock foundation to mould children in a right path. He is the yardstick that measures the achievements and aspirations of the nation. The work and potentialities of a country get evaluated by and through the work of a teacher. They are the real nation-builders. Further, the teacher is the dynamic force of the school in multi-cornered progress of a child. As social engineer, the teacher can socialize and humanise the young by their manly qualities.

He works mainly and contributes for the well-being of children to mould and nourishing them in a proper direction. Tender children always follows the actions, movements and the behaviour exactly displayed the teacher and imbibe all these from the teacher, as teacher's role is very crucial regarding the bring up of the children as other wise they will be deviated and they would be injurious to him/herself, family and society at large being delinquent. Therefore it is not only mandatory but also moral binding, on every teacher to strive heart and soul to raise the children up to highest perfection of mankind with amity and love apart from commitment and morale (leaving aside payment of salaries). They shall impart quality of knowledge.

As long as the teacher fails to attend his job without commitment and disciplaine to impart knowledge, it likely takes another half century to attain the goal of hundred per cent literacy in the country. Presently as per the 2011 census, Andhra Pradesh stands at 31st rank amongst 35 States[28] and uinion territories(7).India stands at 147th rank in the world out of 179 countries as per UNDP Statstics of 2009.The other states like Bihar, Himachal pradehs are also still worse condition in literacy. Even if both Union government and State governments dump and pump up regular flow of money or allocate major part of the budget of the nation to elementary education it is a day-dream to reach the goal. For example, providing all ingredients for making delicious food (quality education) if there is no proper cook (teacher) there is no use of the ingredients so also the status of the schools remain deteriorated as on the other side the private corporate schools are being established with good image and propagation and ultimately they shadow the government schools.

Teacher is a role-model not only to the children but also to the society as teaching is a noble profession. If he fails to attend his duty, ultimately the children will be spoiled and they will become victims probably of hunger, disease, exploitation, poverty and some of them remain vagabonds or they lead meaningless life and there is a scope to become social offenders since the first generation i.e. their parents in most cases are illiterates. Therefore the teacher shall be either side responsible for good or bad. Therefore the appropriate government should be the cane-holder to drive cart in the right path at least for a period of 10 years until to attain the national goal. Further the government should take stern action against the concerned officers as more corruption is deep rooted at all levels (e.g.: An Executive Engineer Mr. Ramesh who was caught by Anti Corruption Bureau (ACB) by taking bribe of Rs. 12,000/- (twelve thousand only) from Rajiv Vidya Commission School Building Contractor, in Sanga Reddy, Medak district in A.P. on 06.01.2012 and there are other similar cases in many states but not ventilated).

Therefore it is suggested that the Central Government will have to take lead for which there are two arguments often arise where to encourage, private unaided schools when the government has no money to set up the needed schools, and that government schools cannot be run like private schools. In this regard there have been excellent studies and reports showing that the government can find money to adopt a common school system which was already recommended by Kotari Commission in 1960 to reduce educational inequalities with a provision of compulsory and totally free education up to Class VIII/XII in the country over the next

10 years. Further, even today the best system of school education in the country is the Central School(s) [Kendriya Vidyalaya, Navodaya Vidyalaya Samithi and Kasturba Gandhi Balika Vidyalaya (KGBV)] which are already dicussed in chapter-1, system run by the Central Government.

The country needs such schools, though some of the vociferous groups as well as state governments in the country taking that it is an attack on the federal structure as quality of education is under concurrent list, for quality of education.

Government of India will have to take lead in this regard instead of rely on State governments mainly on the five reasons:

The first one is the drop out rate is further increased more than 3percent as per the report of ASER 2011 even after lapse of 2years of commencement of RTE Act inspite of schemes supporting like Sarva Siksha Abhiyan (SSA) & Mid-day meal programme are implemented.

Secondly, out of 35(states 28) and UTs (7) only Ten (10) States and UT (viz. Kerala, Lakshadweep, Mizoram, Tripura, Goa, Daman and Diu, Puducherry, Chandigarh, NCT of Delhi and Andaman and Nicobar Islands) have achieved literacy rate of above 85% the target set by the Planning Commission by 2011-2012. The rest of the states have their own glaring weaknesses of the lack of adequate facilities, large scale of absenteeism of teachers, uneven teacher-pupil ratio, lack of local political-will and inadequate supervision and apathetic attitude of local authorities, consequently of the teachers, misappropriation of funds, abysmal quality of education and a obscure view of school system etc.

Thirdly the main objectives of RTE Act are attainment of 100 per cent enrolment, retention without dropouts, impart quality of education, provide infrastructure facilities out of which except enrolment (96.7) the rest of the objectives said above are almost all discouraging the Act.

Fourthly the State Governments are very busy with the local and regional politics and also busy with friendly in-fighting with their dissident colleagues and opposition. Therefore there is no time to them to concentrate on children's education so that they do not make use of educational budget properly released by the Centre. Since the government of India so far in the history of the country allotted large fund of Rs. 2.31 lakh crores for Elementary Education but some of the states are not coming up to utilize due to low level of commitment. The system of education should be imperative purview of the Central Government even to exercise the same above the State system and apparently improve approved standards of the Central government unmindful of concurrent list. Then only literate society can be anticipated in a stipulated time.

Fifthly, the teachers' federations in all most all the states are very strong so that they are in a position to give trouble to concern state governments by way of protesting if any action is iniated over irregular teachers who have mostly strong local base with sufficient political background at gross root level.

There has been financial constraint the government will have to afford by way of earmarking and allocating more budget on par with the National defence budget atleast for a period of 10 years. In this regard Ministry of HRD has already put proposal before planning commission for Elementary Education for Rs. 45,000 crores for annual and 2.31 lakh crores for five year plan of 2012-2017. In this back drop the government of India will have to take lead itself and extend Central school system by allocating further more budget then the instead of state school system to achieve the targeted goal in a conceivable period.

Finally it is suggested to support and encourage NGOs/ Social activists to socialize illiterate parents and deprived sections of the society and also propagate the importance of literacy through electronic media mostly through news reel in all the cinema theatres and T.V. channels. If government do not take stern action for implementation of RTE Act in toto, the private school system will be more strengthened as per the statistics there was 18.7% of children between 6 to 14 years were studying in private schools in the year 2006 whereas in 2011 it was increased to 26.6%. The over all enrolment was increased in private schools for the last five years was 10 percent. Strengthening of corporate and private school system in the country will create further inequality between haves and have-nots as educational inequalities are causes to precipitate other inequalities, ultimately equity and social justice will be a myth to the poor and deprived sections of the society.

Therefore it is advised that the best system of school education in the country is in the above said central schools which certainly cater to the needs of children of deprived and poor sections of the society as we still have a long way to go to attain the goal of complete literate society.

APPENDIX 1

Education of Rural and Tribal Community: An Observation Schedule

Appeal

Dear Parents, NGOs and Teachers,

I hope you might have known well that even after attainment of 65 years of independence, we have not achieved universalization of literacy in our country. If the same trend is continued, we cannot achieve the same in the near future. In this connection, we seek your co-operation, support and encouragement for providing information as respondent(s). This questionnaire is not prepared to point out or to blame any individual or institutions or organizations. The main aim of the study is to achieve the goal of universalization of literacy in a short period of time as a part of National Development.

Prof. K. Vijaya Kumar
Coordinator & Research Unit
Department of Sociology
Andhra University, Visakhapatnam

SI. Individual Details

1) Name of child's Mother :

2) Mother's Education:

3) Name of Father :
4) Father's Education:

5) No. children:

a) Male: b) Female:

6) Name of the Village:

7) Mandal:

8) District:

8)	Respondent's age: a) 15 – 25 years b) 26 – 35 c) 36 – 45 d) 46 – 50 e) 50 years and above	A B C D E
9)	Caste: a) SC b) ST c) BC d) OC	A B C D
10)	Profession: a) Agricultural Labour b) Labour c) Caste Profession d) Others	A B C D
11)	How many people from your family get education in the Government schools: a) Boys: b) Girls:	A B
12)	The class in which your children (boys) are studying a) Primary b) Secondary c) Higher d) Intermediate e) Degree f) Above	A B C D E F
13)	The class in which your children (girls) are studying a) Primary b) Secondary c) Higher d) Intermediate e) Degree f) Above	A B C D E F

II. Your Children's status in the Educational System

14)	Are you taking special interest in the education of your children?	YES NO
15)	Is there a school in your village?	YES NO
16)	If so, what kind of school: a) Primary b) Secondary Education c) Higher Education	A B C
17)	How distant is the school in your village: a) 1-2 km b) 2-3 km c) 3 km d) above 3 km	A B C D

18)	What are the physical facilities available in the school for your children? a) Class-rooms b) Drinking water facilities c) Playground d) Lavatories e) Compound wall f) Electricity.	A B C D E F
19)	Are your children regularly attending the school daily?	YES NO
20)	In case they are not going to school, what are the reasons? a) Agricultural work b) Domestic work c) Looking after infants d) Illness e) Disability to understand the class lesson	A B C D E
21)	In case, of your children are not present in the school, are the teachers bringing that to your notice?	YES NO
22)	Are you satisfied about your children's competence in getting the level of their learning?	YES NO
23)	In case, it is not so, what are the reasons? a) Children's illness b) Lack of Teachers interest c) Because of impact of other students d) Deficiency of their home environment	A B C D
24)	Do you agree that the children's education is spoiled / lagged and indiscipline takes place by the appointment of Contract teachers as they are untrained and also belongs to a strong political and social group in the village?	YES NO

25)	Are the teachers residing in the same village?	YES	NO
26)	Are the teachers coming regularly to the school?	YES	NO
27)	Are the teachers observing regular school times	YES	NO
28)	Are you thinking that the teachers are having proper competency and efficiency in teaching your children	YES	NO
29)	Are you thinking the teachers are observing responsibilities in teaching?	YES	NO
30)	Are you supporting those teachers who are not taking proper responsibility in teaching	YES	NO
31)	Do you complained against any teacher for his irresponsibility?	YES	NO
32)	Were you present in some of the parents meetings in the school?	YES	NO
33)	Were you discussing in parental meetings about your children's education in the school?	YES	NO
34)	Were you aware of your children properly learning in the school regularly?	YES	NO
35)	Are the school management committees overseeing the school discipline?	YES	NO
36)	By sending to school are you thinking that your children are neither studying in the school nor useful for domestic work?	YES	NO

37) Even though the Government is providing incentives like waiver of school fee, giving free books and also providing mid-day meals, why do you opt for domestic work for your children? a) Because of Financial Insecurity b) Because of social disparity c) Learning is not up to the mark — A B C

38) Are you thinking your children are afraid the teachers are giving physical punishment in the school? — YES NO

39) In case your children are not properly progressing in the school are you going to question the teachers? — YES NO

40) The reasons for your children taking back-seat because of the teachers telling so to you; are you convinced for it? — YES NO

41) Recently private schools are prospering more than the Government schools. The private schools in 1993-94 are 12.5 lakh and they went up to 48 lakh in the year 2007-08. And the parents attract the private schools and ultimately losing economically. Are you feeling unhappy about it? — YES NO

42) What are the main reasons for your children joining in private schools instead of Government schools because of a) Teaching is not up to the mark b) Facilities not available c) Prosperity of children's parents d) Teacher's lack moral commitment — A B C

43)	In future, Government schools will be for very poor people, are you feeling the Government schools becoming a nominal tokens of educating the children?	YES	NO
44)	With the recent D.S.C 52 thousand teachers are getting to be recruited and the school assistants as head masters from S.G.T. to school assistants. Are you thinking that the Government schools will be providing better quality of education in the future?	YES	NO
45)	Are you thinking that in case the primary schools will be appointed by women teachers completely?	YES	NO
46)	Are you supporting that the school children can be promoted on the basis of their age?	YES	NO
47)	Are you supporting abolishing public examination in 7th standard exams and giving the natural promotion?	YES	NO
48)	Is the success school is getting access to you approved by Government.	YES	NO
49)	Are you thinking that English medium schools are more useful to your children in future?	YES	NO
50)	Are you thinking that success schools are going to reflect future progress of English medium schools?	YES	NO

51) Is Anganwadi/ Balwadi Centre/ and Pre play school available in your village? YES NO

52) Are the Anganwadi Centres and schools available in different places in your village? YES NO

53) Are your thinking that mid-day meals for your children in the schools will be more useful for your children? YES NO

54) Are your children satisfied for the provision of mid-day meals in the school? YES NO

55) In case you are not happy what are the reasons? a) due to corruption b) Government providing money is not sufficient. c) Teachers are not showing proper interest d) Mahila group members are not cooking properly e) Lack of supervision A B C D E

56) Do you feel that the evil of corruption is very much there in the department of education? YES NO

57) Do you suggest the salaries and promotions linked with performance are given on the basis of the talent, punctuality, sincerity of the teacher and results of the school? YES NO

Optional Questions

58) Do you support the presently on going agitation by parents against the hefty school fee hike imposed by some school managements and their adamant attitude? YES NO

59) Do you feel the present education system (from primary to higher secondary) is in cross roads due to domination by corporate managements?	YES	NO
60) Do you support steps to curb the practice of private unaided schools recognized by the Central Board of Secondary Education (CBSE) and Indian Council of Secondary Education (ICSE)?	YES	NO
61) If yes, do you wish that the Government will have to provide alternative steps for further strengthen and expansion of schools to meet the needs of the society?	YES	NO
62) Do you expect the attainment of hundred percent literacy at least to be reached by 2020?	YES	NO

Open-end Questions

63) What are your suggestions for minimizing dropout and continuing school education in your village?

64) What do you suggest for complete literacy?

References

Report of the Working Group on Secondary and Vocational Education for 11th Five Year Plan (2007-2012)

The Hindu, 5th April 2010 Purandeswari launches education portal

The Hindu, 2nd April 2010 Right to Education launch turns into insipid affair

The Hindu, Sunday, Feb 28, 2010. Child development: role of parents and teachers

The Hindu, Sunday, Feb 28, 2010. Child development: role of parents and teachers

Yamini Aiyar, Avani Kapur and Anit Mukherjee, Unpacking India's Education Budget: PAISA 2010

The Right of Children to Free and Compulsory Education Act, 2009: The Gazette of India Notification (August 27, 2009)

The Elementary Education System in India: Exploring Institutional Structures, Processes and Dynamics / Rashmi Sharma & Vimala Ramachandran (Eds.) - 2009

Education for Rural Development / D.P. Nayar – 2009

India, New Delhi. 2009 "Facing Global and Local Challenges: The New Dynamics for Higher Education" UNESCO [Link]

Sharing Responsibility for Primary Education / Syedah Fawzia Nadeem – 2008

Public Financing and Economics of Education in India / Heman Kr. Panda – 2008

History of Education in India / Suresh C. Ghosh – 2007

Education in India after Independence / Jagdish Chand – 2007

Committees and Commissions: Elementary Education: Select Documents / M.K. Jain – 2007

An Introduction to Elementary Education / Shivaprakasham, M.N. – 2006

Gender, Girls and Women Education / Verma, Mahesh – 2006

Economics of Tribal Primary Education / Latchanna, Gara – 2006

D. P. S. Seth, 2006 "A report on National Knowledge Network" National Knowledge Commission

Annual Status of Education Report (Rural) (ASER) (2005), Pratham Resource Center, Mumbai

Amartya sen (2005): Argumentative Indian, writing on Indian culture, history and identity

Free and Compulsory Education Bill And Other Issues Related to Elementary Education, Report of the Central Advisory Board of Education (CABE) Committee, June 2005 [Link]

Bajpai Nirupam and Sangeeta Goyal (2004) Primary Education in India: Quality and Coverage Issues, CGSD Working Paper No. 11, Working Papers Series, Center on Globalization and Sustainable Development

Reddy Sujata (2004) Status of Learning Achievements in India: A Review of Empirical Research, Azim Premji Foundation.

Aggarwal Y.P., Quality Concerns in Primary Education in Primary: Where is the Problem? National Institute of Educational Planning and Administration, New Delhi.

MHRD. 2004. Selected Educational Statistics: 2002-03. New Delhi, Government of India.

MHRD. 2003. Selected Educational Statistics: 2001-02, New Delhi, Government of India.

MHRD. 2003.: Education in India (Vol. I and Vol. II), 1995-96. New Delhi, Government of India.

Aggarwal Y.P. and Sunita Chugh (2003) Learning Achievement of Slum Children in Delhi, Operations Research and Systems

Management Unit, National Institute of Educational Planning and Administration, New Delhi

MHRD. 2002. *Selected Educational Statistics: 2000-01*. New Delhi, Government of India.

Mehta, Arun C. 2002. Universalisation of Secondary Education: Can It be Achieved in the Near Future?, *Journal of Educational Planning and Administration*. XVII, No. 4, October 2003, pp. 507-528.

Mehta, Arun C. 2002. Education for All in India with Focus on Elementary Education: Current Status, Recent Initiatives and Future Prospects. *NIEPA Occasional Papers*, No. 30, New Delhi.

Mukhopadhyay, Marmar (Ed.). 2002. *Secondary Education: The Challenges Ahead*, National Institute of Educational Planning and Administration, New Delhi.

MHRD. 2001. *Working Group Report on Elementary and Adult Education Tenth Five Year Plan 2002-2007*. Department of Elementary Education and Literacy, Government of India, New Delhi.

MHRD. 2001. *Selected Educational Statistics: 1999-2000*. New Delhi: Government of India.

MHRD. 2000. *Sarva Shiksha Abhiyan: A Peoples Movement for Education for All, Draft Guidelines*. New Delhi: Government of India.

Reddy Sujata (2004) *Status of Learning Achievements in India: A Review of Empirical Research*, Azim Premji Foundation

Varghese, N. V. and Arun C. Mehta. 1999. *Universalisation of Upper Primary Education in India –An Analysis of Present Status and Future Prospects*. National Institute of Educational Planning and Administration, New Delhi.

Varghese, N.V. and Arun C. Mehta (1998), '*Universalisation of Elementary Education- A Study of Upper Primary Education in India*', A Project sponsored by the World Bank, National Institute of Educational Planning and Administration (NIEPA), New Delhi, processed.

Ghosh, P.K. (1998), Disparity and some possible determinant of rural literacy in education, Indian Association or Social Science Institutions.

Mehta, Arun C. 1998. *Education for All in India- Enrolment Projections.* NIEPA and Vikas Publishing House, New Delhi.

NCERT (1998), *Sixth All India Educational Survey Statistics on Schooling Facilities,* New Delhi.

Thorman Mary (1998) *The Quality of Learning: Teaching the 3Rs in the first three grades in E-9 countries,* UNESCO, Paris, France

Mehta, Arun C. (1997,1), *'Indicators of Educational Development: Concept and Definitions',* NIEPA, New Delhi, processed.

Mehta, Arun C. (1997,2), 'Educational Development in India with Focus on Elementary Education', *Occasional Paper No. 24,* September, NIEPA, New Delhi.

Mehta, Arun C. (1997,1), *'Indicators of Educational Development: Concept and Definitions',* NIEPA, New Delhi, processed.

Mehta, Arun C. (1997,2), 'Educational Development in India with Focus on Elementary Education', *Occasional Paper No. 24,* September, NIEPA, New Delhi.

MHRD (1997), *Selected Educational Statistics: 1996-97,* New Delhi: Government of India.

Mehta, Arun C. 1996. 'Reliability of Educational Data in the Context of NCERT Survey'. *Journal of Educational Planning and Administration,* NIEPA. Volume X, No. 1. New Delhi.

Mehta, Arun C. (1996), 'Reliability of Educational Data in the Context of NCERT Survey', *Journal of Educational Planning and Administration,* NIEPA, July 1996, Volume X, No. 1, New Delhi.

Mehta, Arun C. (1995,1), *'EFA in India - Myth and Reality',* Kanishka Publishers and Distributors, New Delhi.

Mehta, Arun C. (1995,2), *'Projections of Student Enrolment and Flows'*, A Project sponsored by the World Bank, National Institute of Educational Planning and Administration (NIEPA), New Delhi, processed.

Mehta, Arun C. (1995,1), *'EFA in India - Myth and Reality'*, Kanishka Publishers and Distributors, New Delhi.

NCERT (1995), *Sixth All India Educational Survey (Provisional Statistics)*, November, New Delhi.

Mehta, A, C (1995) *Education for All*, Delhi: Kanishka publishers and Distributors.

Mujumdar M. and Vidayanathan, A.(1994) Access to Education in India:Retrospect and Prospectm, *Journal of Educational Planning.*

National literacy mission (2000), Guidelines for the Districts Engaged in the Evaluation of Total Literacy Campaign, New Delhi. Directorate of Adult Education, Ministry of Human Resource Development.

Visaria, P, D., Gumber, A.and vasaria, L. (1993),Literacy and Primary education in India:1980-81to 1991:differentials and determinants, *Journal of Planning and Administration*, Vol.7. Mp /1, 13-62.

Director primary education D K Saxena, *The Annual Status of Education Report (ASER)*, 2011, 150 years of University Education in India: Challenges Ahead

J. Ravindra Babu: Universalisation of Elementary Education:A Study of District Primary Education Programme from South India http://www.indiaedu.com/education-india/elementary education.html Elementary Education in India
http://www.educationworldonline.net/index.php/page-article-choice-more-id-639 Cover Story 50 leaders re-shaping Indian education Vinod Raina: Right to Education Finally a Bill in the Parliament

Dr. Saroj Pandey: Para Teacher Scheme and Quality Education for All in India: The Policy Perspectives and Challenges for School Effectiveness

Saswati Chanda: Corporate Social Responsibility, Education and Technology

The Hindu, Krishna Kumar: Why RTE remains a moral dream

The Hindu, Deepa Kurup: Yashpal committee suggests new apex body for higher education

The Hindu, S. Viswanathan RTE Act: combating the lethargy in implementation

The Hindu: Aarti Dhar Child rights panel to monitor RTE implementation

The Hindu, March 28, 2010 RTE Act: Private schools as catalysts? Universalizing Elementary Education in India: Santosh Mehrotra, P. R. Panchmukhi, Ranjana Srivastava, Ravi Srivastava The Crisis of Elementary Education in India Ravi Kumar Public Provisioning for Elementary Education in India Praveen K Jha, Subrat Das, Siba Sankar Mohanty ,Nandan Kumar Jha

Public and Private Partnership in Primary Education in India, A study of unrecognised schools in Haryana Yash Aggarwal

Primary Education in Tribal Areas in India: A Study of Community Participation in Sarva Shiksha Abhiyan — by Srinivasa Rao Vasanta

Scaling up Primary Education Services in Rural India: Public Investment Requirements and Policy Reform Case Studies of Andhra Pradesh and Karnataka

Nirupam Bajpai, Ravindra H. Dholakia and Jeffrey D. Sachs Based on research done during an AIESEC traineeship from January to August 2005 in and around Hyderabad, India ceasar_CRC_in_AP[1] - mbb 2

6 District Primary Education Program

http://planningcommission.nic.in/ plans

Education in the Concurrent List

National Policy on Education, 1986 and Program of Action

National policy on Women 2001

Tenth Five Year Plan (2002-2007)

12th Five year plan (2012-2017)

A.P. Community Participation Act, 1998

Andhra Pradesh Primary Education Project (APPEP)

Operation Blackboard (OBB)

District Institutes of Educational Training (DIET)

District Primary Education Programme (DPEP)

National Programme of Nutritional Support to Primary Education (School Meal Programme) (NPNSPE)

Sarva Shiksha Abhiyan (SSA)

The National Programme for Education of Girls at Elementary (NPEGEL)

Kasturba Gandhi Balika Vidyalaya (KGBV)

Bhatia, K.K., Principles of Education, kalyani publishers, New Delhi

Galab, S chandrasekhera Rao, N., *Women's Self-help Groups, Poverty*

Alleviation and Employment, Economic and Political Weekly, March 22-29

Jean Dreze and Amartya Sen, 2011. *India Development and Participation*

Nabhi's Compilation of Ninth Five Year Plan (1997-2002) A Nabhi

Publication

The Hindu, The War On Litercy, April 2001

Vijaya Kumar and Vanaja, *Status of Women in Andhra Pradesh,* Women in Development, 2004.

Index